MW00680873

Dedication

This book is dedicated to the wonderful people of Traverse City, Michigan. Along with the natural beauty of the region stands the goodness of the people who have made this book possible — not only the people you will meet in this book, but all the people who make Traverse City what it is. We are fortunate to live in this dynamic, active and colorful community. There is a unique "can-do" spirit here that preserves the heritage and resources of the region, yet is unafraid to face the challenges of a wonderful future. These people get things done.

George —
Thanks for all you do
to make northern Michigan
a great place to live and work!
Paul Clark
8/12/97

George —
Great Rotarian, Great
Senator and a genuine
friend. Highest regards
David Oppliger

Acknowledgments

There is an array of people who deserve and have our appreciation for their aid in making this book possible. First of all, we must recognize all you participants who gave so freely of your time and contributions to these pages. Without your help and collaboration, this idea would not have been possible.

To the people at Prism Publications, the definition of publishing style in Northern Michigan, we say thanks. Nile Young, your design talents have made us look better than we deserve. Jon Roth, your ideas about the profiles were the foundation of our success. Thaddius Bedford, your photos bring life to these pages. Josh Marker, we all envy your computer skills and talents. Deborah Wyatt-Fellows, you are the bedrock of the company and we thank you for your input.

Thanks to Charlene Schlueter at the NW Michigan Council of Governments for your help in research. Christina Sexton, Patti Moses, Emily Young and Bonnie Oppliger all put up with us and helped with the endless millions of details.

Finally, a huge thanks to Susie Freedman. Welcome back to Michigan. You are the eleventh-hour miracle worker with ideas that simply sparkle. You have stamped yourself on this project and we are happy to have met and worked with you.

Paul LaPorte
Carol LaPorte
Paul Oppliger

April, 1996

Contents

Introduction

Welcome to Traverse City—Welcome to life in the north lane.

When we started this book, our objective was to catalogue the assets and resources we have found since moving here: the natural beauty, the people, the cultural activities, the opportunities and the energy. The research phase of this project turned into a delightful learning experience for us as well. Now we are ready to share our discoveries with you. On the following pages we will introduce you to the people and the spirit of Traverse City.

We found that life in Traverse City is good — it's not without the normal problems, but overall, this is a really good place to live and work. Generally, people live here by choice. Therefore, they are committed to the area and are dedicated to the well-being of the community. People moving here have discovered the city offers them a unique combination of environment and opportunity. And with the enthusiasm and enterprise living here generates in natives and newcomers alike, Traverse City is no longer a small town.

Traverse City faces both tremendous growth and the issues that accompany it. A recent article in The Traverse City Record-Eagle noted that our Cherry Capital Airport is the fastest growing airport in the country — showing an increase of over 300 % between 1990 and 1995. I became aware of another aspect of that growth recently when the owner of one of the five national rental car companies operating locally told me all his cars were rented. Remembering a time just a few years ago when there were no national rental car companies locally, I guessed he might be talking about ten or 12 cars. "No," he told me, "I have eighty cars out now, and I have another sixty on order."

The combination of technology and good air service makes it easy to live here and work elsewhere. More and more people are either telecommuting to jobs that are location-independent, or they are commuting easily to take advantage of out-of-town opportunities. While this is happening all over the world, the impact of this trend is especially evident

in Traverse City. For the same reason many Californians are moving their electronics-based occupations north to Oregon and Washington, people are coming to this area. If you like the climate and the environment, there is little reason not to live here.

Carol and I moved here in 1990, after living in the metropolitan Detroit area for nearly twenty -three years. Our story is a lot like many others: our children grew up and we began commuting to our place "up north." This continued for more years than we can now believe we ever could have tolerated. Since we decided to move here, we have made many wonderful friends and we have found that we enjoy more cultural activities and a wider variety of restaurants than we did when we lived in the city. There is very little corporate life in Traverse City. Few companies here have a "corporate" feel to them. Instead, what we have found is a variety of interesting people engaged in a wide range of enterprising and curious ways to make a living. Many of the people we have enjoyed meeting are involved in multiple business ventures. We have asked some of them to share their stories with us.

We asked them to tell us what they liked about living and working in Traverse City, the history of their businesses and what they would like to tell someone considering a move to this area.

Each of our thirty-two chapters could be the basis of an entire book by itself. Since we wanted to publish before the end of the millennium and still be current and timely, we decided to ogranize the information into four categories within the chapters: Introductions, Profiles, Directories and Information Boxes.

Through the **Introductions,** you will meet community leaders who were generous enough to share their expertise and give us overviews on a number of specific topics. In the **Profiles,** you will mostly meet people in business. While these folks shared some of the production costs for this project, our book is not meant to be an advertising platform. Instead, we want to introduce you to some of the people and businesses we have come to know and are satisfied with. We have met and dealt with everyone profiled in this book. We hope that after reading about them you will feel like looking them up and saying hello.

The **Directories** and **Information Boxes** were chosen to provide you with information you might not find elsewhere. This information was selected to help you get your feet on the ground in Traverse City. We specifically did not include some directory categories such as attorneys and real estate agents because we feel that these personal relationships can be developed better in other ways.

We have written Life in the North Lane as an intoduction to the region for newcomers and those considering a move "up North." Our desire is to present you with an overall picture of daily life in Traverse City. For more encyclopedic directories, we suggest a number of other resources that, along with this book, will help you begin to find your way. In fact, to give you a head start, the first directory, "Some Orientation Tools," is on the following page.

We hope this book will give you a good look at Traverse City and will help you feel more comfortable in your new surroundings. We hope, too, that through reading about some of the people profiled here, you will begin to understand how it's the people who make Traverse City what it is — a delightful place to live and work.

Welcome to Traverse City. Welcome to life in the north lane.

Paul LaPorte

Some Orientation Tools

Where am I? What's going on? How do I get there?

Here are some directories and resources to help you find your way around and get more acquainted with the people, companies, events and services in the area. If you are serious about becoming familiar with Traverse City, we suggest you start by getting the following:

MAPS—go down to Horizon Books and you find what you need. Right by the cash register, you will find the **Official Four Season Pocket Atlas.** It is a five-county map of the Grand Traverse Region, showing 42 towns and markings for biking, hiking and snowmobile trails and a pretty good outdoor recreation guide. The other one is **The Traverse City Michigan Metropolitan Map** by Arrowhead Publications. You can call Horizon Books at (616) 946-7290.

NPI PHONEGUIDE. You can pick this up at the Chamber of Commerce and a number of local businesses, or contact NPI at 3054 Cass, PO Box 879, Traverse City, MI 49685. Their phone number is: (616) 946-7650, FAX: (616) 946-7809. The front section is jammed full of information on the area — maps, local and county government, information on utilities, etc. They also provide tons of free information in their "Talking Phone Book."

TRAVERSE, Northern Michigan's Magazine. This beautiful monthly publication will acquaint you with the area like no other. Along with editorial coverage of the entire region, you will find a complete monthly calendar of events and the area's most complete dining guide. Pick it up at any newsstand, or call (616) 941-8174 for subscription information.

MEMBERSHIP AND BUSINESS DIRECTORY, Traverse City Area Chamber of Commerce. With this, you can contact any chamber member. They are listed by business category and cross-referenced by name. Contact their office at 202 East Grandview Parkway, PO Box 387, Traverse City, MI 49685. Their phone number is (616) 947-5075, and their FAX number is (616) 946-2565.

THE TRAVERSE CITY RECORD-EAGLE. This is the best way to see what is happening on a day-to-day level. If you live outside of the area, you can have them send you Sundays only. Each Sunday there is summary of the events of the preceding week. Contact them at: 120 West Front Street, Traverse City, MI 49684. There are three phone numbers: 946-2000; classified is 946-2653; circulation is 946-2187.

THE BUSINESS NEWS. This will give you a feel for some of the things going on with local businesses and business people. Pick up a copy at any newsstand or contact them at: A & M Publishing, Inc. 800 Hastings, Suite E, Traverse City, MI 49686. Phones are: (616) 929-7919 and (800) 445-7123. FAX is: (616) 929-7914.
E-Mail: biznews-@traverse.com,
or www.traverse.com/a&m/biznews.html.

Northern Express free at any of several pickup spots around town. This alternative paper has lots of information on events, co-ops, and causes not covered as well as the mainstream publications. For more information, contact them at P.O. Box 209, Traverse City, MI 49685 (616)-947-8787 or on the Internet at: 71632.205@Compuserve.com.

Adventure and Recreation

Chapter 1

Adventure and Recreation

By Robert Downes
Editor, Northern Express

They say that the best things in life are free, and so it is with recreation and sports in Traverse City, a town which packs more free fun within its borders than many small states.

Consider that Traverse City has five beaches within its city limits and two ski hills within the metro area, not to mention two marinas, various sport facilities, hiking and biking trails and a world-class cross-country ski trail. In many ways, this is Recreation City, U.S.A.

Tourists pay hundreds of dollars per week to visit Traverse City, and spend all year savoring their chance to rollerblade, cycle or sail along the bay. But for the lucky residents, these and many other recreation opportunities are available every day of the year. And, almost all of the fun is free. Following is an A-to-Z list of recreation ideas for you to explore:

ADVENTURE: First of all, get yourself into the mindset. You're in Traverse City now, the home of legions of cyclists, runners, skiers, sailors, roller bladers, hikers, bird watchers, windsurfers, beach bums, golfers, kayakers, you name it. Adventure is now your *raison d'etre* (that's "reason for living" for you uncultured types). Think adventure and it will come your way.

BEACHES: Head west from the bustling State Park beach in Acme (tourists mostly) and you'll find two small jewels at the base of Mission Peninsula at East Bay Park and Bryant Park. Another quiet beach that's popular with neighborhood residents is at the Senior Citizens Center on Front Street. The Clinch Park Beach is popular with tourists and is perhaps the best for bikini watching or body-builders, as your gender prefers. Further west are the beach volleyball courts, superseded by West End Beach, which is a popular beach for residents.

BIKING: You're in biking paradise here, with the new Traverse Area Recreation Trail (T.A.R.T.) extending from the west end of Traverse City for 10 miles to Bunker Hill Road in Acme. A new leg is planned for the summer of '96 to the Grand Traverse Resort, which has its own trail system. Yet another new bike path connects the city to Grand Traverse Mall, and future plans call for a recreation path around Boardman Lake, and for connecting T.A.R.T. to the trail through Leelanau County to Suttons Bay.

Some of the best road cycling you'll find heads out Birchwood, on the east side of Mission Peninsula. For off-road cycling, check out the Vasa Trail off Bunker Hill Road in Acme, or in the screaming downhills behind the old State Hospital near Munson.

BIRDWATCHING: For waterfowl, visit the park at Logan's Landing on S. Airport Road. You'll often find hundreds of swans, ducks, geese and other waterfowl there, looking for handouts. Also, some of the area's best birdwatching can be found on the marsh trail at Sabin Pond. (See "Hiking.")

BOATING: Marinas in Greilickville and at Clinch Park offer access to West Bay, with access available to East Bay at a site located approximately 3 miles out on the Old Mission Peninsula. Popular destinations include Power Island in West Bay and the Clinch Park Beach, which is jammed with floating parties throughout the summer.

CIVIC CENTER: This county park is located near the intersection of Garfield and Front and features a popular mile-long track around its perimeter that's perfect for walkers, joggers and roller-bladers. Other facilities include the 25-yard Easling Pool, the Howe Ice Arena, basketball courts, ball fields and a playground.

CROSS COUNTRY SKIING: You can choose from a 3k, 10k, or 25k ski at the VASA Trail which was constructed through volunteer effort in the early '90s. Ski skaters dominate the track, which is the site of a nationally-sanctioned race each February, but there's also a track for "classic" diagonal skiers. Off Bunker Hill Road in Acme. Also, check out the lighted trail at Hickory Hills ski resort on the west side of town, and Michigan's longest lighted trail at the Cross Country Ski Center at the Grand Traverse Resort.

DOWNHILL SKIING: Hickory Hills on the west side of town and Mount Holiday in Acme offer bargain prices compared to the region's full-fledged ski resorts. The hills are moderate in size, but they're perfect for those who don't wish to drive to the resorts, and they are also ideal for families on a budget.

GOLF: Everyone knows Northern Michigan is Golf Nirvana. Courses at Green Hills, Highpointe, the Traverse City Country Club, Elmbrook, Mitchell Creek, and of course, the Grand Traverse Resort are among many in the area, ranging from duffer's delight to world-class.

FISHING: On any day of the week you'll find a resolute group of fishermen probing the waters of the Boardman River at the dam on Union Street. The early morning mists also reveal fishermen in waders at the mouth of the Boardman on W. Grand Traverse, angling for steelhead or salmon. Boardman Lake has a reputation for pike, while Deepwater Point in Acme is popular with those seeking whitefish. And, believe it or not, a six-foot muskie once spooked a pal of mine who was scuba diving near the Holiday Inn.

GYMS: There are at least six major health club/gyms in the metro Traverse City area offering racquetball, aerobics and weight training. There are also various mini-gyms specializing in the martial arts, white collar boxing and aerobic dancing, and private clubs that cater to a specialized clientele, such as gays or advanced body builders.

HIKING: Not even most Traverse City residents realize that they have a hiking paradise just outside the city limits at Sabin Pond. Take Cass Road south to the Sabin Dam parking lot and you'll find a mile-long trail along Sabin and Keystone ponds with gorgeous views, particularly in the fall. Swans nest here and the marshes and woodlands are home to many birds.

HOCKEY/ICE SKATING: The Howe Arena at the Civic Center offers skating opportunities. You'll also find an outdoor rink maintained by the city during the winter months on 14th Street.

JET SKIS: Rentable beachside at the Holiday Inn, Larry's Place and at various hotels along West Bay.

KITE FLYING: The Open Space in downtown Traverse City offers plenty of wind as well as a mecca for local kite enthusiasts.

MUSEUMS: The Dennos Museum Center at Northwestern Michigan College, which opened in 1991, is Traverse City's art museum, offering the work of local and regional artists as well as a permanent collection of Inuit art. For a historical perspective, check out the Con Foster Museum at the Clinch Park Zoo, and its displays of Traverse City's past. Another favorite is the Music House in Acme. Many locals have never been in this fascinating operating display of antique automated musical instruments.

NUDE BEACHES: Are you kidding? You won't find any nude beaches in TC. For *au naturel* sunbathing, head out to Lake Michigan and wander (quite a ways) down Otter Creek Beach, Good Harbor Beach, Cathead Bay or the Empire Bluffs.

PARASAILING: Paradise Parasail and Grand Traverse Parasail offer tethered vistas of the bays throughout the summer.

PEOPLE WATCHING: Stake out a chair outside a downtown restaurant and you'll find folks of all persuasions passing by. The T.A.R.T. trail offers a mobile party on weekends and after work, and the beaches offer good people watching as well. Traverse City's strangest characters can be found roaming the aisles at Meijer's late in the evening, particularly on weekends.

ROLLER-BLADING: You'll see dozens of ecstatic bladers enjoying the T.A.R.T. trail along the bay in the summer, which offers the best blading in the region. Other opportunities include the Civic Center. Local veterans also park at Archie Park on Mission Peninsula and blade out Bluff Road — good for a 10-15 mile cruise along East Bay.

RUNNING: Traverse City's Cherry Festival 15K race is frequently listed as one of the best in the country by Runner's World magazine, and our town is also home to the Bayshore Marathon and 10K, as well as the Frozen Footrace in February, and a 25k trail run each fall along the VASA trail. In short, Traverse City is a great town for runners, with weekly races and camaraderie offered in the summer by the Traverse City Track Club, and gorgeous vistas of the bays along the T.A.R.T. trail. Best bets: along the beaches, at the Civic Center, or out Birchwood on the peninsula.

SEA SERPENT SIGHTINGS & WHALE WATCHING: None seen so far, except in the pages of the Midnight Globe. If you spot one, please inform the editors for next year's edition.

STARGAZING: The college maintains an observatory south of town in the Boardman River Valley, with weekly viewings available through the telescope. For areas free of "light pollution," head to the county park at the tip of Mission Peninsula. Newcomers to Traverse City should keep an eye on the northern night sky for the Aurora Borealis,

which appears at odd intervals. As for UFO sightings, the most recent were to the southeast, near Kingsley.

SWIMMING: The 25-yard Easling Pool at the Civic Center is the biggest pool in the area, offering lap swimming, a kid's area, and sauna. Other pools are available at the Park Place Hotel and the Grand Traverse Resort.

VOLLEYBALL: Like Southern California, Traverse City has a dynamic beach volleyball scene at the courts just west of Clinch Park, downtown. The courts attract those drawn to impromptu games as well as those with near pro ability in the midwestern volleyball league competitions.

WALKING: Without a doubt, the Civic Center attracts the most committed fitness walkers in town. Check also the Mallwalkers program at Grand Traverse Mall, or simply enjoy a stroll past the lumber era mansions of the city's neighborhoods.

WINDSURFING: Either bay is popular, but many boarders seem to prefer a small stretch of beach in Acme near Five Mile Road, about a mile east of the State Park. Being shallow, East Bay has fewer boats to interfere with windsurfers, and there's usually more than enough wind.

TENNIS: Anyone? You'll find courts at Northwestern Michigan College, the high school on Eastern Ave., the junior high schools and at Veterans Memorial Park at Division and Grandview Parkway.

ZOO: The Clinch Park Zoo specializes in Michigan animals and birds, and is particularly popular with children who get a closer look at the animals than they might at a metropolitan zoo. Our favorite is the chatty raven, who frequently caws in a booming voice as you pass by.

Robert Downes is editor of Northern Express, a free arts and entertainment publication, available at more than 400 locations throughout Northern Michigan. The Express offers listings of nightlife and events throughout the region as well as a mix of articles and humor that cater to the unexpected.

"A+ for this delightful in-town course with a history tied to Vern Nelson and his family. They can be proud." — P.L.

Carolyn Olson & Vern Nelson
Elmbrook Golf Course

Elmbrook Golf Course is celebrating its 30th year in operation. It was started in 1966 by Vern Nelson (now 90 years old) and four other businessmen from Traverse City who saw a need for a public golf course in the city. The second 9 holes were added in 1969. It is the only 18 hole course inside the city limits of Traverse City. Elmbrook is a course of high terrain with views of the city and of both bays, with their numerous ridges, valleys and hardwoods. It prides itself on "UpNorth beauty and relaxation."

The first public golf leagues at the course, both men's and women's, were formed in the early 70's. Two of the original leagues are still in existence after 25 years and even include some of the original members! Currently, there are four course-sponsored leagues.

The course received the National Award of Excellence in both 1991 and 1993 from the National Golf Foundation for the promotion of junior golf,

dedication to the growth of public golf and influence in league formation. During Michigan's sesquicentennial, Vern was honored by the National Golf Course Owners for his original idea of creating sand bunkers in the shape of the Great Lakes to promote the "Say yes to Michigan" campaign.

The course has a PGA pro who gives lessons. Families are welcome and the atmosphere is relaxed and friendly. Even though the course has carts, many golfers enjoy the fact that it is very walkable. There is a clubhouse with a pro shop; beverages, snacks and sandwiches are also available. Expansion plans include another nine holes.

Carolyn, Vern's daughter, and members of the Nelson family remain active in operating the course.. They would like people to know that the course is unique because of its proximity to town, its tradition of promoting public golf, its beautiful views and moderate fees.

Carolyn and Vern want to tell new people moving to the area that the quality of life here is unsurpassed. They enjoy the accessibility to the natural beauty of this area and they take great pleasure in getting to know the local business people as well as visitors.

**420 Hammond Road, East
Traverse City, MI 49686
Phone: 946-9180**

"These classes on the NMC campus emphasize a goal of incorporating exercise into your everyday life." — C.L.

Margaret Quinn

Jacki Sorensen Aerobic and Fitness Programs

Jacki Sorensen Aerobic and Fitness Programs have been offered in Northern Michigan since the late 1970's. The franchise has been in existence through Maggie Quinn since 1990. The programs are developed and choreographed nationally, so that the latest research in fitness can be incorporated into the programs providing the safest means for individuals to meet their fitness goals.

Programs are offered through Northwestern Michigan College. Classes include Aerobic Workout, Step Aerobics, Aerobic Dance, Fitness for Older Adults and Weight Strengthening. Personal Coaching services are available to individuals in their own home or club. Students range in age from 18 to 87 and have the option of receiving academic credit.

Our classes differ from other offerings in the area in that we have some students who have been taking classes continually for 15 years. All choreography is reviewed by a medical team to assure the programs are safe. Classes are offered year-round.

Instructors are certified for the aerobic and/or weight strengthening programs. Instructors in Traverse City include Maggie Quinn, Terry Tarnow, Tam Antinozzi and Lynda Smith. Sue Lawry represents the franchise in Petoskey.

Everyone needs to participate in some form of exercise program, every day. Our bodies were developed to be hunters and gatherers. As we look at our sedentary lives, many of the physical ailments we have developed are related to not using our bodies everyday in the manner for which they were designed. Our bodies require a combination of aerobic, endurance, stretching and weight strengthening activities to remain healthy. Through Jacki Sorensen Aerobic and Fitness Programs, individuals can participate in activities that will keep them healthy and productive.

990 Pine Ridge Drive
Traverse City, MI 49686
Phone: 947-0024

"Not just a workout center. They have a full range of services, including personal trainers and physical therapy." — P.L.

Susan Brown
General manager

Lynn Lombard
Clinical Director, Physical Therapy
The Fitness Center

New to the area? Looking for ways to meet new people and make new friends? Here's a good place to start.

If you have been thinking about starting an exercise program, but are not really sure about where to go and don't like that intimidated feeling that you can get from a gym, then The Fitness Center is the place for you. Located in the historic Cigar Box Factory, built in 1920, The Fitness Center is in the heart of downtown Traverse City.

Known as Traverse City's adult fitness facility, our staff includes a wide range of health care professionals: physical therapists, massage therapists, recreational therapists, exercise physiologists and personal trainers. We are here to meet all of your exercise needs.

425 Boardman
Traverse City, MI 49684
Phone: 941-8787

We would like to offer you a FREE 7-day membership and complimentary half-hour consultation. This gives you the opportunity to meet with one of our health professionals, right from the very first visit. This also allows our staff to be able to learn about what you, the consumer, might be interested in.

Once you have decided to become a member, you will be given an initial fitness evaluation, which includes a sub-max bicycle test to determine a target heart rate, a body composition and a general health risk appraisal. This allows us to determine where you are and what areas you may want to work on. After this appointment, you will be scheduled for a personal fitness orientation, during which one of our qualified staff will take you through a one-on-one process to tailor an exercise program specifically for you.

Give us a call or stop by any time to talk with one of our health professionals and to receive your FREE 7-day pass and complimentary consultation. There is no obligation. We look forward to meeting you.

"Almost any day, you can stop in the store and see Bob McLain generating enthusiasm for the products he sells." — *P.L.*

Bob McLain
McLain Cycle and Fitness

All of us at McLain Cycle strive to serve our customers with extensive product knowledge. This is a somewhat dying concept in today's world, with large chain stores and help-yourself marketing. Our store emulates the lifestyle of Northern Michigan and provides the tools for you to experience the best.

We bring the #1 and #2 quality bicycle lines to Northern Michigan: Trek and Schwinn. Lite-speed, Klein and Bontrager complete the line, offering the best in our industry. In addition, we stock an array of parts and accessories, important to any cyclist.

After the last mountain bike event is completed in November, many customers greet the winter weather and strap on their snowshoes. With the variety of snow conditions in Northern Michigan, we have chosen to handle the workhorse Iverson snowshoe and the lightweight technical Atlas brand. Together, these companies provide a full line of models so any conditions and any abilities can be met.

For the customers who enjoy the winter weather in the comfort of their homes, we have home exercise equipment. Treadmills, electronic cycles, stairclimbers and weight stack machines are just a few of the many pieces of fitness equipment that line our large showroom. Schwinn and Spirit dominate this industry and we back these products with a knowledgeable sales and service staff.

We at McLain Cycle are are "addicted to the fun" represented by the products we sell. We organize clinics, weekly mountain bike rides or weekly snowshoe romps. We'll take any excuse to get outside. Our product knowledge was not learned from a book — it's from first-hand experience.

2786 Garfield Road North
Traverse City, MI 49686
Phone: 941-8855
(800) 972-9253

Some Campgrounds in the Traverse City Area

BENZONIA
Vacation Trailer Park - 100 Sites
882-5101
Timberline Campground - 170 lots
882-9548

BEULAH
Turtle Lake Campground - 59 sites
275-7353

CEDAR
Leelanau Pines - 152 sites
228-5742

ELK RAPIDS
Vacation Village Campground - 80 sites
264-8636

EMPIRE
Sleepy Bear Campground - 150 sites
326-5566

FIFE LAKE
Spring Lake State Forest Campground - 32 sites
775-9727

HONOR
Sunny Woods Platte River Campground - 40 sites
325-3952
Platte River State Forest Campground - 26 sites
775-9727

INTERLOCHEN
Interlochen State Park - 550 sites
276-9511
Lake Dubonnet State Campground - 50 sites
775-9727

LAKE ANN
Lake Ann State Forest Campground - 30 sites
775-9727

LAKE LEELANAU
Lake Leelanau RV Park - 166 sites
256-7236

MAYFIELD
Arbutus Lake No. 4 State Forest Campground - 50 sites
775-9727
Scheck's Place State Forest Campground - 31 sites
775-9727

MESICK
Mesick Trailer Park - 270 sites
885-1199
Seaton Creek Campground - 17 sites
775-8539

NORTHPORT
Leelanau State Park - 50 sites
922-5270

OLD MISSION
Old Mission Inn-Campsites - 29 sites
223-7770

ST. JAMES
Beaver Island State Forest Campground - 25 sites
732-3541

SLEEPING BEAR DUNES
D.H. Day Campground, Glen Arbor - 89 sites
Platte River Campground, Honor - 179 sites
326-5134
Veterans Memorial State Forest Campground - 24 sites
775-9727

THOMPSONVILLE
Grass Lake State Forest Campground - 15 sites
775-9727

TRAVERSE CITY
Holiday Park Campgrounds - 154 sites
943-4410
Grand Traverse Camping & RV Resort - 91 sites
269-3203
Ranch Rudolf Campground - 25 sites
947-9529
Yogi Bear's Jellystone Park - 221 sites
947-2770
Traverse City State Park - 343 sites
922-5270

WILLIAMSBURG
Whitewater Park - 40 sites
267-5091
Northern Pines Campground - 60 sites
938-2280

Traverse City Senior Center

Traverse City Senior Center
801 East Front Street
Traverse City, MI 49686
(616) 922-4911

Director: Lori Wells, SDC
Program Coordinator: Diane Connolly
Office Assistant:
Bette Blume, Green Thumb Program

HOURS:
Monday - Friday 9:00 a.m. - 4:00 p.m.
Sunday 1:00 p.m. - 4:00 p.m.

Traverse City Senior Center has "Everything Under the Sun." This is where active people help themselves and help others. Enthusiastic volunteers make things … and make things happen! The Traverse City Senior Center strives to provide services and programs for the active, independent, older adult of the Greater Grand Traverse Area.

PARTICIPATION: Residents of the City of Traverse City, East Bay, Garfield and Peninsula townships can join the Senior Center at no charge. Blair township residents are asked to pay $6.00/12 months. All other residents are asked to pay $12.00/12 months. Membership is necessary to participate in all of our programs except for the noon lunch and travel programs.

Our monthly newsletter with complete details about our program and special events can be found on the back page of the Traverse City Record Eagle's Active Years. This is a free publication and if you would like to receive it, contact us.

We also print our lunch menu monthly which can be picked up at the front desk or call and we will mail it to you.

We also offer information and referral services. If you need a service and don't know where to call, call us and we'll get you the information.

VOLUNTEER OPPORTUNITIES: Senior Center staff relies heavily on the talents and time of our over 200 volunteers. We work hard to fit the skills of the volunteer with our needs. Contact staff if interested in being part of our volunteer crew.

Call today to find out more about becoming a member!

REGULAR PROGRAMMING:

MOVIES: Every Wednesday at 1:30 p.m. we show a movie in our lounge

BIRTHDAY CELEBRATION: The first Friday of every month we serve cake and ice cream for lunch and celebrate with those having a birthday that month.

MEDICARE & MEDICAID COUNSELING: The third Wednesday of every month, by appointment, you can get assistance from trained volunteers in filing claims or completing paperwork for these programs.

MASSAGES: Monthly a 15-minute body massage is offered compliments of "Hands On" massage therapists. A $3 donation is suggested. Appointments are necessary.

DANCES: Every other Friday night at 8:30 p.m. we have live music and refreshments for just $2.00. We also offer at least one dinner dance a month. Check schedule for details.

LUNCH: Served daily at 12 noon. Cost is just $1.50 for those 60 + and $4.00 for all others. Reservations required 24 hours in advance. Please call 947-5285.

EXERCISE: Mondays at 10:00 a.m. we offer a light stretching exercise program. This program is also shown on TCTV Channel 2 Monday-Wednesday and Friday mornings at 10:00 a.m. and Tuesdays & Thursdays at 2:00 p.m.

COSTUME JEWELRY REPAIR: The first Friday of every month, Miner's North will repair costume jewelry free of charge.

KITCHEN BAND: This renowned group practices at our Center every Thursday morning from 10:30-11:30 a.m.

HOBBY GROUP: Share your talents with one another every Monday from 11:00 a.m. - 2:00 p.m.

DINING OUT WITH MATURE MINGLERS: The third Thursday we meet at a local restaurant and share company. Couples, singles, everyone welcome. Dinner and transportation is on you.

SINGLE SENIORS OVER SIXTY: First Tuesday at 5:30 p.m. this group meets for a potluck supper and feature program or gathering. The third Saturday they also meet to eat out at a local restaurant. After dinner they meet back at the Center for a movie, cards or whatever suits them.

CARDS: You do not need partners to play. Different game played daily at 1:30 p.m. Need to register for game at front desk when coming in. Monday-Double Euchre; Tuesday-Euchre; Wednesday-Double Pinochle: Thursday-Bridge & Pinochle: Fridays-Double Euchre. Evening games are also played at 7:00 p.m.: Mondays & Thursdays-Duplicate Bridge; Fridays & Sundays-Euchre.

BLOOD PRESSURE CHECKS: A nurse is at the Center the first Monday and Wednesday of every month for a free screening.

FOOT CARE CLINIC: Nurses are at the Center the 2nd & 4th Tuesday of every month for foot care. Appointments are necessary. Cost is $11.50.

TRAVEL: We offer an extensive travel program in partnership with Good Company Tours. We have day trips, extended tours and over seas adventures. If we're not headed in your direction, let us know, we welcome suggestions for new destinations.

GROUP MEETINGS:

Parkinson's Group
    4th Wednesday, 10:00 a.m.

Pineneedler's Quilting Club
    2nd Wednesday, 7:00 p.m.

Traverse Area Scandinavian Society
    1st Wednesday, 7:00 p.m.

Retired School Personnel
    1st Tuesday, 1:00 p.m.

Ballroom Dance Club
    Every Tuesday ,7:00 p.m.

Grand Traverse Area Rock & Mineral
    3rd Tuesday, 7:00 p.m.

Newcomers Bridge-Ladies
    2nd Thursday,10:00 a.m.

Newcomers Bridge-Men
    Alt. Wednesdays, 1:30 p.m.

Traverse Bay Embroiderers

3rd Wednesday, 7:00 p.m.

A.A.R.P.
    1st Wednesday, 12:00 p.m.

Breather's Support Group
    2nd Wednesday, 2:00 p.m.

Stocks 'R Us Investment Club
    2nd Tuesday, 9:00 a.m.

Winners Take All Investment Club
    1st Tuesday, 9:00 a.m.

FUNDING: The Traverse City Senior Center is a department of the City of Traverse City and we receive the majority of our funding from them. We also receive a grant from the Grand Traverse County Commission on Aging, pro rata shares from Blair, East Bay, Garfield and Peninsula townships. The Senior Center also relies on the generous donations of our members and friends. For more information about making a contribution to the Senior Center, contact the Director.

ADVISORY BOARD: A group of members of the Center meet every other month on the 2nd Wednesday at 10:00 a.m. to discuss the direction of the Senior Center. All members are encouraged to attend and anyone interested in becoming a member of the Board is asked to contact the Director.

Northwestern Michigan Artists and Craftsmen

Here's an art center with classes and activities of all sorts. It is in the building that once housed the "All Faiths Chapel," a Traverse City landmark on the grounds of the old State Hospital. Membership has a number of advantages including discounts at local art supplies stores. Classes are offered in: painting, watercolors, photography, drawing, carving, portraits, pastels, polymer clay, and many others. Call them for a class schedule. Better yet, go over there and visit. It is an impressive facility in our area. Take a class.

720 South Elmwood
Traverse City, MI 49684
941-9488

This list of area golf courses is maintained by the Traverse City Area Chamber of Commerce and is reprinted here with their permission. Annually, the Chamber updates the list and publishes a brochure showing current rates. For a copy, contact the Chamber of Commerce.

A-GA-MING
Phone: 616-264-5081
Course: 18 holes, 6735 yards, Cart mandatory
Location: McLachlin Rd., nine miles N of Elk Rapids, off US-31.

ANTRIM DELLS
Phone: 616-599-2679
Course: 18 holes, 6670 yards,
Carts mandatory until 5 p.m.
Location: US-31 at Atwood.

CEDAR HILLS
Phone: 616-947-8237
Course: 9 holes, Par 3; 9 holes, Executive Course.
Location: 7525 Cedar Run Road, Traverse City.

CRYSTAL MOUNTAIN RESORT
Phone: 616-378-2000
Course: 27 holes, 4983 - 6752 yards
Location: M-115, Thompsonville.

DUNES GOLF CLUB
Phone: 616-326-5390
Course: 18 holes, 5957 yards
Location: M-72, Empire.

ELMBROOK GOLF COURSE
Phone: 616-946-9180
Course: 18 holes, 6319 yards
Location: 420 Hammond Road, Traverse City.

GRAND TRAVERSE RESORT—SPRUCE RUN
Phone: 1-800-748-0303, or 616-938-2100 - ext 3675
Course: 18 holes, 6899 yards
Location: US 31 North, Acme.

GRAND TRAVERSE RESORT—THE BEAR
Phone: 1-800-748-0303, or 616-938-2100 - ext 3675
Course: 18 holes, 7177 yards
Location: US 31 North, Acme.

GREEN HILLS
Phone: 616-946-2975
Course: 9 holes, 3353
Location: 2411 W. Silver Lake Road, Traverse City.

HIGH POINTE GOLF CLUB
Phone: 800-753-7888 or 616-267-9900
Course: 18 holes, 6849 yards
Location: 5555 Arnold Road, Williamsburg.

INTERLOCHEN
Phone: 616-275-7311
Course: 18 holes, 6040 yards
Location: 12 miles SW of T.C. on US-31, South.

MATHESON GREENS
Phone: 1-800-443-6883 or 616-386-5171
Course: 18 holes, 6609 yards
Location: Matheson Rd. at Swede Rd., Northport.

MISTWOOD GOLF COURSE
Phone: 616-275-5500
Course: 18 holes, 6715 yards, Practice Range.
Location:7568 Sweet Lake Rd., Lake Ann

SHANTY CREEK-THE LEGEND GOLF COURSE
Phone: 1-800-678-4111
Course: 18 holes, 6764 yards, Cart mandatory.
Location: M-88 on Shanty Creek Rd., Bellaire.

SHANTY CREEK-THE SCHUSS MOUNTAIN GOLF COURSE
Phone: 1-800-678-4111
Course:18 holes, 6922 yards, Cart mandatory.
Location: M-88 on Shanty Creek Rd., Bellaire.

THE SHANTY CREEK GOLF COURSE
Phone: 1-800-678-4111
Course: 18 holes, 6276 yards, Cart mandatory.
Location: M-88 on Shanty Creek Rd., Bellaire.

SUGAR LOAF RESORT
Phone: 616-228-1870
Course: 18 holes, 6813 yards
Location: 18 miles NW of Traverse City. Take M-72 W 7 miles; right on County Rd 651 and follow signs.

TWIN BIRCH GOLF COURSE
Phone: 616-258-9691
Course: 18 holes, 6,133 yards
Location: 1030 Highway 612 NE Kalkaska

VERONICA VALLEY GOLF COURSE
Phone: 616-256-9449
Course: 9 holes
Location: 4341 S. Lake Leelanau Drive (Co. Rd. 641).

Chamber of Commerce

Chamber of Commerce

By Hal VanSumeren
Executive Director, Traverse City Area Chamber of Commerce

My first day in Traverse City was January 3rd, 1962. There was a foot of snow on the ground and the snowbanks in some places were three to four feet high. My first impression as I was being driven from the airport to the Park Place Hotel was that this was the most beautiful place I had ever seen. Today, 34 years later, having seen the mountains, the desert and the seashore, the statement still stands.

"Easy for him to say — he's paid to feel that way", you might think. Fair enough, but let's look at the evidence. Traverse City, the county seat of Grand Traverse County, is almost at the geographic center of the Grand Traverse Region. The other counties in the region are Antrim, Benzie, Kalkaska, and Leelanau. Grand Traverse County, the largest of the five, accounts for roughly 50% of the total population with 70,000 residents. The population of Traverse City is approximately 16,000.

Many people who now call Traverse City home, probably first saw the area as summer tourists. They may have noted some things that made a distinct impression, like Grand Traverse Bay, the beautiful beaches and open shoreline, a downtown that is alive and vibrant, and a community that cares about how it looks. They surely were impressed with the almost nightly events at the Interlochen Center for the Arts, with concerts featuring performers from Willie Nelson to the Chicago Symphony. And while there is fast food aplenty, they could enjoy one-of-a-kind, specialty, upscale and gourmet restaurants scattered throughout the five county region. The week-long National Cherry Festival, attracting nearly a half a million visitors makes for many fond memories, as well.

What visitors don't always observe however, are things like Munson Medical Center with its state-of-the-art cancer treatment program, daily open heart surgeries, and a medical community that rivals the best in the state. Public, private, parochial and future charter schools are well run and planned and are supported by the community.

While there are a few corporate headquarters in Traverse City, the area boasts major employers like Munson Medical Center with 3,000 employees, Sara Lee bakeries with 1,000 and many upscale resorts employing hundreds of people year-round. However, small businesses, dominated by retail and service companies, provide the bulk of employment opportunities.

The Traverse City Area Chamber of Commerce, with over 2,800 members, is well supported by the business community. The Chamber's priorities include: quality of life issues, an educational system that produces students with marketable skills, an economic development program that creates jobs in the community and an awareness of the changing health care needs of its residents.

Quality of life issues however, relate to all Chamber

goals. Because so many people are attracted to the area for its natural beauty, it's only fitting that preserving this natural resource would be high on the Chamber's agenda. To that end, the Chamber takes a highly visible role in dealing with growth management issues. The Chamber's resources are directed at projects that preserve, enhance and restore the natural beauty of the area. By supporting sound planning policies, the Chamber creates more economic opportunity for the citizens of Traverse City.

Many opportunities for involvement in civic activities abound in Traverse City. Newcomers will find an open door and an outstretched hand welcoming their participation. Traverse City, the retail, wholesale, and financial center of Northern Michigan is like nowhere else.

The Grand Traverse Bay region contains natural resources of unparalleled beauty. The water, woods, beaches, and hills are an important part of our daily life. For many, these cherished resources are a major reason for living, vacationing, or investing in this area.

Special Member Benefit Programs

Traverse City Area Chamber of Commerce members can take advantage of these member benefit programs.

BLUE CROSS/BLUE SHIELD
Group Health, Life & Disability programs

AUTO OWNERS GROUP DISCOUNT
(10% above and beyond the company's customary discounts based on individual factors) on personal auto, home and excess liability (umbrella) insurance

AGENCY SERVICES USA
Discounted long distance telecommunications rates, equipment discounts, and additional value-added benefits

AT&T BENEFITS
Discounted long distance telecommunications rates and additional value-added services

UNEMPLOYMENT SERVICES, INC.
Program designed to assist employers in controlling and reducing unemployment costs

J.A. YEAGER PERSONNEL ASSESSMENT
Tools designed to assist in making better hiring and placement decisions

US SIGNAL
Discounted long distance telecommunications rates and additional value-added services

AIRBORNE EXPRESS
Discounted overnight air shipping rates

GRAND TRAVERSE INTERNET
Discounted access to the Internet

For more information on Chamber benefits, please contact the Chamber of Commerce offices at 947-5075.

Don't miss these important networking events:

- •Good Morning, Traverse City!
- •Business After Hours

Call the Chamber of Commerce Office for details and schedules.

Business Assistance Programs

This is an overview of the business assistance services available to individuals seeking to expand their business operations, start a new business, or maintain the viability of an existing business in the Traverse Bay region.

Additional information regarding the services of a specific office or offices listed below may be obtained by calling the contact person indicated.

TRAVERSE BAY ECONOMIC DEVELOPMENT CORPORATION: Provides area marketing, retention and expansion services, financing, industrial park development and marketing, sites and buildings inventories, economic and demographic data, and coordinates delivery of services by supporting agencies.

Charles Blankenship, 946-1596.
TC Area Chamber of Commerce
Box 387, TC, MI 49685-0387

SMALL BUSINESS DEVELOPMENT CENTER: Provides free business counseling services on all aspects of business planning and management. The Center also offers special programming, networking and resource referral opportunities.

Matthew Meadors, 947-5075.
TC Area Chamber of Commerce,
Box 387, TC, MI 49685-0387

TRAVERSE BAY ENTERPRISE FORUM: Links potential private investors and professional service providers with individuals seeking equity financing to start or expand operations. The Enterprise Forum facilitates an alternative source of capital when traditional sources are not available.

Matthew Meadors, 947-5075.
TC Area Chamber of Commerce,
Box 387, TC, MI 49685-0387

SCORE (SERVICE CORPS OF RETIRED EXECUTIVES): Provides free business counseling by men and women who have had successful business careers as company executives or owners of their own businesses.

Pat Hobson, 947-5075.
TC Area Chamber of Commerce,
Box 387, TC, MI 49685-0387

NORTHWEST MICHIGAN PRIVATE INDUSTRY COUNCIL: The Local Procurement Office provides technical assistance to businesses interested in marketing to federal and state governments.— Jim Haslinger, 929-5036.

Employment, recruitment, placement and training assistance and labor market information.—Deborah Vogel, 929-5078.

Small Business financing and financial counseling services.—Richard Beldin, 929-5017.

Northwest Michigan Private Industry Council,
P.O. Box 506, TC, MI 49685-0506

TRAVERSE BAY ECONOMIC DEVELOPMENT OFFICE: Provides business retention and expansion assistance and markets industrial property in the Airport Industrial Park.

Jo Rudino, 922-4440.
City of Traverse City,
400 Boardman Ave., TC, MI 49684

ENTREPRENEUR DEVELOPMENT PROGRAM: Provides individual business planning assistance and consultation in areas of strategic planning, marketing, organization and finance for new and existing small business.

Richard Wolin, 922-1124.
Northwestern Michigan College,
1701 E. Front Street, TC, MI 49684

CENTER FOR BUSINESS AND INDUSTRY (CBI): Provides training and consulting for local businesses. Services include needs analysis, employee assessment, customized training, entry-level job skills training, employee upgrading, personal growth seminars, teleconferences, leadership development programs, market research, grant-writing assistance, project management, technical consulting, and technology transfer assistance. CBI is a regional affiliate of the Michigan Manufacturing Technology Center.

Cheryl Throop, 922-1715.
Northwestern Michigan College,
1701 E. Front Street, TC, MI 49684

Cultural Activities

Chapter 3

Cultural Activities

Eugene A. Jenneman
Director, Dennos Museum Center

Culture abounds in the region, as much as natural beauty. It is within the splendor of nature itself that the region's leading international arts organization was created - The Interlochen Center for the Arts. Chartered in 1927, the center has grown to claim the title "World Center for Arts Education." The Inter-

lochen Center for the Arts offers arts education opportunities throughout the year. The Arts Academy offers a full academic program with emphasis on the visual and performing arts for students from grades 9 through post-graduate studies. The summer Arts Camp draws students from around the world who come together to share the universal language of music and celebrate the joy of creative expression. The Interlochen Arts Festival hosts hundreds of performances from international superstars in Kresge and Corson Auditoriums to faculty and student recitals in the Dendrinos Recital Hall. Interlochen also covers the air waves on WIAA, Interlochen Public Radio broadcasting to northwest lower Michigan and eastern Wisconsin. The station, which broadcasts continuously with a format of classical music and news, boasts the highest per capita listener support among public radio stations in the United States.

Community involvement is the hallmark of culture in Traverse City. A major example of this involvement is found in the Old Town Playhouse, which has been producing plays since 1959. Volunteers from around the five-county area present eleven theatrical productions annually. This community is committed to providing educational workshops in all aspects of theatrical production with the goal of keeping theater a vital part of the cultural scene in the region.

Since 1951, the Traverse Symphony Orchestra (TSO) has brought together dedicated musicians from the region to produce major performances of symphonic music. Begun as a community orchestra of amateurs, the organization has matured into an organization of professional performers who come from a wide variety of backgrounds with a common love of great music. The TSO performs in locations throughout the area and serves all of northern lower Michigan as the only professional orchestra north of Grand Rapids. Each year, the TSO offers a subscription season of five concerts plus a special Christmas concert and a summer concert series. The concerts often feature guest artists of national and international stature.

Dedicated to serving the youth of Northern Michigan, the TSO offers school and family concerts. Through these concerts, young people are introduced to fine music and encouraged to become the performers and audiences of the future.

Two important arts groups which have recognized and supported the needs of regional visual artists are the Traverse Area Arts Council and the Northwest Michigan Artists and Craftsmen. The Traverse Area Arts Council, in addition to providing exhibition opportunities for regional artists in its gallery, produces a regional newsletter on arts happenings in the area and serves as the regional re-granting agency for the Michigan Council for the Arts and Cultural Affairs. The Northwest Michigan Artists and Craftsmen serves area artists with workshops conducted by nationally recognized artists, and offers exhibition and sales opportunities through its gallery exhibitions and numerous special events, including the annual Traverse Bay Outdoor Art Fair on the campus of Northwestern Michigan College.

Dancers will find a home with the Dance Arts Academy which has provided professional training in the region since 1981. The Academy is the home of Company Dance Traverse (CDT). CDT presents concerts by local and visiting professional dancers and choreographers at numerous venues throughout the Grand Traverse area.

Those who enjoy dance will find additional opportunities to perform with the group Pedestrians Unhinged.

The newest cultural facility to appear on the Grand Traverse arts scene is the Dennos Museum Center on the campus of Northwestern Michigan College. The facility grew out of a desire to have gallery and performance space on campus which would provide the community with a first class facility to host important art exhibitions, and house the college's growing collection of Inuit art from the Canadian Arctic.

Opened in 1991, the Dennos Museum Center has become a major cultural center for northwest lower Michigan and the state. The 40,000 square foot center features a "hands on" Discovery Gallery, a gallery of Inuit art, and offers changing art exhibitions from other museums and individual artists of national significance, while hosting a variety of concerts in its 367 seat Milliken Auditorium. The auditorium is the home of several concert series including Jazz at the Museum, produced by the Northern Michigan Jazz Society; the Dancing Bear Music Series, produced by the Dennos Museum Center; NMC Presents, produced by the NMC Music Department; and the concerts of the Encore society of Music, a regional woodwinds ensemble.

The arts play a significant role in the daily lives of people in this area. A review of any publication in the area listing arts events reveals a broad range of offerings appealing to a variety of artistic interests and tastes. The organizations mentioned above, plus many other smaller groups and individuals, contribute to this wealth of offerings.

The Grand Traverse region is fortunate to have such an active arts community. It is equally fortunate to have a supportive audience for the offerings of the community. This combination enables the arts to be a vital part of the quality of life in this area.

"You may see your friends or neighbors perform here. A great showcase for local talent and a fun night out." — C.L.

Joseph Paul Bertucci
Old Town Playhouse

The Old Town Playhouse, now in its 36th season, is one of Michigan's most respected civic theatres. Each year, the volunteers of the Traverse City Civic Players present a total of eleven theatrical productions. Three musicals and three nonmusical plays are fully staged in the Mainstage 350-seat auditorium. A black box theatre, seating up to 100, is home to three Studio Theatre plays and two shows for children.

The theatre is also deeply committed to education. In addition to presenting workshops in acting, auditioning, lighting, and other aspects of production, it is home to the Traverse City Intermediate School District Theatre Tech Intern Program.

The Playhouse is known for the professional quality of its artistry. Recent offerings have included highly acclaimed productions of "The King and I," "I Hate Hamlet," "Lost in Yonkers," "The Sound of Music," "Little Shop of Horrors," "The Taming of the Shrew," "Jeffrey," and "Fiddler on The Roof," as well as premier productions of original scripts by local authors.

Old Town Playhouse
148 E. Eighth Street
P.O. Box 262
Traverse City, MI 49685
Phone: 947-2210

"Barry has made a significant commitment to this community. We should all help, since we will all benefit. Wonderful, top rate performances." — C.L.

Barry Cole
Michigan Ensemble Theatre & Expert in Residence Program

Since its inception in 1991, Michigan Ensemble Theatre (MET), Northern Michigan's only professional theatre company, has dazzled area audiences with everything from an unforgettable version of the Broadway blockbuster, "A Chorus Line!" to a sold-out production of "Forever Plaid." MET's growing reputation for quality enabled it to be chosen to stage the very first independent production of the phenomenally successful "Plaid," prior to any public release of performance rights.

In April, 1996, MET owner and president, Barry Cole purchased the historic State Theatre in downtown Traverse City and is holding it in public trust

205 Wellington
Traverse City, MI 49686
Phone: 929-7260

while the community considers the opportunity to convert it into a performing arts center. If sufficient funds are raised, the building could become a permanent home for the not-for-profit MET, the Traverse Symphony Orchestra, and numerous other cultural events. During summer and fall of 1996, MET will hold a special two-show season in the present facility.

MET has also launched an Expert in Residence Program that underwrites collaborative efforts by area arts groups to bring prominent experts into the region to share their knowledge and enthusiasm for their fields with students, arts participants and the public. MET absorbs a significant portion of the costs incurred and provides housing, educational and reception space in the historic MET house, located in downtown Traverse City.

Call for more information on the Expert in Residence Program.

"A real treasure! Go alone or take your guests on this spectacular and fascinating musical performance tour." — P.L.

The Music House at Harmony Village
David Stiffler, Executive Director

Many residents, both newcomers and old-timers, join our out-of-town visitors each year in a fascinating visit to the Music House. This is a performing museum, featuring a large collection of rare restored antique musical instruments in turn-of-the-century settings. It has been serving the public since 1983, open every day except during the mid-winter months.

Each year, thousands of guests enjoy hour-long guided tours, hearing music from fine music boxes, nickelodeons, Gershwin at the reproducing piano and many other wondrous treasures of a golden age of entertainment. The centerpiece of the collection is the Mortier dance organ, with its 30 foot wide carved facade. This remarkable instrument from Belgium provides big band sounds of a bygone era.

One of our interesting restoration projects is a 1929 American LaFrance fire engine. This truck was purchased new in Traverse City and served for over thirty years as an important part of the Traverse City Fire Department. It was housed in the old fire house on Union Street where the Firehouse Fair now operates. We will be using it as a parade vehicle, fitted with some antique outdoor musical instruments. You can look for us in local and regional parades and festivals.

The Music House is a non-profit organization, established, supported and growing largely through the efforts of several hundred volunteers and donors. Although it is a facility one might expect to find in an urban setting, the cultural environment and talented people in the Grand Traverse area make this location appropriate. We are happy to offer a unique, quality cultural asset to the community which is also a major benefit for tourism.

We invite you to come for a visit.

7377 US-31 North, Box 297
Acme, MI 49610
Phone: 938-9300
FAX: 938-3650

Museums in the Area

DENNOS MUSEUM CENTER
Changing exhibits, hands-on exhibit, permanent Inuit (Eskimo) prints and sculpture; Mon-Sat. 10-5pm, Sun 1-5pm: $2 Adults, $1 Children, $6 Families, Northwestern Michigan College, 1701 E. Front St.; 922-1028

CON FOSTER MUSEUM & CLINCH PARK ZOO
Water recreation of the past, exhibit includes ice shanties and old bathing suits. Seven days, 10-4:30pm; 922-4905

LEELANAU HISTORICAL MUSEUM
Historical displays about early settlement of and life on the Leelanau Peninsula, including a hands-on display of old toys. 10-4 Tues.-Sat., $1 Adults, $.50 Children; 203 E. Cedar St., Leland. 256-7475.

EMPIRE AREA MUSEUM
Replica of a turn-of-the-century saloon, parlor, kitchen and sewing room and on-site barn, blacksmith shop, railroad display and one-room schoolhouse. Open Mon.-Sat. 10-4pm, Sun. 1-4pm; closed Wednesdays. Donations accepted. In Empire on M-22.

SOUTH MANITOU VISITOR'S CENTER
On South Manitou Island. National Park Service museum depicts history of the island, its settlers, and inhabitants, daily noon-3pm, Free; 326-5134.

THE MUSIC HOUSE
Restored automated and rare musical instruments. Mon-Sat 10-4pm; Sun 1-5pm. Adults $6, Children $2. North of Acme, 7377 US 31 N; 938-9300.

SLEEPING BEAR POINT COAST GUARD STATION MARITIME MUSEUM
History of US Coast Guard lifesaving and services. Weekdays 1-4:30pm, Sat.-Sun. 10:30-5pm; Free. In Sleeping Bear Dunes National Lakeshore, M-109 near Glen Haven; 326-5134.

THIS OLE FARM MUSEUM
Livestock farm setting with blacksmith shop and woodworking, logging and farm displays. Reservations required. 11459 Pavlis Road Buckley; 269-3672.

FIFE LAKE AREA HISTORICAL MUSEUM
Historical exhibits from lumbering to early farming, including replica kitchen, parlor, bedroom, general store, barber shop, and school room. Wed.-Sat. 10-4pm; free; State Street, Fife Lake.

ELK RAPIDS HISTORICAL MUSEUM
Historical exhibits include photos, paperwork, books, an 1800s piano, and the township's 1883 jail. Tue.-Fri. 2-4pm; Sat.-Sun. 1-4pm; Free; Lower level of renovated township hall, 401 River Street, Elk Rapids.

BENZIE AREA HISTORICAL MUSEUM
Housed in a century-old church building. Features artifacts pertaining to pioneers who carved a living from northern Michigan wilderness. Tue.-Sat. 1-4pm. Traverse Avenue, a block west of US 31. 882-5539.

GUNTZVILLER'S SPIRIT OF THE WOODS MUSEUM
North American wildlife and Native American artifacts in a diorama setting. $2 Adults, $1 Student; Open seven days. US 31, 2 miles south of Elk Rapids; 264-5597.

WALTER E. HASTINGS NATURE MUSEUM
Wildlife photos, collections of rocks and minerals, and Native American tools and handiwork. Free. Tue.-Sat. 8am-6pm, Sun. 1:30-5pm. One mile beyond WIAA at Interlochen Center for the Arts, Interlochen.

Here is a sampling of some of the series you will enjoy at the Dennos Museum.

Dancing Bear Music
Series & Special Events
Guitar at the Museum Series
NMC Faculty in Concert
NMC Music Benefit Concerts
NMC Ensembles on Stage
NMC Student Showcases

For information, call the Dennos Box office: 922-1553

Downtown Traverse City

Chapter 4

Downtown Traverse City

Bryan J. Crough
*Executive Director, Traverse City
Downtown Development Authority*

"In the beginning the word was timber."

Opening words, *Queen City of the North*
by Lawrence Wakefield

As you stand atop the historic Park Place Hotel downtown Traverse City and look out over a downtown blessed with the Boardman River meandering not once, but twice, through the Central Business District, it is hard to imagine the early days when the river carried timber from Traverse City to Chicago.

Traverse City's downtown, consistently ranked as one of the best downtowns in the Midwest, is a testament to the history of the region while also serving as the heart of a fast-growing regional center. Well-maintained buildings from the turn of the century house nearly 200 unique, mostly locally-owned, retail and service businesses. But this is more than a collection of retail shops. Located at the southern end of Grand Traverse Bay, the downtown features a recreational and cultural environment that is an attraction itself. The downtown area is also the civic center of our community, housing a renovated historic Courthouse, our Governmental Center, Visitors Center and library.

Clinch Park Beach and Marina, the Con Foster Museum, Clinch Park Zoo and the bay-side park called the Open Space all exist as a part of a city commitment to maintain publicly-owned bay frontage. The Traverse Area Recreational Trail, a non-motorized path, crosses through downtown as it makes its way along the bay from Acme to Leelanau County. The Open Space serves as a passive, open air park year-round, and is also the base for the National Cherry Festival held in July every year.

I am not a native, but after 15 years I am at least a "local." I moved here when the downtown was recovering from the impact of the first mall in the region. There were those who thought our downtown might not survive. After all, where is there a downtown still thriving after a mall came to town? But eventually, the market caught up with the additional retail space and the downtown began to thrive again. Today, we have several new malls and Walmart is breaking ground south of town. But there are no real retail vacancies downtown, new construction is underway and the small-town charm remains.

The most important thing I can impart about our downtown is this: We have a downtown that reminds everyone of the downtown they remember from their past. Our downtown has survived perhaps because the merchants and civic leaders had the experience of other cities to learn from. The sidewalks are well-maintained and tree-lined with a pedestrian scale that speaks of the past. The merchants are trained in contemporary service techniques and work together in a fashion that is rare. Downtown's organizational structure includes a traditional Downtown Development Authority (DDA), and one of the oldest and most successful merchants' organizations, the Downtown Traverse City Association (DTCA). Almost every one of the merchants voluntarily assesses themselves to support marketing and promotional efforts. The downtown features events year-round, but the most successful is the "Friday Night Live" series. On Friday evenings in late July and August, the streets are closed to traffic, and locals gather to enjoy food, music and each others' company. If you need a "fix" of small-town nostalgia, this event will provide it!

The retail mix downtown has changed over time so that it now contains a surprisingly diverse collection ranging from the unique to the traditional. While many of the traditional downtown anchors like Montgomery Wards and JC Penney's are gone, Milliken's Department Store remains and is joined by the recently re-located 16,000 square foot Horizon Book store. Horizon Books' move into the former Penney's space in 1992 was a signal that downtown, even in the face of over a million square feet of new retail space in the region, was not going to die like so many others. The bookstore contains a coffee bar and is a local gathering place. Home furnishings, specialty foods, clothing and accessories are all available downtown. And of course, given our tourism base, there are unique gift shops, galleries and T-shirt stores in abundance.

One aspect of downtown that remains unchanged, however, is respect for the community's history. The historic Park Place Hotel, which has roots in the late 1870's, was rebuilt in the 1930's, and is a ten story tribute to the community's past. The City Opera House located above storefronts on our main street was built in 1891, and now operates as a community hall and rental facility. Our library is a 1904 Carnegie facility sited along the Boardman river. The well-maintained Traverse City State Bank, built in 1903 and now owned by old Kent Bank, is one of Traverse City's sky-line features. In recent years historic buildings like the former city fire station and the candy factory have gone through renovations to make them usable again for retail activities.

We are not without our challenges. In order to face the massive additions of retail business outside our city limits we must be constantly moving to make better and more intensive use of our precious land downtown. That must be accomplished without destroying the unique small-town character we have worked so hard to maintain. We anticipate building parking decks in the near future, but recognize that these structures must blend with the environment and be integrated into our retail and office center. We realize that traffic congestion must be addressed, but not in such a way to discourage pedestrians.

I think a pleasant discovery newcomers find when moving to Traverse City, especially as it relates to downtown, is that there IS a downtown: A downtown where you can work, enjoy lunch at a picnic table on the bay or savor an ice cream cone along the river; a downtown you might bike or roller-blade through on your way along beautiful Grand Traverse Bay; a downtown where you can bring your visitors to shop and dine; a downtown where you can dance in the street on a warm summer Friday evening; a downtown where you can join your neighbors singing carols in front of a giant Christmas tree; a downtown where Santa is presented the key to the city by the Mayor after arriving in a vintage fire truck — a downtown you will fiercely defend. Not everyone is as passionate as I about our community's center, but I will bet you, too, in a short time will love this downtown. Directory of DDA Members

"Custom design, excellent repair service, and downtown location make this jewelry store a favorite. George and Laurie have energy and style." — C.L.

George & Laurie Wildman
Federico's Jewelry

I am the third generation in my family to own a business in Traverse City. Federico's, the fine jewelry store that I operate with my wife, Laurie, was founded in 1986 by my parents, Anthony and Marian Federico. The store has moved once since opening and is presently located on Front Street, downtown. I believe strongly in maintaining the downtown as a viable business center, and I foresee that this business will always remain downtown.

The store has recently undergone a remodeling which was done with the intention of giving the customer a more comfortable setting in which to shop. Often, repair work can be done in a short time and there is a place to relax while that is being done. Service is important to us. We recognize that new customers may feel uncomfortable leaving jewelry to be repaired when they first move to a community so we offer to let customers observe the repair process. Two goldsmith artisans work full time at the store, and one has his table in the front window so people can watch the jewelry-making process. Free parking behind the store allows a customer to drop off or pick up something quickly, if desired.

Creativity is an important part of this jewelry business. I believe that one's jewelry should be individual and unique and we custom design much of our work. Pieces can be created from an idea or a picture that a customer brings in. The first step in the design process is an appointment with the client. Then, a wax model is made up for the client's approval before the piece is cast. Our focus is on current and contemporary design, but we can make pieces in any style. Our shopping trips to the fine gem markets in New York assure that very high quality stones are readily available. We also carry Howard Miller grandfather clocks and Concord watches and we have plans to expand into other lines of fine jewelry. Our emphasis is on quality, and we will continue growth in the custom design aspect of the business.

We love living in Traverse City. We are especially happy about the growth of the arts in the area and we enjoy the proximity to Interlochen. Our home is close to downtown, and we hope that Traverse City's small town feeling will be maintained. We hope that people who move to the area will be supportive of the local business community so that it remains strong.

156 E. Front Street
Traverse City, MI 49684
Phone: 946-4252

"This shop is loaded with wonderful gift items. When you need a special present for someone (or yourself) this is the place to go. Godiva choclates!" — C.L.

Jim & Irene Beall
My Favorite Things & Peppercorn

Hi! We are Jim & Irene Beall, and we would like to welcome you to our gallery and gift shop, My Favorite Things, and our gourmet kitchen store, Peppercorn. Both stores are located in the heart of beautiful Downtown Traverse City, nestled among a variety of specialty shops and great restaurants.

We started My Favorite Things in 1981 in an outlying small town. The business grew, and in 1988 we relocated to Downtown Traverse City. In 1993, we opened Peppercorn. Three years later, both are going strong and have become the stores the local residents make sure they show to their out-of-town guests.

We buy carefully at trade shows throughout the U.S. We look for those items that other stores don't carry, and as a result, have become the stores where people comment, "You just don't find these things anyplace else." While our emphasis is to appeal to local residents, our merchandise lines are very popular with tourists. We have a strong repeat business from downstate visitors, many of whom would not visit Traverse City without stopping at our stores. At My Favorite Things, we offer Godiva Chocolates. At Peppercorn we have a wine tasting room where we taste and sell Chateau Grand Traverse wines, a locally grown and bottled wine.

We love this area. It is scenic and beautiful, and the bay looks different everyday. While Traverse City is growing, it still retains its friendly and hometown atmosphere of which the downtown is a central focus. Business is good, and because of our tourist season, it's like having Christmas twice a year. It is slower in the winter months following Christmas, but for other businesses, the winter season is strong. We take advantage of the slower times to travel to shows, complete those projects there hasn't been time for and to catch our breath before the summer season arrives.

Our personal philosophy is to always keep moving forward. Try new things, be daring, keep life interesting and enjoyable.

143 E. Front Street
Traverse City, MI 49684
Phone: 929-9665

"A definitely unique inventory. You'll need to go more than once just to absorb all this. We love it!" — C.L.

Molly Johnson
Guy Morrison
Firehouse Fair

fixtures. Customers love the old fireman's pole and Molly or Guy can easily be convinced to give kids, young or old, a treat by activating the fireman on the pole.

Molly was restoring dolls and doing repairs on antique doll houses at The Doll Hospital in Berkeley, Michigan, when she offered to spend some time helping her dad open the store in Traverse City. She decided to stay, and now does the buying. Her interest in antique dolls is evident, although the eclectic mix of merchandise is not concentrated in any one area.

"People are initially confused and intrigued when they enter the store," Molly said, "and that's just the way we want it." She feels there is a great interest in things both ancient and nostalgic as the end of the century approaches. People are looking back as they think about the year 2000.

Guy and his wife, Lyn, live on the Old Mission Peninsula. Molly and her husband, Tom, enjoy the relaxed lifestyle Traverse City has to offer. Even though some things take longer, there is plenty to do. They think people seem happier here. Molly is delighted with the activities available for her child: the beach, parks, art classes and nursery schools.

W e want a store that is crammed with beautiful things — nostalgia with a sense of humor."

This is how Molly Johnson described the vision her father, Guy Morrison, had when he was planning to open this unique and fascinating downtown store. This gift store is great fun, and as Molly says, " It's the only place in town where you can get a rubber chicken and a Picasso in the same store."

Firehouse Fair is located in the old Traverse City fire house on Union Street. Constructed in the 1890's, the building served as a fire hall until the mid-1970's. Since then, the building has housed a number of tenants, including Habitat for Humanity and others. It sat vacant for nine years before Guy Morrison decided to restore the building and convert it into this unusual store.

Guy is a commercial photographer, working mostly with automotive clients and their advertising agencies around the country. He bought the old fire hall in 1993 and spent over a year restoring it prior to opening. There is a single apartment above the store. He designed the massive doors for the building, the distinctive Dalmatian logo and the light

**118 Cass Street
Traverse City, MI 49684
Phone: 935-4442**

"Our favorite bookstore anywhere. We love to go in the evening for coffee and book browsing. It's a Traverse City treasure!" — C.L.

Vic Herman
Horizon Books

Horizon Books has been a core business in downtown Traverse City since its formation in 1960. Vic Herman and his family started the business and have been supporters of the growth and development of a strong viable downtown. The business started with 800 square feet, was expanded twice in its original location, and in 1993, moved across the street to a vacated, 12,000 sq. ft. department store. Two other stores were opened in Northern Michigan — Petoskey in the mid-70's and Cadillac in 1990.

The community seems to feel an emotional ownership toward this store as evidenced by the spontaneous volunteer effort that occurred during the move in 1993. Over 125 people spent the day moving the entire inventory of books across the street to the new location and stocked the shelves to get the store back in operation as quickly as possible. The Hermans were both pleased and amazed.

Customers love the vibrancy offered in the store's selections — Vic has always enjoyed ordering material that provokes discussion. All material is computerized and if a book is not in stock, the staff will check its availability and order it. The staff is enthusiastic and well versed in helping the customer.

243 E. Front Street
Traverse City, MI 49684
Phone: 946-7290

Joining the Horizon Encore Club allows the customer a 10% discount on many items, and the coffee shop makes this a great gathering spot. With long store hours, it's a great place to stop anytime to relax. Seating around the fireplace and the various bay views encourage people to linger and browse.

The store offers several group activities, including writers' and poetry support groups, a reading discussion group and a children's hour. The mezzanine is the center for multi-media materials. Vic is enthused about the growth of electronic publishing and envisions a strong emphasis on educational materials. The lower level will eventually be renovated to include a performance area.

Vic is strong advocate of keeping the small downtown feeling of Traverse City. The Hermans live just a few blocks from town and walk to work. They love the community and especially the feeling of a central gathering spot — downtown. By keeping the rampant growth on the outskirts of the downtown, they feel that we can retain the small town feeling loved by so many people who move to Traverse City.

"Browsing here is a treat. All the dealers are friendly and helpful and we always find what we are looking for." — C.L.

Frank & Carol Leonard
Wilson's Antiques

The Wilson name in Traverse City has always been equated with fine furniture, so it seems appropriate that it should be the name of the antique store on Union. In 1914, Frank Leonard's grandfather started the company in the Taylor Printing location and, in 1918, moved the business to its present location. As you browse through this old building looking for a treasure, remember to think of the history here. In the 1930's, the high school basketball team played its games on the third floor, and in 1955, the entire building was damaged by fire.

Today, Frank and his wife Carol continue to sell furniture from the location, but now it's antique furniture. The store is home to 45 antique dealers who display their wares. Each dealer works two days per month. It's a huge place — 22,000 square feet — and it is filled, on all four levels, with quality pieces. It's a great place to browse and, because of its downtown location, is often filled with tourists on rainy days. Parking in the back makes it easy to both shop and load up purchases. The dealers are highly reputable and stand behind the authenticity of their antiques. They are not just local dealers. Frank says he has dealers in the store from the Detroit area, Lansing, Petoskey and even Florida. Customers from all around the country frequent the store and a number of designers use the place as a source for their clients. The store is well kept and clean, making it a delight to explore.

Frank has lived his entire life on the Old Mission Peninsula and can't imagine being anywhere else. He may have a 15 mile commute, but he feels it's worth it because he is surrounded by so much natural beauty at home. From a business standpoint, the Leonards love getting to know their customers. Frank sees many positive changes in the area such as people who have moved here to create opportunities in sports and social activities that weren't available when he was a child. Now his children can take advantage of them.

123-125 South Union
Traverse City, MI 49684
Phone: 946-4177

"Head to Cali's for fun and unique apparel.
The accessories are great, especially the earrings." — C.L.

Alison Knowles
Cali's Cottons

Welcome. I'd like to introduce myself. I'm Alison Knowles of Cali's Cottons. I moved to Traverse City twelve years ago. Shortly thereafter, I opened my little shop on Union Street, downtown. Our natural fiber clothing and our unique selection of jewelry were a good fit for this area's simpler lifestyle. We soon became Traverse City's original boutique. I was happily housed in our Union Street location for eight years. Then, when my first child was born, I needed more space so we re-located to our spot on the East end of Front Street.

Even with the enlargement of the shop, we still maintain the intimate feeling that Cali's has become known for. At our present location we carry a diverse selection of natural fiber clothing, more jewelry and wonderful sundries for your home and person. You'll notice the difference on your first visit with the personal service we provide, and in our attention to detail in the clothing and accessories we carry. Our atmosphere is unhurried and friendly. The eclectic mix of one-of-a-kind finds is sure to delight your senses.

We invite you to come in and browse — you'll probably meet a few of your neighbors. We look forward to meeting you!

**242 E. Front Street
Traverse City, MI 49684
Phone: 947-0633**

Downtown Events Calendar

Every year, the DTCA sponsors a number of events. Following is a list of the events that were scheduled at the time of this publication. Many thanks to the DTCA for providing this information.

JUNE, 1996
7-28 Traverse Area Arts Council(TAAC) Gallery Small Summer Group Show
8 Bay Day - A Watershed Festival, 10am-5pm at Maritime Academy
9 Ribs, Bibs, Tall Ships & Kids for Big Brothers, Big Sisters, Open Space
22 Olde Towne Craft Bazaar, Union Street, Old Town
22 Koins for Kids for Child & Family Services, throughout downtown
22 Harley Owners Group Father Fred Fundraiser

JULY
5-26 TAAC Gallery Small Summer Group Show
6-13 National Cherry Festival (Blue Angels July 6-7)
7 Cherry Festival Arts & Crafts Fair, 10am-7pm on Union Street
20-8/4 Summer Rails Model Railroad Exhibit, 12-8pm, City Opera House, $1
24 Sidewalk Art Chalk Making Workshop for Artists
26 Friday Night Live, 5:30-9pm 100 & 200 blocks of E. Front. Streets close to traffic & open for music, games, food, & fun.

AUGUST
2-30 TAAC Gallery Small Summer Group Show
2 Street Sale and FNL, 8am-9pm 100 & 200 blocks of E. Front
3 100 S. Union Sidewalk Art
4 Artists Market at the Farmers Market Lot, Cass and Grandview Parkway
9 Friday Night Live, 5:30-9pm 100 & 200 blocks of E. Front
10 100 S. Union Sidewalk Art
11 Artists Market

16 Friday Night Live, 5:30-9pm 100 & 200 blocks of E. Front
17 100 S. Union Sidewalk Art
18 Artists Market
23 Friday Night Live, 5:30-9pm 100 & 200 blocks of E. Front
24 Downtown Art Fair, 10am-5pm, 100 E. Front St. 100 S. Union Sidewalk Art
25 Artists Market
30 Friday Night Live, 5:30-9pm 100 & 200 blocks of E. Front
31 100 S. Union Sidewalk Art

SEPTEMBER
6-27 TAAC Gallery All Media Juried Show "In Your Dreams"
7 2nd Annual Cherry Classic Downtown Car Show, 10am-5pm
27-28 Questers Antique Seminar, City Opera House

OCTOBER
4-25 TAAC Gallery Third Biennial Print Show
19-31 Haunted Opera House at the City Opera House

NOVEMBER
1-29 TAAC Gallery All Media Juried Show "It's About Time"
23 Window Unwrapping and Holiday Stroll
29 Santa's Arrival & Tree Lighting, 5:30-9pm 100 & 200 blocks of E. Front

DECEMBER
8 Kids Shopping Day and Clinch Park Zoo Christmas for the Animals
14 Romance Night, Valentine's Day in December
20-1/5 Festival of Trains at the City Opera House

FEBRUARY, 1997
15 3rd Annual Downtown Chili Cook-Off, City Opera House, 12-3pm

DTCA Members

A Step Above, 217 1/2 E. Front St.
ABCD's, 430 E. Front St., 946-2112
Accents, 140 E. Front/Arcade 941-1737
All American Sports Col., 158 E. Front St. 933-5339
All That Jazz126 Boardman 946-1537
American Spoon Foods, 230 E. Front St. 935-4480
Americana Collection, 224 E. Front St. 933-0297
Anamalia, 140 E. Front St.
Andrew Kan Travel Service, 135 E. Front St. 946-1690
Angelic Images, 140 E. Front/Arcade 946-9019
Annie's, 247 E. Front St. 946-6201, 941-7166
Attitude T's, 161 E. Front St. 946-3957
Auto Service Ctr-Goodyear, 436 W. Front St. 922-2600
Backcountry Outfitters, 227 E. Front St. 946-1339
Bananarama, 127 E. Front St. 941-0057
Bartling's, 225 E. Front St. 946-8002
Bavarian Village Ski/Golf, 107 E. Front St. 941-1999
Bay Bridal Boutique, 109 S. Union #206 929-2636
Bear Affair Activewear, 140 E. Front/Arcade 941-4346
Belstone Gallery & Gifts, 321 E. Front St. 946-0610
Ben Franklin Crafts, 101 E. Front St. 929-0606
Bill Dwyer Co., 120 S. Union St. 941-8422
Bilmar Sports Inc., 211 E. Front St. 947-8005
Bittersweet Gifts, 525 W. Front St. 941-8077
Bookie Joint, 120 S. Union St. 946-8862
Brady's Bar, 401 S. Union 946-8153
Burritoville, 236 E. Front St.
Cali's Cottons, 242 E. Front St. 947-0633 947-8745
Camera Shop, 114 E. Front St. 946-7150
Captain's Quarters, 151 E. Front St. 946-7066
Carlson's Fish Market, 511 W. Front St. 941-9392
Cathie's Tote And Dine, 104 Cass St. 929-4771
Cedar Creek Interiors, 415 S. Union St.
Celebrations, 126 Lake Ave. 941-4554
Chef's In, 519 W. Front St. 941-1144
Children's World, 140 E. Front/Arcade 946-3450
Christian Science Reading, 118 S. Union 947-6293
Christopher-Jon, 441 E. Front St. 947-6944
City Bike Shop, 322 S. Union St. 947-1312
Coins & Collectibles, 129 E. State St. 947-3940
Conch Connection, 330 E. Front St. 922-0221
Cousin Jenny's, 129 S. Union St. 941-7821
Custer's Last Stamp, 123 E. Front St.935-3700
D.J. Kelly's, 120 Park St.941-4550
Dandelion Inc., 130 E. Front St. 933-4340 933-4346
DeYoung's Wallpaper/Paint, 234 E. Front St. 946-8021
Dill's of Michigan, 423 S. Union St. 947-7534
Dillinger's Pub, 121 S. Union St. 941-2276
Dillon's, 153 E. Front St. 941-1616
Diversions, 140 E. Front/Arcade 946-6500
Doug Murdick's Fudge, 116 E. Front St. 947-4841
Downtown Big Boy, 161 E. Front St. 941-2020

Eb.A.Shae, 137 E. Front St. 947-0708
Evergreen Gallery, 531 W. Front St. 929-9522
Everts Jewelers, 222 E. Front St. 941-7231
Eye Designs, 324 E. Front St. 946-0560
Fascinations, 140 E. Front/Arcade 922-0051
Fashions for Two, 118 S. Union 941-2015
Federico Jewelers Ltd., 156 E. Front St. 946-4252
Field Crafts, 129 1/2 E. Front St. 941-4440
Fivenson Food Equipment, 324 S. Union St. 946-7760
Folgarelli Import Market, 424 W. Front St. 941-7651
Fun Factory, 408 S. Union
Futons and More, 150 E. Front St. 922-6757
Gold & Silver Center, 126 E. Front St. 947-3363
Golden Shoes, 122 E. Front St. 947-6924
Good Harbor Chocolates, 111 W. Front St. 935-4166
Good News Music, 140 E. Front/Arcade 946-1230
Grand Bay Kite Co., 121 E. Front St. 929-0607
Grand Traverse Auto, 124 W. Front St. 922-2000
Great Frame Up, 145 E. Front St. 946-9302
Habersham, 427 S. Union 929-2666
Hair Quarters, 509 S. Union 947-6666
Harbor Wear, 125 E. Front St. 935-4688
Hibbard's-Plantasia, 312 S. Union St. 946-6460
Hickory Stitches, 417 S. Union 946-6050
Higher Self, 328 E. Front St. 941-5805
Hocus Pocus, 140 E. Front/Arcade 941-0556
Holiday Inn, 615 E. Front St. 947-3700
Horizon Books Inc., 243 E. Front St. 946-7290 946-2545
Id, 212 E. Front St. 947-0821
Impres Salon, 420 S. Union St. 941-1027
Instant Framer, 445 E. Front St. 947-8908
J&S Hamburg, 302 W. Front St. 947-6409
Jack's Party Mart, 448 E. Front St. 947-6170
Justin Parish Salons, 518 E. Front St. 946-9171
Karen's Uniforms, 116 S. Union St. 941-1960
Kay's, 219 E. Front St. 941-7505
Kilwin's Chocolate Shoppe, 129 E. Front St. 946-2403
Kinney's Pioneer Service, 128 S. Union 946-7180
Kitchen & Co., 122 Cass 938-4044
Kroneberger's, 121 E. Front #106 922-8723
Krouse Tire, 310 W. Front St. 946-1710
Bo-Beer / Kuch's Deli, 542 W. Front St. 947-6779
Kurtz Music & Sound, 237 E. Front St. 947-3730
La Cuisine Amical, 229 E. Front St. 941-8888 941-8893
Leaping Lizard, 207 E. Front St. 935-4470
Left Bank Cafe, 439 E. Front St. 929-9060
L'il Bo's Bar, 540 W. Front St. 946-6925
Lost Art Yarn Shoppe, 123 E. Front St. 941-1263
Lutfy's Hallmark Shop, 209 E. Front St. 947-1040
MTA Travel, 336 E. Front St. 946-8030
Main Street Inn, 618 E. Front St. 929-0410
Martinek's Jewelers, 217 E. Front St. 946-4664

Mary's Kitchen Port, 539 W. Front St. 941-0525
Max's Service, 135 E. State St. 947-6830
Maxbauer's Market, 407 S. Union St. 947-7698
Michigan Rag Co., 104 E. Front St. 947-8722
Milliken's, 204 E. Front St. 947-5140
Milliken's Man, 206 E. Front St. 947-5140
Miner's North Jewelers, 157 E. Front St. 946-8528
Mode's Bum Steer, 125 E. State St. 947-9832 946-3249
Modern Cleaners, 501 W. Front St. 946-8013
Mr. Bill's Shirt Co., 228 E. Front St. 941-1022
Muffin Tin & Sundries, 115 Wellington St. 929-7915
My Favorite Things, 143 E. Front St. 929-9665
Nautical Works, 102 E. Front St. 929-3774
Nesbitt's Hardware, 417 S. Union 947-5434
New Attitudes, 220 E. Front St. 922-2262
New Moon Records & Tapes, 240 E. Front St. 941-1035
Nolan's Tobacco, 336 E. Front St. 946-2640
Nutcracker, 205 E. Front St. 947-3121
Old Town Kid Stuff, 418 S. Union St. 941-0410
Old Town Optical, 515 S. Union 946-0333
Olde Towne Hair, 412 S. Union
Omelette Shoppe, 124 Cass 946-0912
One Hour Martinizing, 115 Pine St. 946-4990
Paesano's Pizza, 447 E. Front St. 941-5740
Painted Door Gallery, 108 S. Union St. 929-4988
Park Place Hotel, 300 E. State St. 946-5000
Passageways Travel, P.O. Box 512 947-0880
Pavlova Day Salon, 114 S. Union 941-5707
Peddler's Corner, 426 W. Front St. 947-1198
Peek-A-Boo, 140 E. Front/Arcade 933-4991
Peppercorn, 226 E. Front St. 941-4146
Petertyl Drugs & Gifts, 111 E. Front St. 946-4830
Petty Stuff, 119 S. Union 933-4060
Plamondon Shoes, 144 E. Front St. 947-5091
Poppycock's, 128 E. Front St. 941-7632
Pratt's, 215 E. Front St. 946-2020
Professional Office Sup., 148 E. Front St. 946-5727
Progress Laundry, 329 E. State St. 946-8480
Pure Essence Salon, 414 E. Front St. 935-1808
Randy's Olde Towne, 430 S. Union 947-0939
Raven's Child, 516 E. Front St. 941-8552
Ray's Coffeehouse, 129 E. Front St. 929-1006
Riecker's Outdoor Gallery, 134 E. Front St. 946-0414
Robertson's Barber Shop, 109 S. Union St. 946-8392
S & J Pasta Company, 221 E. State 922-7732

Screen Plus, 308 E. Front St. 947-1977
Selkirk's, 302 E. Front St. 946-0366
She, 154 E. Front St. 929-1444
Snap Quick Print, 131 E. State St. 946-4702
So Many Books, 140 E. Front/Arcade 922-5916
Soaps & Scents, 121 E. Front St. 946-3543
Spring Hollow, 414 S. Union 946-2578
St. Julian Wine, 127 E. Front St. 933-6120
State Theatre, 233 E. Front St. 947-9684
Stereo Shoppe, 110 E. Front St. 946-1340
Stewart-Zacks, 118 E. Front St. 947-2322
Stone Soup II, 115 E. Front St. 941-1190
Strom's Career Apparel, 217A Lake Ave. 941-5447
Studio 101, 101 W. Front St. 946-7953
Subway Sandwiches, 136 E. Front St. 929-7972
Sundance Soccer, 114 E. Front St. 941-9640
T.C. Athletic Club, 428 E. Front St. 929-7247
Taylor Printing, 127 S. Union St. 946-7101
The Blind Site, 219 1/2 E. Front 941-1500
The Clipper, 443 E. Front St. 947-6894
The Copy Shop, 514 E. Front St. 947-2080
The Firehouse Fair, 118 Cass 935-4442
The Recklace Necklace, 140 E. Front/Arcade 922-2102
The Styles Inn, 411 S. Union 947-3512
The Vintage Bean, 406 S. Union 933-0942
Thirlby Automotive, 231 E. 8th St. 947-8120
Timbuktu Station, 238 E. Front St. 947-9665
Toy Harbor, 221 E. Front St. 946-1131
Trains & Things Hobbies, 106 E. Front St. 947-1353
Traverse City Bakery/Cafe, 149 E. Front St. 946-1516
Traverse City Shirt Co., 223 E. Front St. 929-3352
Traverse Country Store, 218 E. Front St. 941-0961
Trinkets, 102 S. Union St. 947-9401
Trophey Trolley, 152 E. Front St. 922-8755
Twin Bay Sportscards, 311 E. State St. 941-5811
U & I Lounge, 214 E. Front St. 946-8932
Union Street Station, 117 S. Union St. 941-1930
Up North Traders, 155 E. Front St. 935-0264
Verbenas, 140 E. Front/Arcade 941-0628
Votruba Leather Goods, 112 E. Front St. 947-5615
Weathervane, 108 E. Front St. 947-2460
Whimsicality, 502 E. Front St. 941-1444
Wildflowers, 332 E. Front St. 935-1516
Wilson's Antiques, 123 S. Union 946-4177
Wooden Gallery, 116 E. Front St. 941-0823

Education

Chapter 5

Education

Timothy Quinn
President, Northwestern Michigan College

Education in the Grand Traverse region is distinguished by its spirit of commitment and collaboration. Cooperative partnerships are visible and viable at every level, among the schools themselves, and with business, industry, government, agencies and individuals.

Because the citizens have made education a priority, this area has a variety of excellent public and private institutions. Now, faced with significant growth and change, northwest Michigan understands the need to keep education at the top of the list in order to preserve its unique quality of life.

One major recent initiative which demonstrates the cooperative nature of education is the University Center at Northwestern Michigan College (NMC). Early in 1992, a group of 135 community leaders from throughout Antrim, Benzie, Grand Traverse, Kalkaska and Leelanau counties gathered to discuss how to meet the higher education needs of the 21st Century. The following year, they recommended the creation of a "University Center" at the two-year NMC which would involve a number of four-year Michigan universities and colleges in a partnership with NMC and the region's public schools to provide bachelor's and advanced degrees to area residents—right here in Northern Michigan. An $8.8 million fund-raising campaign was another

successful collaborative venture— the University Center opened in the fall of 1995.

The "Founders 21 Committee" was modeled on the original grassroots effort which established NMC in 1951 to meet the higher education needs of that time. Just as in the 1950's, this region is still geographically isolated from four-year institutions, a barrier which keeps many people from completing their education. Today, however, technology can travel the miles that people cannot. Thus, "Project Interconnect" was part of the University Center program—a distance education network which provides two-way audio/video interactive classrooms in 15 area high schools as well as at NMC and the institutions in partnership with the University Center.

Michael McIntyre, superintendent of the Traverse Bay Area Intermediate School District, said, "A high degree of collaboration among the K-Adult education providers within the region along with state-of-the-art voice, video and data technologies will continue to rank the quality of education in this five-county region among the very best in the state. These assets are enhanced by a sense of pride among area residents and a commitment from business leaders to provide access for every citizen to learning experiences which lead to successful employment."

Other cooperative ventures include the School to Work program which seeks to provide meaningful career preparation for all young people; the consolidation of occupational programs between NMC and Traverse Bay Area Intermediate School District (TBA) to achieve a more seamless learning experience and shared resources; and coordination of millage campaigns to maximize support of the whole educational program.

Dr. Peter Wharton, superintendent of Traverse City Area Public Schools, said, "The direct involvement and collaboration of all area educational organizations, parents, business and other community members is an essential component to maintain progress and prepare our students for their adult lives. We share with the community the responsibility of preparing our youth to meet the challenges of life complicated by a rapidly changing society. Our sphere of responsibility encompasses the academic, vocational, social, and cultural aspects of students' lives. We must educate students in ways that encourage them to respond with wisdom and maturity."

The challenges which the Grand Traverse region faces are primarily related to growth and change. Our school systems must encourage local citizens to prepare for growth and provide the resources which support enlightened decisions and creative responses. This collaboration has never been more essential in this era of diminishing resources and increasing expectations. Looking ahead, the Grand Traverse region has many reasons to be confident about its educational institutions.

Mary Oosterhouse, superintendent of the Grand Traverse Area Catholic Schools, said, "Education in the Grand Traverse area is seen as a community effort; therefore, all of us, public and private, work together to educate the children of this 'village'." Small enough to provide meaningful involvement and large enough to provide academic excellence, our schools and college are a growing resource for this growing region.

"Not simply daycare! Pam has built a diverse program of classes and activities with a full measure of computer education." — *P.L.*

Pamela Yeager
Alphabet Soup Pre-School and Day Care Center

M y husband, John, and I moved to Traverse City from the Ann Arbor area in 1989. The move was not a difficult one since John's consulting clients were not dependent on where we lived, and I was able to put my real estate broker's license to good use immediately. Once settled, we began looking for another business to buy.

In 1992, we bought Aunt Barb's Daycare and changed the name to Alphabet Soup Pre-School and Day Care Center. Because of my background in early Ed teaching and the desire to further test my management skills, we decided this might be a good fit. The day after we changed the name, the enrollment began to accelerate.

We focused our own philosophy for the business and changed it from one of day care to one of education. By doing so, we challenged our staff to make the best use of the time the children were in our center. We also wanted to enrich the children with experiences that often seem to be in short supply in our working-parent society.

We recognize that the uniqueness of Alphabet Soup

is dependent on the staff we hire. This means hiring a staff educated in the habits of young children and understanding of their learning capabilities. With the aid of pre-employment testing, we select staff members who meet our high standards. Our enlightened staff have helped us add a number of new programs to our curriculum including: summer day camps, pre-kindergarten classes, kindergarten classes, MST Techno Kids, adult computer classes and camps and Super Saturday classes.

Traverse City is a wonderful place to leap into a new business. This really is a community of risk-takers and entrepreneurs who show support for those who want to make a difference in the area. My advice to prospective business owners is to know your capabilities and resources. Establishing solid contacts in the community before relocating is also helpful. To succeed, you must continually nurture and grow your business to meet the needs of our ever-changing community.

222 E. 14th Street
Traverse City, MI 49684
Phone: 941-1330

"We really need a new library in Traverse City. Three cheers for Dick and CFL for spearheading this initiative." — P.L.

A New Library for Traverse City

Richard F. Rosser

C itizens for Libraries (CFL), a group of volunteers, was organized in the summer of 1995. Our objective is to bring a new district library to Grand Traverse County through a proposal to be presented to county voters in the middle of September, 1996. This grassroots effort is a fascinating example of the extraordinary civic spirit evident in so many public projects in or around Traverse City. An amazing amount of energy is directed toward the improvement of the Traverse region on a wide range of fronts. One indication is the number of major fund raising drives currently underway.

When we first considered Traverse City as a retirement location, we drove by the Carnegie library on 6th Street. I assumed at the time that this was a small branch building. Later, I learned that I had

Citizens for Libraries
2161 Harbor Reach Drive
Traverse City, MI 49686
Phone: 223-4243

seen the library. Not surprisingly, I also learned that many long time residents have been frustrated for years with this facility. People have been embarrassed to show out-of-town guests their library, built in 1905 with a "modern" wing added in 1965.

The contrasts with progress elsewhere were dramatic. We have a beautiful new museum and a fine center for undergraduate and graduate study at the college with a new high school in the offing. But nothing had been done to bring a modern library to our region, in spite of the extraordinary usage of the hopelessly outdated 6th Street facility. There currently are 19,000 active cardholders. We expect that number will grow substantially when the new facility is completed.

The new library will be at least three times the size of the current library and will combine the latest technology with more traditional library materials. As far as we can see into the future, books, magazines, journals and newspapers will be needed. Children must have space for story hour programs, high school students need space to research papers and study, as do people of all ages engaging in life long learning. The computer can do some things very well, but it will never substitute for a library — the one free educational institution for all citizens.

The *Traverse City Record-Eagle* editorialized about the need for a new initiative in March 1995, noting, after listing the progress in so many other fields, that it was finally time to do something about the library. The League of Women Voters had also been monitoring the situation for many years and was ready to help organize an initiative for a new library. In August 1995, CFL was organized to serve as a adjunct resource for the Library Board. CFL assists in planning, analysis, fund raising, public relations and political campaigning.

At this writing, we are about halfway through our year-long effort to organize. Committees are in place and we have over 400 volunteers working with us. Many of these volunteers are recent arrivals in Traverse City, almost all having used newer library facilities in their previous homes. Many of our volunteers are retired senior citizens, public spirited and still very active. At least half of our key positions are held by seniors.

Our first task is to get a "yes" vote in September. Two earlier proposals to raise capital and increase operating millage were soundly defeated in 1991. Next, we will build a new main district library. The cost of this will be approximately $6 million.

After that, we will find a new use for the Carnegie building — possibly as a headquarters for deserving non-profit organizations such as the historical society, genealogical groups, the Maritime Heritage Alliance, etc. The future of the Carnegie building was a bitter and divisive issue in 1991, with residents wanting to preserve "their" library, and citizens elsewhere in the county wanting a totally new main building.

We want to locate the one main library in or near downtown and we currently have an option on property on Boardman Lake near Eighth Street and Woodmere. Since this will be the county building used by more people than any other, it must be located close to other governmental buildings. We also do not want the library to contribute to further urban sprawl.

We will link the main library electronically with the member libraries, the schools and the college to maximize service and reduce duplication. This integration has been a serious concern for many citizens who wonder why we need "all these libraries." Once state-of-the-art linkage is in place, we may consider new branches or new facilities elsewhere

We will be asking benefactors from our region for as much as $2 million (including the site cost) that the voters will need to approve a bond proposal of as little as $6 million. This is considerably less than the proposal that was turned down in 1991, and this "bargain" will have a powerful appeal. Such philanthropy will be in the great tradition of Andrew Carnegie who financed the original building, and Perry Hannah, a local entrepreneur, who made a gift of the land.

Please contact us if you would like to help with building the new library for this vibrant community of ours.

ABOUT OUR LIBRARY
from Citizens for Libraries

LIBRARY FAST FACTS

The Traverse Area District Library (TADL) system covers Grand Traverse County and Elmwood Township, and has 22,000 users served by the Sixth Street main Library in Traverse City, The East Bay Branch, and member libraries on Old Mission Peninsula, Interlochen, Kingsley and Fife Lake. The Sixth Street main library is used by more area residents of all ages than any other public building in the area.

The main library was last expanded in 1965. Between 1965 and 1995, the population of Grand Traverse County nearly doubled, and continues to grow.

In 1965, 80,000 items were checked out. In 1995, circulation has grown to 500,000 items, a six-fold increase.

In Grand Traverse County, library funding at present costs a family living in an average priced home only $23 per year; the price of a night out at the movies and less than the cost of one new hardcover book.

Every year, Americans visit their libraries 3.5 billion times and check out an average of six books. More children take part in summer reading programs than play Little League baseball.

QUESTIONS AND ANSWERS

Why does the Grand Traverse Community need to upgrade its main library?

The district's Sixth Street library was built in 1905 and was last expanded and modernized 30 years ago. The main library is far too small for our community's present and future use.

Why not expand the present facility?

The site is too small for expansion. Parking space is grossly inadequate.

What will happen to the Carnegie Library building?

The TADL board, city officials, and Citizens for Libraries are studying ways to preserve this architectural treasure and find new uses for it compatible with library purposes.

Where would a new library be located?

Traverse City is the cultural core of this area. Our sense of community and neighborhood focuses the site search in or near downtown. (At this writing, a tentative site has been selected south of the corner of Eighth Street and Woodmere, overlooking the north end of Boardman Lake.)

How would a new library be funded?

Bond issues, operating millages and private gifts. How much will be needed depends on the size of the new facility and the kinds of modern services the community wants. Member libraries may also need more money for operations and physical improvement.

How can I help?

For information, call 922-9696.

ELK RAPIDS SCHOOLS
707 E. 3rd, Elk Rapids, 264-8692

GLEN LAKE COMMUNITY SCHOOLS
3375 W. County Road, Maple City, 334-3061

GRAND TRAVERSE CATHOLIC SCHOOLS
941-5621 (Executive Director's Office)
123 E. 11th, 946-8100

KALKASKA PUBLIC SCHOOLS
Birch Elementary School, 309 N. Birch, 258-8629

KINGSLEY AREA SCHOOLS
Blair Street, 263-5161

LEELANAU SCHOOL THE
Glenn Arbor, 334-3072

LELAND PUBLIC SCHOOL
Pearl, Leland, 256-9857

LIVING GOD CHRISTIAN SCHOOL
1514 Birmely, 946-5276

MANCELONA PUBLIC SCHOOLS
112 St. Johns Avenue, Mancelona, 587-5401

MIGRANT SCHOOL PROGRAMS
701 S. Elmwood, 946-6660

MONTESSORI ELEMENTARY SCHOOL
967 Elm St., Suttons Bay, 271-4454

NORTHPORT PUBLIC SCHOOLS
104 Wing, Northport, 386-5153

PATHFINDER SCHOOL THE
11930 S. West Bay Shore Drive, 946-7820

ST. MARY'S SCHOOL
310 St. Mary, Lake Leelanau, 256-9636

SEVENTH-DAY ADVENTIST SCHOOL
5625 Gray Road, 947-4640

SUTTONS BAY PUBLIC SCHOOLS
310 Elm, Suttons Bay, 271-3846

TRINITY LUTHERAN SCHOOL
1003 S. Maple, 946-2721

TRAVERSE BAY AREA INTERMEDIATE SCHOOL DISTRICT ADMINISTRATION
Traverse City, 922-6200

CAREER TECH CENTER
880 Parsons Road, Traverse City, 922-6273

SPECIAL EDUCATION SERVICES
Traverse City, 922-6200

TRAVERSE CITY AREA PUBLIC SCHOOLS
922-6400

ELEMENTARY SCHOOLS

BERTHA VOS
3722 Shore Drive, Acme, 938-4466

BLAIR
1625 Sawyer, Traverse City, 943-8655

CENTRAL GRADE SCHOOL
301 W. 7th Street, Traverse City, 922-6505

CHERRY KNOLL
1800 3 Mile Road, N., Traverse City, 922-6515

COURTADE
1111 Rasho Road, Traverse City, 922-6585

EAST BAY
3962 3 Mile Road, N., Traverse City, 922-6525

EASTERN
1600 Eastern Avenue, Traverse City, 922-6530

GLENN LOOMIS
1009 Oak Street, Traverse City, 922-6535

INTERLOCHEN
S. M-137, Interlochen, 276-9561

LONG LAKE
7738 N. Long Lake Rd., Traverse City, 922-6540

NORRIS
10781 E. Cherry Bend Rd., Traverse City, 922-6545

OAK PARK
301 S. Garfield Ave., Traverse City, 922-6550

OLD MISSION PENINSULA
2735 Island View Road, Old Mission, 223-4234

ST. FRANCIS ELEMENTARY
130 E. 10th Street, 946-5961

SABIN
2075 Cass Road, Traverse City, 922-6555

SILVER LAKE
5858 Culver Road, Traverse City, 943-4353

TRAVERSE HEIGHTS
933 Rose, Traverse City, 922-6560

WESTWOODS
1500 Fisher Road, Traverse City, 922-6580

WILLOW HILL
1250 Hill, Traverse City, 922-6565

MIDDLE AND JUNIOR HIGH SCHOOLS

EAST JUNIOR HIGH SCHOOL
1776 3 Mile Road, N., Traverse City, 922-8800

WEST JUNIOR HIGH SCHOOL
3950 W. Silver Lake, Traverse City, 922-6700

IMMACULATE CONCEPTION MIDDLE SCHOOL
218 Vine, 947-1252

HIGH SCHOOLS

TC SENIOR HIGH SCHOOL
1150 Milliken Drive, Traverse City, 922-6600

ST. FRANCIS HIGH SCHOOL
123 E. 11th Street, 946-8038

COLLEGES & UNIVERSITIES

CENTRAL MICHIGAN UNIVERSITY
Traverse City Office
2200 Dendrinos Drive, 922-0537

ENTERPRISE LEARNING LAB
1701 E. Front Street, 929-3751

FERRIS STATE UNIVERSITY OFFICE
Campus Program
1701 E. Front Street, 922-1734

MICHIGAN STATE UNIVERSITY
812 S. Garfield Avenue, 929-3902

NORWESTERN MICHIGAN COLLEGE & UNIVERSITY CENTER
1701 E. Front Street, 922-1000

Employment

Employment

Bill Echlin
Traverse City Record-Eagle

The employment picture in the Grand Traverse Area, while generally good, has been steadily improving over the past several years. In 1995, the jobless rate in Grand Traverse County, the largest job market in the region, hovered around six percent, slightly above the state and national averages. That is a distinct improvement over past decades when the unemployment rate was consistently much higher than state and national rates and the job market was whipped through severe seasonal and cyclical swings.

Thanks in part to a vigorous jobs development program created by the Traverse Bay Economic Development Corp. — and a steadily growing population — the area has seen a strong growth in a number of sectors. Much of that has been fueled by a growing manufacturing base. Another important factor has been the emergence of Traverse City and surrounding communities as the hub in northern lower Michigan for health care, higher education, tourism, financial and professional services and wholesale and retail trade.

Traverse City and Grand Traverse County are the dominant job markets for the five-county Grand Traverse Bay region as illustrated by commuting patterns. Nearly 40 percent of the workers in Benzie, Kalkaska, and Antrim counties find their jobs in Grand Traverse County and that figure rises to more than 50 percent + for the workers living in Leelanau County. Only eight percent of Grand Traverse County workers are employed outside of their county.

If there is a downside to living and working in the Grand Traverse area, it would have to be that pay levels are below the state and national averages — but that gap is narrowing. This trend should continue if the projections of labor force availability and job growth by the Traverse Bay Development Corp. are accurate. The organization sees annual unemployment rates steadily falling over the next 10 years to an estimated 4.7 percent. As the supply of available workers shrinks in respect to jobs growth, it is expected that wages and benefits will rise. Even so, the slightly cynical motto often heard in the region, that "A view of the bay is worth half the pay," will probably remain true to a degree. Grand Traverse pay levels are about 10 percent below Michigan averages, especially for lower-skill, non-management positions.

The Grand Traverse Area was ahead of the national trend in terms of the economic shift from a manufacturing to a services-based economy. Nearly three quarters of all jobs are in the services sector while manufacturing employs less than one fifth of the workforce. Unlike the national trend, however, manufacturing in the area has been growing significantly over the past several years. That has been partly due to the rebounding health of the auto sector and the increase in orders to local parts suppliers. This growth spurt also has been related to new start-ups in the high-tech areas, rising export sales by local producers and a fast-expanding rubber and plastics industry.

One of the blessings of a fast-growing economy is that nearly anyone with basic skills and good work habits can find a job. In fact, employers have been complaining for the past several years that they can't find enough qualified people. That applies all the way from entry-level, low-skilled positions to high-pay, high-skill jobs. Many have resorted to advertising in downstate papers in an effort to induce qualified people to move to the area.

Here's a brief look at the job market situation sector by sector:

CONSTRUCTION: Thanks to high demand for housing, new schools being built, a booming retail sector that is adding millions of square feet of store space, and a major highway expansion program, the construction industry is in the middle of a major jobs expansion. In December, 1995, at a low point in the year for building activity, construction companies in Grand Traverse County employed 225 more people than a year earlier — a 6.4 percent jobs growth. All indicators are that construction will continue to be a vigorous sector of the economy.

MANUFACTURING: Here the picture is somewhat less positive in the short run but more optimistic over the next several years. Because of a slowdown in sales growth in the auto industry in 1995, which is expected to continue into 1996, manufacturing jobs growth has been negligible, especially in the areas of metalworking, casting, light assembly and small electrical components. The upside is local manufacturing operations are quickly modernizing and diversifying with many qualifying as tier-one auto suppliers, meaning they have a better chance in the future to gain new orders from automakers. Another positive factor is the growth of high-valued-added operations which are not as sensitive to transportation cost factors as are low-value, commodity producers. Being on the far end of the transportation network to major markets has, to some degree, worked against the manufacturing sector in the area but that diminishes in importance as industry shifts to higher-value-added work.

Demand for high-skilled labor in this sector is strong and will likely continue to be. Tool and die workers, pattern makers, engineers and designers can command pay and benefit levels nearly as high as some metro markets in Michigan. Unskilled labor, on the other hand, will earn less in the Grand Traverse area than in larger, more unionized cities.

SERVICE PRODUCING INDUSTRIES: Growth is occurring in nearly all areas of services work from retail store clerk jobs to bank executive and resort manager positions. Retail trade in 1995 added nearly 600 new jobs in Grand Traverse County, compared to a year earlier, while health care, lodging and other private services created nearly 900 new jobs in the same period — a 5.6 percent growth rate.

Some Employment Resources

EMPLOYMENT AGENCIES

Management Recruiters International, Inc.
120 Boardman
929-2195

The Resource Group
12935 West Bayshore Drive
941-5063

Sales Consultants of Traverse City
124 N. Division Street
935-4000

EMPLOYMENT CONTRACTORS— TEMPORARY HELP

Kelly Temporary Services
3155 Logan Valley
947-8532

Manpower Temporary Services
441 W. Front Street
947-3840

Old Town Employment Services
420 S. Division
935-4127

Physicians Management Service Organization
109 E. Front Street
935-0400

TC Temps
401 W. Front Street
947-1001

EMPLOYMENT SCREENING

J. A. Yeager and Associates
6445 Mission Ridge
946-8378

EMPLOYEE LEASING

Simplified Employment Services
432 Bay East Drive
929-0807

EMPLOYMENT TRAINING

JOBNET
1144 Boon Street
929-5098

Private Industry Council
2200 Dendrinos Drive
929-5000

Financial Services

Financial Services

Susan Bondy
President, Bondy Financial Services

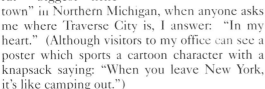

When I first moved here, my New York friends asked: "Where on Earth is Traverse City?" To which I would reply: "Oh, about 250 miles beyond the 'Resume Speed' sign after leaving Detroit."

After seven years of living in this wonderful "biggest little town" in Northern Michigan, when anyone asks me where Traverse City is, I answer: "In my heart." (Although visitors to my office can see a poster which sports a cartoon character with a knapsack saying: "When you leave New York, it's like camping out.")

In spite of the long winters, adjusting to Traverse City was much easier than I thought it would be. Within one year, I had as many friends here as I left behind in New York, and my professional career continued to grow.

My nationally syndicated financial column "Bondy on Money" continued to be transmitted to my Los Angeles syndicate via computer just as it was in New York, Toledo and Detroit. The

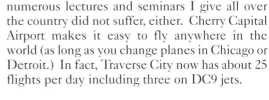

numerous lectures and seminars I give all over the country did not suffer, either. Cherry Capital Airport makes it easy to fly anywhere in the world (as long as you change planes in Chicago or Detroit.) In fact, Traverse City now has about 25 flights per day including three on DC9 jets.

Financial and investment services in the Traverse City area are abundant and varied including: bank trust departments, full service as well as discount brokerage firms, independent money management firms, insurance brokers and agents, financial advisors and fee-only financial planners.

With the advent of sophisticated communications and computer technologies, investment services no longer need to be located in major money centers. At times being far away from the "maddening crowds" can actually help professionals keep their cool.

And there is one other advantage to living in Traverse City: you end up knowing many of the players personally.

There has been only one drawback to my own move to Traverse City — neither "Good Morning America" nor "The Today Show" has asked me back since they re-classified me as geographically undesirable - their designation for: "No longer living in Manhattan."

Well, too bad. I'm left with the beautiful views, wonderful friends, clean air, pure water, a caring community, stimulating cultural events, a sense of personal safety and a growing business.

"This CPA firm has a solid history of service in the TC business community. Their sterling reputation is well deserved."—P.L.

George J. Freeman, Jr.,

Managing Partner
Gavigan, Burkhart,
Freeman & Co. , P.L.L.C.

Gavigan, Burkhart Freeman & Co is the largest public accounting firm in Northern Michigan and we have been a part of the growing Traverse City community for over seventeen years. As Traverse City's client base has grown and prospered, so has Gavigan, Burkhart. The firm has grown to a total staff of 30, with offices located in Traverse City and Gaylord, and we are still growing.

"Service and Quality" sets Gavigan, Burkhart apart from all other accounting firms. The firm is composed of a team of dedicated professionals, each with special industry skills and areas of expertise. We believe in the philosophy of providing sound business skills and judgment combined with close personal attention in charting a successful course for our clients.

Tell your friends and relatives who are in the accounting profession that we are continually looking for good people! The Traverse City community provides a family-oriented atmosphere with a wide variety of year-round activities. Traverse City residents are friendly and the beauty of the area is unsurpassed. The unique combination of industry, service and tourism found here provides a means for career opportunities and earning potential in a fantastic place to live.

We welcome you to the Grand Traverse region! We are confident that you will experience an enjoyable and prosperous future here.

1010 South Garfield
Traverse City, MI 49686
Phone: 947-7800

"Not only is Randy doing a great job here for Baird, but he and his wife ride a couple of the classiest motorcycles in the county."—P.L.

Randall J. Kiessel,

Portfolio Manager
Robert W. Baird & Company, Inc.

Being part of the fourth generation of Kiessels to settle in northwestern lower Michigan, I am fortunate to live and do business in a community of family and trustworthiness. With fifteen years in the securities industry, I am a first vice president and branch manager in the Traverse City office of Robert W. Baird & Company, Inc. I coordinate a team of individuals in providing portfolio management services to a diversified group of investors, business owners and professionals.

Our investment philosophy is based upon a successful investment program consisting of fact finding, setting objectives and planning. We build upon this foundation by implementing and maintaining the financial plan and making adjustments as necessary.

The investment process consists of each client's portfolio being individually structured and managed. We use an asset allocation model, prudent security selection and a strict adherence to our investment discipline to help clients achieve their results.

My background includes working as a CPA in a national firm, and as the director of training for a major investment company in New York City. I am active locally with various civic matters.

I look forward to meeting you and assisting you in realizing your financial goals. Doing business in the community where you live leads to a sense of well being and trust. Sit back. Enjoy the cherries and the view and leave the market watching to us!

1001 Bay Street
Traverse City, MI 49684
Phone: 933-6050
(800) 793-6379

Financial

ACCOUNTING FIRMS

Dennis, Gartland & Niergarth, PC
415 Munson, P.O. Box 947
Traverse City, MI 49685
Phone/Fax: 946-1722/946-2762

Gavigan Burkhart Freeman & Co.
1010 S. Garfield Ave.
Traverse City, MI 49686
Phone/Fax: 947-7800/947-0348

Weber Curtin & Drake, PC
880 Munson Ave., Suite B
Traverse City, MI 49685
Phone/Fax: 947-6795/947-0680

Fuller, Somero & Pahssen, PLC
201 E. Seventeenth Street
Traverse City, MI 49684
Phone/Fax: 946-6652/946-3638

Plante & Moran, LLP
10850 Traverse Hwy., Suite 1100
Traverse City, MI 49684
Phone/Fax: 947-0090/947-2541

J.L. Stephan Co., PC CPAs
862 E. Eighth Street
Traverse City, MI 49686
Phone/Fax: 941-7600/941-1996

Kalcher, Vanderwal & Torrey, PC
923 S. Garfield Ave., Suite 3
Traverse City, MI 49686
Phone/Fax: 946-2300/DND

Schepers & Hofstra, PC
10850 Traverse Hwy., Suite 3315
Traverse City, MI 49684
Phone/Fax: 935-1850/935-1943

Budget Tax
1305 E. Eighth Street
Traverse City, MI 49686
Phone/Fax: 941-8224/941-0695

Coleman & Company CPAs
12935 W. Bayshore Drive
Traverse City, MI 49684
Phone/Fax: 929-3991/941-5079

Gaudette & Company
733 E. Eighth Street
Traverse City, MI 49686
Phone/Fax: 946-8930/946-1377

Jarvis, Vanderzouwen & Kindlinger, PC
3886 Cass Road, P.O. Box 2310
Traverse City, MI 49685-2310
Phone/Fax: 947-9260/947-1658

J & B Tax & Bookkeeping Co., Inc.
3350 Wyson Road
Traverse City, MI 49684
Phone/Fax: 941-9098/941-9022

Northern Associates
1305 E. Eighth Street
Traverse City, MI 49686
Phone/Fax: 941-8220/941-0695

SOME LOCAL BANKS

Empire Bank Corporation
1227 E. Front Street
Traverse City, MI 49684
922-2111
James Dutmers Jr., Larry F. Kennedy/922-5621

First of America Bank
901 S. Garfield
Traverse City, MI 49685
935-1111
Edward Arbut, Mary DuFort/935-1244

NBD Bank-Traverse City
250 E. Front Street
Traverse City, MI 49685
922-2400
D.A. Wolf, Lorraine Sudekum/922-2481

Northwestern Savings Bank & Trust
625 S. Garfield
Traverse City, MI 49686
947-5490
Harvey Calcutt, Jeff Bach/947-5490

Old Kent Bank-Grand Traverse
102 W. Front Street
Traverse City, MI 49685
922-4240
John Paul Jr., Larry Ehrlinger/922-4196

Republic Bank
534 E. Front Street
Traverse City, MI 49684
933-5626
Constance Deneweth, Andy Sabatine/933-5626

Sault Bank
1241 E. Eighth Street
Traverse City, MI 49684
929-2431
Paul Sabatine, Lloyd Scoby/929-5220

SOME LOCAL INVESTMENT BROKERS

A.G. Edwards & Sons
415 Munson Avenue
Traverse City, MI 49686
Phone/Fax: 946-1630/946-1240
John Gillen

American Express Financial Advisors, Inc.
814-A South Garfield
Traverse City, MI 49686
Phone/Fax: 935-1457/935-3949
Bill Peddie

Edward D. Jones & Co.
512 W. 14th Street
Traverse City, MI 49684
Phone/Fax: 947-1123/947-1024
Jim Mellinger

Edward D. Jones & Co.
408 St. Joseph
Suttons Bay, MI 49682
Phone/Fax: 271-4866/none

First of Michigan Capital Corp.
10850 Traverse Ghighway, Suite 1103
Traverse City, MI 49684
Phone/Fax: 947-2200/947-7047
JayBatcha/William Corbett

Harbay, Kessef & Company
945 E. Eighth Street
Traverse City, MI 49686
Phone/Fax: 941-4447/941-5086
Thomas Cosgrove

Matrix Group Financial Services
4620 N. U.S. 31 N.
Traverse City, MI 49686
Phone/Fax: 938-3200/none
Joel Magner

Merrill Lynch
12935 S. West Bayshore Drive
Traverse City, MI 49684
Phone/Fax:922-0770/922-3338
Jim Favors

Paine Webber Inc.
109 E. Front Street, Suite 203
Traverse City, MI 49685
Phone/Fax: 235-9031/922-3044
William Grombala

Prudential Securities
880 Munson Ave., Suite H
Traverse City, MI 49686
Phone/Fax: 929-4700/none
Laurence Oliver

Robert W. Baird & Co. Inc.
1001 Bay St., Suite B
Traverse City, MI 49684
Phone/Fax: 933-6050/933-6055
Randall Kiessel

Roney & Co.
522 E. Front Street
Traverse City, MI 49686
Phone/Fax: 946-3650/946-4968
Jeff Pasche

Smith Barney
300 Grandview Parkway
Traverse City, MI 49684
Phone/Fax: 941-7200/941-5820
Edward Maier/Branko Gegich

Stifel, Nicolaus & Co. Inc.
223 E. State Street
Traverse City, MI 49684
Phone/Fax: 946-2550/946-0408
Jack Stegenga

Financial

SOME LOCAL FINANCIAL COUNSELORS

Bondy Financial Services Corp.
810 Hastings Street
Traverse City, MI 49686
Phone/Fax: 929-4500/946-0274
Susan Bondy

Dennis E. LeJeune, Investment Counsel
12935 W. Bayshore Drive, Suite 200
Traverse City, MI 49684
Phone/Fax: 922-0525/922-5025
Dennis LeJeune

Financial & Investment Management Group
417 St. Joseph Street
Suttons Bay, MI 49682
Phone/Fax: 271-3915/271-4087
Paul Sutherland/Tom Bender

Harbay, Kessef & Co.
945 E. Eighth St.
Traverse City, MI 49686
Phone/Fax: 941-4447/941-5086

Horvain Pension & Financial Services Inc.
338 E. Front
Traverse City, MI 49684
Phone/Fax: 922-0170/922-0169

John B. Watkins, CFA
407 S. Main
Leland, MI 49654
Phone/Fax: 256-7282/none
John Watkins

Old Kent Bank
120 W. Front Street
Traverse City, MI 49684
Phone/Fax: 922-5515/922-5529
Dennis Piskor

Securities Management & Timing Inc.
620 Woodmere, Suite B
Traverse City, MI 49684
Phone/Fax: 947-8200/947-0236
Craig Pauly/Richard Pauly

Thomas G. Bickersteth & Associates
215 Bridge Street
Charlevoix, MI 49720
Phone/Fax: 547-4602/547-0834
Thomas Bickersteth

SOME LOCAL CREDIT UNIONS

Credit Union One
1202 Veterans Drive
Traverse City, MI 49684
941-7330
Armando Cavazos
(Open through cooperatives and affiliates.)

East Traverse Catholic Federal
3797 Veterans Drive
Traverse City, MI 49684
946-6655
Len Classens
(Open to members of Catholic parishes in Grand Traverse or Leelanau counties.)

Members Credit Union
3745 N. U.S. 31 S.
Traverse City, MI 49685
929-2000
Jackilyn Ravis
(Open to governmental employees, employees of member businesses and relatives of members.)

Northwest Consumers Federal
2948 Garfield Road N.
Traverse City, MI 49686
947-7600
Robert Bray
(Open to employees and family members of small businesses within a 25 mile radius of the credit union and attorneys in Grand Traverse, Leelanau and Antrim counties.)

T.B.A. Education Credit Union
537 Bay Street
Traverse City, MI 49686
946-7090
David Yeomans
(Open to employees, retirees, trustees, volunteers, alumni and board members of Northwestern Michigan College, schools served by the Traverse Bay Intermediate School District and employees of Central Lake Public Schools.)

Food

Chapter 8

"Prevo's service is noteworthy. Carry-out service is a treat. Fresh flowers and videos add to the convenience."—P.L.

David and Dan Prevo

Prevo's Family Markets

In 1943, the first Prevo's market was opened on Eighth Street in Traverse City by my grandparents, Harry and Ethel Prevo. It was a modest 1,000 square foot store that offered the growing neighborhood fresh produce (hard to get in those days), meats and groceries. After returning from service in World War II, my father, Ray, joined the company and contributed to its growth. Over the next few years, additions were made bringing the store to its present day size of over 19,000 square feet.

My brother, Dan, and I began working in the store in our early teens and officially joined the management team in 1972 when our grandparents retired. In 1977, the second Prevo's Family Market was built at Chums Corners. In 1983, our father, Ray Prevo, retired and so brought forth the third generation of Prevo's ownership. Today, there are seven stores around northern Michigan.

The services we offer have expanded to meet the lifestyles of the 90's.

Prevo's has very high standards when it comes to selecting associates who will serve our customers. Our associates enjoy excellent pay and benefits, flexible hours, paid vacations, bonus days and holidays. Career opportunities and advancement are available for those who demonstrate superior customer service.

We have seen strong growth since our beginning. We believe our success has been due, in large part, to our philosophy of customer importance and providing our customers with the right products and services.

Prevo's Mission Statement

Prevo's Family Markets are dedicated to creating and keeping customers by offering quality, freshness, selection and value in a clean shopping environment to achieve 100% customer satisfaction. To fulfill our mission we will provide our associates with a safe working environment, the training, resources and leadership necessary to successfully achieve service excellence.

4146 U.S. 31 South
Traverse City, MI 49684
Phone: 943-9941
(800) 868-9941

"A classy kitchen shop. Gourmet foods and cooking utensils along with unique take-outs. Don't miss the desserts."—C.L.

Mary's Kitchen Port
Mary Boudjalis
Mike Boudjalis

Mary's Kitchen Port is Traverse City's first - and only - combination kitchen, specialty food and gourmet take-out store. The business originated as "Catering by Mary," a full-service catering operation I started in 1971.

In 1977, I opened a cooking school and kitchen shop on Jefferson Road in Traverse City. In 1981, My son, Mike, and I incorporated our business and moved to the current West Front Street location. The full-service catering business was dissolved; food service and specialty foods were added to the Mary's Kitchen Port collection of products and services.

At Mary's Kitchen Port you will find the very finest lines of kitchen tools and equipment; outstanding food products from around the world; one of the largest selections of cookbooks in Northern Michigan; and delicious, innovative and original food creations from our kitchen.

The market for our products and services is far smaller than it would be in a more cosmopolitan area. For instance, we know the holiday season is the only time we can sell good Russian caviar (of course, fifteen years ago the holiday season was the only time we could sell pate...now it is an everyday purchase). To do business in that cosmopolitan arena would certainly increase our financial gains. But then, we would forego the quality of life as we know it on beautiful Grand Traverse Bay.

At Mary's Kitchen Port we strive to make each visit a pleasant experience and adventure for our customers. There is always something new being offered to tempt your taste buds or bring out your culinary skills.

> **539 West Front Street**
> **Traverse City, 49684**
> **941-0525**

"For four generations, the Carlson family has been providing this area with fresh fish. Whitefish and perch are our favorites."—P.L.

Mark Carlson
Carlson's Fish Market

The lake is my heritage.

My family has been in the commercial fishing business in this area since the early 1900's, when my great grandfather, Nels, and his son, Will Carlson, founded the company in Leland in an area now known as Fishtown. My brother, Bill, and I are the fourth generation in the business, operating fish and seafood markets serving the Grand Traverse/Leelanau area. My niece, Shannon Bumgardner, is the manager of our store and is fifth generation.

In 1977, we expanded from one location in Fishtown to a second location in Traverse City. The Traverse City operation was moved to the present downtown location in 1986. Over the years, the region has grown, and the demand for quality fish and seafood has surpassed that growth. From the early 70's through the 80's, we served mostly wholesale customers. With the population

**511 W. Front Street
Traverse City, MI 49684
Phone: 941-9392**

growth, the competition began to move in from the large downstate wholesale supply houses. These wholesalers began shrinking the profit margins in their effort to gain customer base. Dwindling profits on the wholesale side has caused this part of our business to take a back seat to our flourishing retail trade. This comes at the same time the public is becoming more and more aware of the health and nutritional value of seafood.

It is our objective to supply those who want the very best fresh fish and seafood available. Through hard work, determination and a "Customer is always right" attitude on the part of our staff, we will continue to strive for this goal.

After traveling around the country, there is no other place I'd rather live. Because of the seasonal nature of retail business in this area, many people, including myself, are involved in two or three different ways to make a living. I sell real estate with Coldwell Banker in Leland. I guess that's the price we pay for living as close to Paradise as you will find in North America.

"Hot stuff! That's all they carry and you can taste any of it before you buy."—P.L.

Tim Crawford
Calido Chile Traders

Calido Chile Traders is an exciting, wonderfully unique store, complete with an awesome array of over 500 varieties of salsas, sauces, oils, vinegars, seasonings, mixes, etc. that delight the taste buds of our customers. We opened our Traverse City store in August, 1995 in the Grand Traverse Mall.

Our products run the gamut on the Heat Gauge from "Wimpy" to "Snappy" to "Fiery" to the ultimate "Meltdown." The Heat Gauge is prominently shown in the store so you can get an idea of how hot any product is. The unapologetic chile-head, will experience "HOT 'n SPICY" like never before, because at Chile Traders, our motto is: "Try it before you buy it." Our tasting table is a highlight of the store. It is not unusual to find customers gathered around, making delightful sounds of warm satisfaction.

We carry our own line of quality gourmet products including the award-winning Mesquite Smoked Jalapeno salsa, "Pain is Good" hot sauce, Bloody Mary and Marga "Rita" mixes,

Hott Nutts (... If you've got the guts, we've got the nuts!) and more. We also carry a wide array of culinary items, cookbooks, aprons, chile-wear, and novelty items.

We have stores in three regional shopping centers in Michigan. However, Traverse City has undoubtedly been the most rewarding for my wife and me in conjunction with the "real" people and relationships we've been fortunate to make here.

As a businessman and as an individual, I believe we are all faced with a deluge of challenges in the 90's and beyond. However, these challenges and their results are, quite simply, buffered by the good will of the people we have met in Traverse City. This is a unique and vibrant city, offering a healthy business climate as well as a vitally healthy, values-oriented haven for our family.

Grand Traverse Mall
929-7122

"A TC favorite for the fun atmosphere and ethnic food supplies. Open olive barrels and a wavy wood floor are part of the charm."—C.L.

Donna Folgarelli
Folgarelli's Import Market

Folgarelli's Market was established in 1978 by my parents, B.J. (Fox) and Marge Folgarelli in an attempt to combat boredom after retirement. Little did they know that what they were starting was a long-term family run business that would grow to receive national acknowledgment.

I have been a resident of Traverse City since 1972, and I took over the store when my parents retired. Since the market opened, it has seen remarkable growth, especially in the past five years. This can be attributed to many reasons, but mostly to a creative buying approach, accompanied by the incredible population growth in the area. Folgarelli's Market is now the largest

specialty foods store in Northern Michigan, specializing in foods, wine and beer from around the world.

The market has a strong background in Italian foods — from imported olive oil to a large selection of imported meats and cheeses. We take pride in having the largest selection of imported specialty goods in the area, comparable to many markets in the Detroit, Grand Rapids or Chicago areas. We keep a competitive edge by spending the time to search out new products to keep the market supplied with the goods our customers want.

Traverse City is becoming one of the best places in the State of Michigan to do business. The city is growing rapidly and supplying extraordinary business opportunities while allowing the pleasure of living in "God's Country." Traverse City has allowed my family and me the lifestyle that most people consider a vacation.

> 424 W. Front Street
> Traverse City, MI 49684
> 941-7651

Fun Things to Do

Chapter 9

Chapter 9

Fun Things to Do

Are you looking for something fun to do? Here's a list of over a hundred things going on in the area. There's something here for everyone—guaranteed.

1. Check out the view from the top of the Park Place Hotel. Take the elevator to the top and either have drinks or dinner there. It is the best high view of the downtown area.

2. Drive out to Leland for the Wine Festival in June.

3. Go to Dill's in Old Town for karoke for kids (and adults) that is pretty much a hoot with Laura, the karoke princess, in command. Pair it with their Friday night fish fry for a great time.

4. Smooch the Moose at Sleder's Tavern. Then have a buffalo burger at this old-fashioned neighborhood tavern. They claim it's the oldest continuously operating tavern in Michigan.

5. Go on a picnic. Stop at Mary's Kitchen Port for carry-out, then drive to the Northport light house or to the end of Old Mission Peninsula. There are picnic areas at each spot. From there, you'll get the idea of why the area was initially called *Le Grand Traverse*.

6. Take a hike or go mountain biking in the Sand Lakes Quiet Area. Ski there in the winter.

7. Check out the VASA trail for hiking or cross-country skiing. Go watch the races there in the winter — competitors from all over the world.

8. Go smelt fishing in the spring.

9. For another wonderful view, climb to the second floor of Horizon Books and go to the area between "Poetry" and "Performing Arts". Grab any book within ten feet and take a seat at the table there and either browse through the book or just look out the window at the bay. If you had any question about why you moved here before, you won't anymore.

10. Attend any function at the Opera House. While you're there, check out the restoration project.

11. Go to see Classic Boat Rendezvous in Suttons Bay in June.

12. If marathons are your thing, enter the Bayshore Marathon in May. It leaves from Northwestern Michigan College.

13. Drive up to East Jordan for the Fiddler's Jamboree in March.

14. Hike the dunes near Glen Arbor. Then go for a swim in Lake Michigan or one of the inland lakes.

15. Go to the NMC Bar-B-Q on the last Sunday in May prior to the Memorial Day weekend. You will meet friends and neighbors, have a buffalo burger and benefit the college.

16. Bike around Torch Lake in the Cherry Blossom Pedal around Mother's Day in May.

17. Go the Clinch Park Zoo. While you're there, take a ride on the train and walk around to find the talking crow. You will think the person next to you just said "hello" to you, but you will turn and there won't be anybody there. It's the crow.

18. Learn more about the Coast Guard at Coast Guard Days at the Maritime Museum in Glen Arbor in August.

19. Watch for details on the Friendly Garden Club tour in the summer, then go with a friend to enjoy some of TC's finest gardens.

20. Visit the Music House in Acme. It will cost about the same as a movie and you will have memories that will last forever. This wonderful collection of antique automated musical instruments makes for a very entertaining museum visit.

21. Enjoy a summertime drink on the deck at The Elk River Inn, on the river in Elk Rapids or at Larry's Place, located across the highway from the State Park.

22. Go para-sailing over the Bay in the summer. Just look up to find the para-sail and drive to their departing point.

23. Plan and go on a winery tour. You can make a full day of wine tasting-just be sure you have a designated driver.

24. Go watch the Michigan Open in June at the Grand Traverse Resort.

25. Take an Adult-Ed class at NMC-a great winter activity.

26. Have fun at Northport Harbor Days in July.

27. Eat at Round's Restaurant on Eighth and Garfield. If you don't go there for a great breakfast, you might try their lunch. Where else can you find a bologna sandwich on the menu?

28. Spend a day at the Renaissance Fair on a Sunday late in August. It is a fund-raiser for the Grand Traverse Medical Care Facility with medieval theme costumes, food, games and contests. A whole family treat.

29. Energize with a walk around the Civic Center track (one mile), then go for a good cup of coffee at Ray's, Good Harbor or Horizon Books.

30. Meet friends at Interlochen before a summer concert and have a picnic. There are picnic tables just outside the auditorium, or you can have one on the tailgate. Then enjoy the show.

31. Go on the Home Tour in the fall to benefit the TSO.

32. Drive out to the Old Mission Tavern on the Peninsula in the winter time for a "Starving Artist" dinner. Last season, this was two delicious dinners for $9.95. Call them or watch for details.

33. Drive up to Boyne City for the National Morel Mushroom Festival in May. If that's too far to go, then go morel hunting on your own.

34. Try ice fishing.

35. Visit and have a taste at TC Brewing, the new micro-brewery in Elk Rapids.

36. Check out the art fairs in the summer-Suttons Bay, Old Town and NMC are a few to enjoy.

37. See the star show at the Rogers Observatory on Birmley Road.

38. Enjoy "The Messiah" at Central Methodist Church in December. Better yet, participate in it.

39. Find the 45th parallel marker. At that point, you will be half way between the Equator and The North Pole.

40. Go to the Northwestern Michigan Fair in August. The Fairgrounds are south of Traverse City, near Chums Corners.

41. Set aside a Saturday in early November for the Christmas bazaars. Most take place on the same day.

42. Watch the sunset from Chateau Chantal or Chateau Grand Traverse, then go to the Boathouse for dinner.

43. Go to the Howe Arena for the annual Ice Show. All local talent, in March — a great show.

44. Enjoy the Traverse Symphony Orchestra Christmas Concert in early December.

45. Go to the Downtown Farmer's Market in the summer for fresh produce, fruit, cut and dried flowers and fresh baked goods from area growers. It is held in the parking area between the parkway and the river, between Cass and Union on Saturday and Wednesday mornings. Traditionally opens on Mother's Day and closes in October.

46. Check out the jazz series at the Dennos Museum.

47. Visit the historic Hannah House on Sixth Street. It is now the Reynolds-Jonkhoff Funeral Home. Occasionally, they are open for tours. Afterwards, take a walk around the neighborhood and see the Victorian architecture.

48. Go to the Gladhander Auction at St. Francis School in October. Dress up for a fancy meal and bid on thousands of items. A good way to spend an evening, spend some money and raise money for the Catholic Schools.

49. Do the same thing for the Pathfinder School in Leelanau County at the annual Pathfunder Auction.

50. Take your kids to see the Haunted House at the Opera House in October.

51. Go down to Frankfort for the Blueberry Festival in August.

52. Visit the Old Engine Show in Buckley in August. Be careful — its a guy thing. Steam engines and thrashers of every description. Also, food, music and fun.

53. Support the Michigan Winter Special Olympics by your attendance at Sugar Loaf Resort in February.

54. Ride around town at Christmas time to see the elaborate house decorations. A must: drive out M72 toward Empire and stay on 669 to see the most elaborate home decorations in the area.

55. Spend a day antiquing. There are great dealers in the area.

56. Watch the NORBA Bike Races at Shanty Creek

57. Go downtown for the Friday Night Live events in July, August and December. While you're there, have dinner at La Cuisine Amical (outside in the summer).

58. Have dinner at Hattie's in Suttons Bay and get out in time for a movie at The Bay. Each is unique and you will enjoy both.

59. Go to a home football game in the fall at Thirlby Field. Great spirit and fun and the whole facility is in the process of being rebuilt and expanded.

60. Have apple cider at Hitchpoint Cider Mill in Williamsburg in the fall, see the one-of-a-kind horse-drawn mill and have a fresh donut to go with it. Buy a pumpkin from any roadside stand on the way home.

61. Explore Leland's Fishtown and shops. Watch the river activity while you have lunch on the deck at The Cove.

62. Ice skate at the city rink on 14th Street in the winter, then go to Marifil's bakery for a treat.

63. Ride down Cairn Highway near Kewadin and see the monument. There is a stone there from every county in Michigan.

64. Ride your bike or skate the full length of the TART Trail, from Greilickville to Acme. Or, go the other way.

65. Watch the swans from Logan's Landing on Boardman Lake.

66. Rent a canoe and ride down the Crystal, Platte, Manistee or Boardman River.

67. If you're really hungry, go to Boone's Long Lake Inn and have a steak. Unbelievable!

68. See the old wooden boats downtown on the Boardman River during their annual gathering.

69. Get some great bargains at the Downtown Street Sale in August.

70. Ride out the Old Mission Peninsula around Mother's Day and see the cherry blossoms. Chateau Chantal has a "blessing of the blossoms" in mid-May.

71. Go to The Festival of Trees during the holidays at the Dennos Museum.

72. Ask the people at Wild Birds Unlimited about going on an owl watch some night. They are held at the Pyatt Lake Natural Area.

73. Watch a summer sunset from the patio at Bowers Harbor Inn.

74. Go to Ranch Rudolf for a winter sleigh ride.

75. Visit the Dennos Museum to see whatever is on display and tour the permanent hands-on exhibits.

76. Volunteer as a Cherry Ambassador for the National Cherry Festival. You will have to pay for the opportunity to volunteer, but there are three great parties. You will do some work, meet a bunch of people and

have a ton of fun doing it.

77. Tour The Grand Traverse Resort between Thanksgiving and Christmas and see the decorations. Have a drink or dinner at The Trillium.

78. Take a romantic carriage ride around Downtown in the summer.

79. Take the ferry from Leland to South Manitou Island for a day trip. Be sure to pack a picnic and everything else you'll need for the day, since there are no services on the island. Enjoy the many trails, the lighthouse and old farms.

80. Check out a new gym. They all have a one-time rate.

81. Tour the Parade of Homes in June. It's a look at lots of new homes built by area builders.

82. Drive to Omena and visit the Tamarack Art Gallery.

83. If gambling is your thing, drive out to the casino at Peshawbestown. Buffet meals at the new restaurant there have already gotten a good reputation.

84. Play tourist and take a ride on the Malabar, a beautiful schooner that sails the bay.

85. If cigars are your thing, stop in Nolan's Tobacco Shop on East Front Street and have a smoke. There is always some stimulating conversation going on there. You will meet some local philosophers and have an opportunity to learn something new or share your opinion.

86. Go to the Rotary Show. Every year, near the end of April, the local Rotary Club puts on a variety show at Lars Hockstad Auditorium as their major fund-raiser for the year. A low ticket price gets you in on lots of fun and funds some important community projects.

87. Drive out to Cedar for the annual Polka Fest

around the Fourth of July weekend.

88. Watch the hang gliders over the dunes near Frankfort any summer day with good weather and strong updrafts.

89. Go to the Old Town Theatre for any production.

90. Take a hot air balloon ride.

91. Take your kids on a carousel ride at the Grand Traverse Mall.

92. Jump on the Manitou Island Transit ferry at Leland for a cocktail ride at sunset.

93. Visit the Hocus Pocus shop above the Arcade on Front Street for magic stuff and costumes.

94. Pick your own fruit: berries, cherries, or apples in season.

95. Tend a plot at the Community Garden on West Front and Cedar Run Road.

96. Drive over to Grayling for the AuSable River Festival and Canoe Marathon in July

97. Rent a pontoon boat from one of the marinas on Elk Lake or another inland lake.

98. Cut your own Christmas tree at one of the tree farms in the area.

99. Experience The Stone Circle, an evening of poetry and music around a campfire, ten miles north of Elk Rapids on Friday and Saturday nights in the summer.

100. Compare good old-fashioned hamburgers. Try Don's Drive-In at US-31 and Four Mile and J& S on Front Street, downtown.

101. Go to the circus. The Hanneford Circus usually tours through the area in March or April.

102. Take your kids to Story Hour at the Library or Horizon Books.

103. Morning, noon or night, take a drive up Wayne Street and see West Bay, downtown, East Bay and beyond. Not a better view in the midwest.

104. Go to the National Park Visitors Center in Empire, watch the ten-minute video, tour the center and then take the Pierce Stocking Drive where you can view Big and Litle Glen Lake, Lake Michigan and the Manitou Islands.

105. Enjoy the holiday festivites by going to a madrigal dinner-both the Presbyterian Church and the Park Place have great ones.

106. If you're a cigar smoker, go to one of the area cigar nights-Hattie's and the Park Place each have one.

107. Dress in your favorite animal costume and join in the Earth Day parade in the spring. It's in downtown Traverse City.

108. Listen to the Traverse Symphony Orchestra when they play at the Open Space in the summer and watch the sunset over West Bay. It is a great place for a picnic.

Garbage, Trash & Recycling

Chapter 10

Garbage, Trash & Recycling

David G. Knudsen

Division Manager, Ken's Landfill
United Waste Systems of Northern Michigan

Welcome to Northern Michigan. The beauty you find here is unsurpassed. The four seasons offer every individual a variety of activities. Take a springtime tour on Old Mission Peninsula when the cherry blossoms are in full bloom and stop to sample some fine wines. Or perhaps, taking an autumn walk in the woods with all of nature's glorious colors surrounding you might sound appealing. Do you enjoy winter activities? Well Northern Michigan offers some of the finest skiing in the Midwest for the cross country, ski boarding, or downhill enthusiast. Perhaps a solitary excursion on snow shoes through the Sand Lakes Quiet Area is more to your liking. And what about summer? That's the time when we all share the area's best qualities with visitors from around the world.

Regardless of the season, people, activities and events create a challenge for the management of solid waste in our beautiful area. It's a challenge that neither industry nor government takes lightly.

Back in 1988, Grand Traverse County officials felt a strong need to study solid waste and alternative programs for managing it. Specifically, they studied increasing recycling opportunities and regulating the waste stream. Suffice it to say that private industry and government regulators did not always agree on how to best achieve the goals of 25% recycling of the non-organic waste stream and 75% of the organic waste stream.

After spending over $200,000 of a state grant, Grand Traverse County developed a program in conjunction with a consulting firm. The plan was presented to the local units of government in late 1990. For the next four years, several "hot" topics from both sides were discussed, mediated, challenged and then discussed again.

Finally, in late 1995, Grand Traverse County Ordinance No. 17 was adopted with the proposed rules and regulation changes, with a start-up date of October 1, 1995 for curbside recycling service and all other provisions of the ordinance.

Ordinance No. 17 is a document of some 50 pages that outlines the "Intergovernmental Resolution," "Intergovernmental Contract," "County Ordinance" and the "Rules & Regulations" for the system. Anyone wishing to review it can contact me or the County Solid Waste Coordinator for a copy.

For those of you wishing a condensed version, please allow me this opportunity to simplify it. The Intergovernmental Resolution and Contract grants the Board of Public Works (BPW) the authority to establish the system for managing solid waste on behalf of the Local Units of Government or Townships. Through this system, all haulers would need to be licensed with the County of Grand Traverse in order to be eligible to provide service in the county. Every landfill would need to be designated by the County as a facility eligible to accept waste from the County. Further, this "designation" requires the facility to collect a county surcharge that is levied on all solid waste delivered to it from the county to fund the system. This surcharge is collected by the designated facility and paid to the County on a quarterly basis. The haulers pay the designated facility the surcharge through increased fees to both the residential and commercial customer on a volume basis.

The Rules and Regulations outline the project and system goals including: Targeted & Banned Materials, Collection Service Requirements, Fees, Rates and Charges for Collection Services, Designated Facilities, Enforcement and finally, the Program Management and Administration. Whew! So much for smaller government. By now you may be asking yourself: "What does it mean for me?"

First of all, all haulers wishing to provide service in Grand Traverse County must be licensed. There are currently seven licensed haulers. You may wish to talk to a neighbor or business associate for referrals or look up "HAULERS" in the yellow pages under Rubbish Removal and call for information. Also, find out if you're located inside the "Curbside District" where curbside recycling is being offered.

As a resident of Grand Traverse County wishing to have your solid waste disposed of and recycling material collected and properly managed, here are your options:

•Choose a "Full Service" package, which may include a 90-gallon tote for trash, or it may allow for a set number of bags, if a tote is not offered. Also included in the package is a recycling bin used for gathering your properly prepared materials. Both trash and recycling service is provided for on the same day, once per week. Different service providers may each have a different day of service. Different providers may charge different rates.

•Choose a "Budget Bag" option where you pay a flat fee per bag. Recycling service would be provided for an additional charge.

•Choose to haul your own trash to a "Designated Facility" and pay a fee. Again, recycling service at your curb would be available for an additional charge.

•Choose to haul your own trash or have your "Budget Bag" serviced at the curb and haul your recyclables to a FREE recycle drop-off location. There are nine different drop-off locations.

As an industry, our greatest challenge is meeting the customer's needs and expectations, today and into the future. We need to provide the services you require at a competitive rate. We must be responsible to the environment and ensure the integrity of our free enterprise and open market system.

We will all be challenged to help meet the goals set forth on both the local and state level. They can only be achieved through the cooperative efforts of industry, government and consumers. We would like to help educated consumers who see the benefits of reducing, reusing and recycling.

QUESTIONS?
For information on recycling or drop-off stations, call the recycling Hotline: 922-2052.

RECYCLING TIPS

PAPER PRODUCTS

What to Recycle: Newspapers, magazines, catalogs, office paper, telephone books, all clean cardboard and junk mail.

Hints: Keep each paper product separate in a bag or bundle the material and "Put it in the Bin!"

What NOT to recycle: Box liners, waxed cardboard and soiled paper.

GLASS JARS & BOTTLES

What to Recycle: Clear, brown or green jars & bottles, food and beverage containers

Hints: Rinse clean and remove lids. Labels are acceptable, but remove all metal from glass.

What NOT to recycle: Pyrex, ceramics, light bulbs and window glass

#2 HDPE PLASTICS

What to Recycle: Clean plastic milk, juice and water jugs, detergent, bleach, and fabric softener jugs, shampoo and liquid soap bottles (containers with a seam across the bottom)

Hints: Rinse clean and remove all excessive residue or contents.

What NOT to recycle: cottage cheese or yogurt containers, plant trays, toys and other food containers. (Containers with a dimple on the bottom)

ALUMINUM

What to Recycle: Clean aluminum foil and cans, lawn chairs (remove webbing) TV antennae

Hints: Rinse clean all foil and cans. When in doubt, check with a magnet to see if object is magnetic (aluminum is not magnetic)

TIN (STEEL) CANS

What to Recycle: Food and beverage containers, aerosol and paint cans (if empty)

Hints: Remove both ends and flatten cans. Clean, empty and remove labels. Colored cans and painted labels are acceptable.

What NOT to recycle: Any containers with excessive residue or contents.

YARD WASTE

What to Recycle: Grass clippings, leaves, and small brush

DROP-OFF LOCATIONS

GARFIELD TOWNSHIP
United Waste Station, Cass Road*
GTP Center, Premier Street
KPS Landfill, Cedar Run Road

ACME TOWNSHIP
US 31 North, at Bunker Hill Road

EAST BAY TOWNSHIP
Transfer Station at Rasho Road

PENINSULA TOWNSHIP
Transfer Station on Devil's Dive Road*

CHUM'S CORNERS
Prevo's

FIFE LAKE VILLAGE
Village Hall

KINGSLEY
KMP Hall

*These locations accept yard waste for a per bag fee.

COMPOSTING TIPS

COMPOSTABLE MATERIALS

Tree leaves, sod, grass & hedge clippings
Hay, straw, weeks, wood ashes
Shredded newspaper, chopped corn stalks and cobs
Most kitchen waste and plant refuse

NON-COMPOSTABLE MATERIALS

Grease
Fat, meat scraps
Dairy products

HOW TO PREPARE YOUR COMPOSTING RECIPE

1. Layer one part green materials with two parts brown materials. One third of the pile is green materials: grass, weeds, spent flowers, bouquets, fruit and vegetable garden scraps. Two thirds of the compost pile is brown materials: dry leaves, dead brown plants, straw, sawdust, pine needles, chopped wood, brush and corncobs.

2. Sprinkle a half-inch of soil or mature compost every few layers to provide the microorganisms necessary for the decomposition process.

3. Add water to keep the pile as damp as a moist sponge.

4. Mix or turn periodically with a garden fork.

Composting is easy to customize to suit your needs and is a wonderful nutrient for your garden.

Government

Government

K. Ross Childs

County Administrator
Grand Traverse County

*O*ur success is that we still have trout in the streams, says Maureen Kennedy Templeton, Drain Commissioner of Michigan's Grand Traverse County, which has launched intense efforts to protect rivers and streams in areas like the Mitchell Creek watershed. This once rural basin is growing fast as retirees, families and businesses are lured by its beauty.

Opening words, National Geographic article "Learning to Tread Softly" February 1996.

Government at all levels: county, township, city and villages shares a vision to provide its citizens with competent, courteous and easily assessable services comparable to the initiatives highlighted in the above statement. Future residents can expect "one stop shopping" for the normal everyday functions relating to city and county government at a single facility known as the Governmental Center. This was not the case when Grand Traverse County was organized in 1851.

Brief history of Grand Traverse County:

In the early fur trading days, the French described the nine-mile voyager trail along the shore at the foot of Grand Traverse Bay as Le Grand Traverse or "the long crossing." Originally named Omena, probably meaning "the point beyond," the county was a part of Mackinaw, but was organized by an act approved on April 7, 1851, as Grand Traverse County. Traverse City was incorporated as a village by the Act of Legislature in 1881, and on April 30, 1895 was incorporated as a City under a special charter. The territory west of Grand Traverse Bay was called Leelanau and to the east, Omena. The Grand Traverse Area was part of Omena.

The first meeting of the Board of Supervisors was held at the store of Cowles and Campbell, in the town of Peninsula on July 27, 1853. The county building was erected in 1854 and destroyed by fire approximately eight years later. As of June 10, 1861, there were two buildings located in the public square known as the Courthouse and Jail, but the courthouse burned down and the jail was of little value.

On the 24th day of June, 1898 the Grand Traverse County Board of Supervisors entered into an agreement with contractor Jordan E. Gibson of Indiana for the construction of the present courthouse building on the grounds known as the "Courthouse Square" to be completed before May 1, 1899.

The present-day City-County Governmental Center was completed in 1979 and continues to be the focal point of governmental functions for its residents. Its integrated design assists both policy makers and their employees to interact and exchange information more easily than anywhere else within the State of Michigan.

Residents may find the following services available on the main floor:

Tax Payments
Utility Billings
Dog Licenses
Recording of Deeds and Mortgages
Birth, Death and Marriage Records
Assumed Names (registering a business)
Passports
Partnership Certificates and other Professional Registrations
Real Estate Transfers (deeds and mortgages)
Assessments
Land Information (maps, addresses, sales)

The remaining floors provide access to planning, personnel, administration, aging, veterans, city building inspection, solid waste and the site for City and County Commission meetings. The facility is also home to many appointed boards, commissioners and not-for-profit groups who hold in excess of 200 meetings per year there.

The success and acceptance of the combined services at the Governmental Center prompted the construction of the Law Enforcement Center which again centralized police functions. Centralized dispatch and records enables the officers in both departments to access and share information and coordinate their work effort. The end result is improved law enforcement services for the community.

The Grand Traverse County Courthouse was originally constructed in 1899. The Courthouse contained county governmental and judicial functions through the 1970's. Continued pressure to crowd more functions into already overburdened space had rendered the Courthouse ineffective in meeting the County's needs. Deteriorating outside, uninspiring and inefficient inside, the Courthouse presented the County with the inevitable dilemma: to destroy the old building despite its historical and

architectural stature, replacing it with a new building; or to conserve the building within the framework of a restored exterior with the addition of contemporary environmental systems and the appropriate use of interior space.

The County chose to conserve the building after several years of public debate. To solve the problem of inadequate space, the County initiated a two phase strategy. First, plan and construct a new facility housing only governmental functions for the expanded needs of both city and county. Second, embark on a conservation program for the Courthouse to house judicial functions only. This strategy freed the Courthouse from space demands that no longer could be satisfied within the existing building shell, and it permitted the development of a program that would protect and upgrade a landmark building.

Judicial-related services for Circuit Court, District Court and Friend of the Court are available at the Courthouse, while Probate Court and Juvenile services are located on the third floor of the Governmental Center. The public also has availability of the most complete law library north of Grand Rapids on the upper floor of the Courthouse.

Health services for the Counties of Benzie, Grand Traverse, and Leelanau are provided from a new facility called the Public Services Center at 2325 South Garfield Road. They include:

Prenatal and Infant Services
WIC Food Coupons
Well Child Health Screening
Communicable Diseases
Immunizations
Reproductive health services
Anonymous AIDS Testing
Health Education Services
Animal Control
Food Service Sanitation
Well and Septic Evaluations

This facility also provides related services through the Construction Code, Drain Commission and Soil Erosion and Public Works Departments. The single point of contact for building, soil erosion, sewer and water and well and septic covers the majority of jurisdictions within the County. Traverse City, Garfield and Green Lake Townships are serviced at their local level.

A state-of-the-art Medical Care Facility will be available by 1998. The facility will contain 201 long term care beds, 32 bed Early State Alzheimer's Respite Care residence and an Intergenerational Day Care Center. This project is currently under contract and will be constructed in compliance with Historical regulations on the Grand Traverse Commons (formally the State Hospital grounds). Grand Traverse County and Munson Medical Center are jointly providing Traverse City's first parking facility to compliment the Medical Campus.

I know that you will find bright, warm and courteous individuals waiting to service your needs at all levels of local government. You will be truly amazed at the quality and the availability of your local government.

Northwestern Michigan Council of Governments

Alton. M "Bud" Shipstead

The Northwest Michigan Council of Governments is a public organization made up of ten member counties: Antrim, Benzie, Charlevoix, Emmet, Grand Traverse, Kalkaska, Leelanau, Manistee, Missaukee and Wexford. It was formed in 1973 to give the counties a vehicle for "economy of scale" in delivering various services, addressing common needs across county lines, and providing a stronger voice for Northwest Michigan. The Board of Directors consists of the ten chief elected officials (county board chairpersons).

It is typical across the country for rural counties to group together in consortiums in order to receive certain federal, state and private grants that require a minimum population base. An organization such as the Council of Governments also allows the region to provide specialized professional and technical functions that no individual county could afford to do alone. It also gives the counties a forum for addressing common problems and issues in a neutral setting. Another primary role the Council of Governments plays is that of community leadership in pursuing progressive new direc-

P.O. Box 506
Traverse City, MI 49685-0506
Phone 929-5000

tions in public services and human services.

Over the years, the organization's focus and programs have changed according to the region's needs, as well as federal and state trends. Currently, the Council of Governments has five main service categories: employment and training, economic development, data research and information services, regional planning, and community corrections. These services are outlined below. Some programs are operated by Council of Governments staff; others are contracted out by the agency to a variety of community organizations with the council of Governments acting in an administrative oversight role. A wide variety of individuals, businesses, agencies and governmental units take advantage of the Council of Governments' services.

The Northwest Michigan Council of Governments maintains a headquarters office in Traverse City and has staff members working in the other counties on a daily basis. It also has eight JOBNET Centers throughout the region for access to all the employment and training programs. People may stop in at any JOBNET Center or call (800)442-1074 for employment and training services through JOBNET. They may call (616) 929-5000 or (800) 692-7774 for the main Council of Governments office.

WHAT IS THE COUNCIL OF GOVERNMENTS?

A ten-county public organization, supported by a combination of many different sources: federal, state and local public funds, plus private foundations and contributions; approximately $6 million annual budget.

EMPLOYMENT & TRAINING

Administrative entity for JTPA and Work First

Coordinating and oversight agency for the JOB-NET system, providing:

Job Training

Employment Counseling

Job Search Assistance

Job Placement Assistance

Occupational Information, Assessment and Testing

Welfare-to-Work Placement

Basic Workplace Academic Skills - reading, math, language arts, computer orientation

Employer Assistance in finding, training and retaining employees

Special Services for youth, migrants, veterans, disabled, and older workers

Many other Employment and Training Services, as needed by individual customers

JOBNET Centers are provided for customer access to workforce development and economic development services in:

Petoskey	Cadillac
Charlevoix	Manistee
Bellaire	Benzonia
Kalkaska	Traverse City

ECONOMIC DEVELOPMENT

Small business assistance: business planning, financial packaging, governmental loans.

Procurement Technical Assistance Center: assistance in bidding for governmental contracts and finding export opportunities, to expand markets and create/retain local jobs.

Community Commitment Fund: small business start-up training and micro-loans for entrepreneurs.

DATA RESEARCH SERVICES

Regional census repository

Economic and population data provided for public and private needs

REGIONAL PLANNING

Coordinate and support common planning activities across multiple counties, including:

Water quality/watershed planning, activities and education

Computer mapping of a wide variety of public and private uses.

Technical assistance for state and local transportation planning activities

Greenways development (recreation and conservation corridors)

Local ordinances regarding water resources, soil erosion and sedimentation, zoning, waste management, etc.

Communication and sharing among counties for economies of scale

COMMUNITY CORRECTIONS

Administrative entity for the counties' community corrections programs: work release, home tether, etc.

Planning, reporting and technical assistance

Where to Vote

If you are new to the area and don't know where to vote, let this information help you find your way. If you have questions, just call the County Clerk's office at: 922-4760.

CITY OF TRAVERSE CITY

Precinct # 1 Fire Station, 510 W. Front
Precinct # 3 Central Grade School, 301 W. 7th Street
Precinct # 4 Willow Hill School, 1250 Hill Street

(Leelanau County)
Precinct # 7 Traverse Heights School 933 Rose Street
Precinct # 8 Civic Center, 1125 W. Civic Center Drive
Precinct # 9 Eastern School, 1600 Eastern
Precinct #10 Glenn Loomis School, 1009 S. Oak Street

ACME TOWNSHIP

Precinct # 1 Township Hall, 6042 Acme Road

BLAIR TOWNSHIP

Precinct # 1 Township Hall, 2121 Hwy. 633, Grawn
Precinct # 2 Township Hall, 2121 Hwy. 633, Grawn

EAST BAY TOWNSHIP

Precinct # 1 Township Hall, 1965 Three Mile Road
Precinct # 2 Fire Hall, 110 High Lake Road
Precinct # 3 Fire Hall, 110 High Lake Road
Precinct # 4 Township Hall, 1965 Three Mile Road

FIFE LAKE TOWNSHIP

Precinct # 1   Township Hall, 134 Morgan Street, Fife Lake

GARFIELD TOWNSHIP

Precinct # 1 Silver Lake School, 5858 Culver
Precinct # 2 Garfield Twp. Hall, 3848 Veterans Drive
Precinct # 3 Garfield Fire Hall, 3400 Veterans Drive
Precinct # 4 Garfield Fire Hall, 3400 Veterans Drive
Precinct # 5 Garfield Twp. Hall, 3848 Veterans Drive

GRANT TOWNSHIP

Precinct # 1 Township Hall, 8986 David Road, Buckley

GREEN LAKE TOWNSHIP

Precinct # 1 Township Hall, 9394 10th St., Interlochen

LONG LAKE TOWNSHIP

Precinct # 1 Fire Station, 8870 N. Long Lake Road
Precinct # 2 Fire Station, 8870 N. Long Lake Road

MAYFIELD TOWNSHIP

Precinct # 1 Township Hall, 3010 Center Road, Kingsley

PARADISE TOWNSHIP

Precinct # 1 KMP Building, Blair St., Kingsley

PENINSULA TOWNSHIP

Precinct # 1 Township Hall, 13235 Center Road
Precinct # 2 Fire Hall, 8150 Center Road

UNION TOWNSHIP

Precinct # 1 Township Hall, 5020 Fife Lake Road

WHITEWATER TOWNSHIP

Precinct #1 Township Hall, 5777 Vinton Rd., Williamsburg

Health Care

Chapter 12

Health Care

Jay Hooper
President & CEO, NorthMed, HMO

Rolling hills covered with flowering cherry trees, long beautiful beaches outlining our bays and lakes and a summer tourist season that attracts over 300,000 people each year are some of the features that make Traverse City unique. For most people, health care issues are the furthest thing from their minds when discussing the "uniqueness" of an area blessed with such natural beauty. However, health care is an issue that positions Traverse City far ahead of other rural areas in Michigan. With health care facilities comparable to those provided in larger urban areas like Ann Arbor or Grand Rapids, patients are willing to travel from as far away as West Branch and Sault Saint Marie to receive medical attention in Traverse City.

Traverse City's Munson Medical Center, the largest hospital in Northern Michigan, is among the most cost effective, high quality health care facilities in the state. Serving the area with 368 inpatient beds and 26 bassinets, Munson has the region's largest medical staff with over 250 physicians. Nearly 27,000 patients were treated in the Emergency Department and 1,800 babies were born in the maternity unit in 1995.

Health care does not merely pertain to hospitals and centers providing medical services. There are over 70 family physicians offering care through private practices; over 30 psychologists and psychiatrists; close to 20 centers and family physicians that provide services for patients seeking chiropractic care; and many holistic and self-healing services.

Overall, the health care services in Traverse City meet a variety of medical needs. The comprehensive health care services and programs include: a family practice residency program, midwifery services, a cancer center, eye and ear centers, a comprehensive cardiac program, drug and alcohol treatment programs, speech and hearing clinics, home health services, community service programs, a poison prevention center, plastic surgery services, allergy and sinus centers, and many other programs and services. The only two services not provided in the Traverse City area are organ transplants and burn specialists. These services are usually provided only in highly populated areas where the rate of occurrence increases due to the large number of people.

Traverse City residents also have access to North Flight, Inc., an advanced life support (ALS) air and ground emergency medical transportation system, consisting of a helicopter and fixed wing aircraft. ALS provides scene responses and inter-hospital transports within a 22 county Northern Michigan service area. This guarantees medical services to a large number of people over a vast area of geography.

Traditional values are important to the residents of Traverse City, and traditional health care coverage is equally as important. From more traditional coverage like Blue Cross/Blue Shield, to managed care options like NorthMed HMO, a locally owned and operated company, residents have their choice of health care coverage.

The future holds many exciting prospects for the Traverse City region. Continued growth has created the need for better health care services, and Traverse City is stepping up to the challenge. Since the Traverse City State Hospital closed in 1988 due to a shift in the treatment of mentally ill patients, community leaders and Munson Medical Center have created a re-development plan for the property. Munson is planning to expand by opening a fam-

ily practice residency and community re-development plans centering on progressive elderly care are under consideration. Grand Traverse County recently broke ground for a new County medical care facility on the property.

The Traverse City area is currently one of the fastest growing regions in the state. The availability of first-rate health care services continues to be a key feature to the vitality and quality of life in this region.

Local Health Care

PHYSICIANS REFERRAL SERVICE

Even if you are not new to the area, and need the name of a doctor, call the Physicians Referral Service at: 935-6507

AREA HOSPITALS AND CLINICS

Leelanau Memorial Hospital
215 S. High Street
Northport, MI 49670
386-5101
Long-term Care

Munson Medical Center
1105 Sixth Street
Traverse City, MI 49684
935-5000
Total health care delivery

Munson Medcare Walk-In
Munson Ave. W. of Eighth Street
Traverse City, MI 49684
935-9000
Full walk-in services for non-life-threatening illness/injury

Paul Oliver Memorial Hospital
224 Park Ave.
Frankfort, MI 49635
352-9621
Long-term care

Urgent Care/Burns Clinic
844 E. Front Street
Traverse City, MI 49686
929-1234
Pre-employment physicals, drug & breath alcohol testing, school and sports physicals, worker's compensation

"A state-of-the-art dental practice with a professional and friendly staff. Beautiful gardens and bird feeders relax you while you're in the chair."—C.L.

Edward Kouhout, D.D.S.
Dentist

I remember when I was in dental school at the University of Detroit, reading an article about a young boy who had just won an essay contest. The assignment was to describe the most beautiful thing these students had ever seen. The winner wrote "My Mother's Smile." I remember being struck by the simplicity and power of those words. Today, after 27 years as a dentist, I have honed my professional skills to be able to enhance the beauty of the human smile.

Being a dentist in Traverse City has been personally and professionally rewarding. The people here have a higher "Dental IQ," they take better care of themselves, and demand the best oral care they can get. My area of specialization is cosmetic dentistry. My patients expect to have their teeth for a lifetime. Years ago, that wasn't the case. In 1900, the average life expectancy in America was 47 years. By the year 2000 the average American will look forward to an 80-year lifetime. These patients want and expect their teeth to last and look good. That's where I come in.

Aesthetic dentistry and preventative oral care is the foundation of my practice. My patients' treatment plan is based on what we know today and what we will know tomorrow. I've never lost my enthusiasm or commitment to life long learning. Each day brings new and rewarding challenges, doing the best I can for my patients and family.

After 27 years of practice, I look forward to tomorrow. Part of that stems from the good fortune of living and working in Traverse City.

4124 Cedar Run Road
Traverse City, MI 49684
Phone: 947-3530

"These physicians are dedicated to keeping your eyes healthy. Glasses and contacts are available at the clinic."—C.L.

Kenneth H. Musson, M.D., M.S., F.A.C.S.

Grand Traverse Ophthalmology Clinic, P.C.

T raverse City is well known for the availability of high quality medical care. Grand Traverse Ophthalmology Clinic is a single specialty group practice devoted to eye care. Our practice is the continuation of ophthalmology services that began fifty years ago by John G. Beall, M.D., the first board certified ophthalmologist in Northern Michigan. We are the oldest established comprehensive medical eye care practice in the Grand Traverse region.

We are board certified specialists who are doctors of medicine working with certified assistants, technicians, and opticians. We provide a broad range of general ophthalmological services, including treatment of medical and surgical disorders for infants, children and adults. This includes glaucoma, diabetic eye disease, cataract, injuries, infections, ocular plastic surgery, in-office laser surgery, refractive corneal surgery and routine examinations for glasses and contact lenses.

We are doctors of medicine first and specialists second. Our philosophy is to act as the patient's advocate and adviser in the ever-increasingly complex world of health care. We work with you and your other medical providers to assist in solving your health problems.

**1105 E. Front Street
Traverse City, MI 49684
947-6246**

"Dr. Bob has great patient rapport with kids and adults. He makes you want to smile."—P.L.

Dr. Robert S. Portenga
Orthodontist

Welcome to Northern Michigan and your new home in this beautiful region. You will find that this area is not only rich in natural resources, but that it also is able to provide you with outstanding retail, cultural and professional services. The health care community has a reputation for excellence delivered in a caring atmosphere.

I established my orthodontic practice in Traverse City in 1973, after attending Albion College and graduating from the University of Michigan Dental School, with both a DDS and MS in orthodontics. The technological changes in orthodontics during the past 20+ years has been staggering, and our office has constantly been a leader in bringing these improvements to our patients.

We have treated newborns with cleft problems and believe strongly in interceptive treatment at an early age to prevent severe problems from fully manifesting themselves. Although we enjoy treating the traditional young patient when permanent teeth have just erupted, the adult segment of our practice is a challenging and exciting part of our busy day.

We are in the business of creating self-confidence and personal satisfaction in addition to straight teeth. Each patient becomes a part of our family and hopefully will remember us for a long time. We have a staff of well-trained, dedicated professionals who take pride in their work and enjoy meeting the needs of others. We try to create an atmosphere of professional excellence and fun that makes our patients eager for their visits with us.

Since patients today are very health conscious, we are here to help you achieve your desire to have a happy, healthy smile. We welcome new patients and look forward to meeting you to discuss your family's orthodontic needs.

432 Munson Place
Traverse City, MI 49686
Phone: 947-3570

"This HMO is doing a great job in service and their growth is testimony to their success."—P.L.

Jay Hooper
President & CEO, NorthMed HMO

What makes moving to Traverse City special is recognizing the appreciation that locals have for this beautiful region, and then gaining the appreciation yourself. NorthMed and the people of the Traverse City region welcome you to an area full of natural wonders and delight.

What makes NorthMed unique among HMOs in northern Michigan? We're your neighbors. As a health care organization, we grew up here. The founders of NorthMed understood the realities of serving a rural area, and built an organization to serve the community. Our bottom line is the health of the community in which we live.

Since 1986, NorthMed has grown to be the largest HMO in Northern Michigan. More than 16,000 members belong to NorthMed, more than any other plan in the area. And 95% of area physicians participate with NorthMed, a rate higher than any other plan in the region. Our growth is a direct result of our commitment to the highest quality service to our members and the skills of our health care providers. NorthMed ensures that your concerns about health care end when you choose to join our family of care.

NorthMed provides its members with emergency services anywhere, diagnostic procedures such as lab tests and x-rays, outpatient and inpatient surgeries, home health care, discounts on health clubs and fitness programs, and health education programs not traditionally covered by insurance plans. Some additional advantages of the NorthMed plan include no deductibles, limited out-of-pocket expenses, simplified rules for changing doctors, and no claim forms to file.

In a fast-paced, sometimes complicated world of juggling the needs of family, work, and everything in between, the last thing you need is a roundabout path to health care when you're in need of service. Our goal at NorthMed is to make obtaining health care as simple as possible.

NorthMed is here to serve the residents of Traverse City through caring and convenient services at competitive rates.

**109 E. Front St., Suite 204
Traverse City, MI 49684
Phone: 935-0500**

History

History

Larry Wakefield
Traverse City Historian

Most Northern Michigan towns grew up around a sawmill—pine timber gave them birth. Traverse City was no exception. It got started in 1847, when Captain Harry Boardman, a prosperous farmer near Naperville, Illinois, bought 200 acres of virgin pine timber at the foot of Grand Traverse Bay, and furnished his son, Horace, with the means to build a sawmill there. Horace and two or three hired hands sailed north from Chicago in his father's sloop, "Lady of the Lake," and arrived on the site in early June.

With the help of local Indians they finished the sawmill in October of that same year. It stood on the small creek (successively known as Mill Creek, Asylum Creek, and Kids Creek) that empties into the Boardman River at its western loop at Wadsworth Street. The only other settlement in the vast wilderness for miles around was an Indian mission near the tip of the peninsula that separates the two arms of Grand Traverse Bay. It had been established in 1849, by a Presbyterian missionary, Reverend Peter Dougherty, in 1839.

The little Boardman mill continued to operate through the winter of 1850-51, but results were disappointing. With its single muley saw, the mill was slow and inefficient, and when the price of lumber plummeted in 1850, Captain Boardman (the military title was honorary) decided to sell. He found a buyer in the newly organized Chicago lumber firm of Hannah, Lay & Company and its three youthful partners, Perry Hannah, Albert Tracy Lay and James Morgan. Eager to develop their own standing timber resources, Hannah and William Morgan accompanied Captain Boardman to Grand Traverse Bay aboard the schooner, "Venus," in the spring of 1851 and closed the deal. For $4,500, they acquired the sawmill and several small buildings and the 200 acres upon which Traverse City now stands.

It is said that Captain Boardman was astonished upon arrival to find the mill shut down and all hands playing cards. Horace's explanation that he'd given the men a day off because of a threat of rain convinced the Captain that his decision to sell the property was wise.

The company lost no time in building a much larger steam mill on the Bay just west of the river's mouth. Over the next thirty-five years it would harvest more than 400 million feet of pine lumber in the Boardman River valley. The lumber was shipped to Chicago in the company's own bottoms—some of it was used to rebuild Chicago after the Great Fire of 1871—and great wealth flowed into the pockets of all four partners. (William Morgan had been added to the partnership in 1852.)

For the first few years, Hannah and Lay alternated every six months as company head in Chicago and Traverse City, but after 1855, Hannah took sole charge of the company in Traverse City and Tracy Lay remained in the Windy City.

The village was laid out by Tracy Lay in 1852, and was granted a post office in 1853. During the winter, the mail was carried weekly from Manistee in a backpack by an Indian called Old Joe. The first school was established in 1853 with 15-year-old Helen Goodale, daughter of Traverse City's first physician, David C. Goodale, as teacher. It was housed in a little log shanty, formerly a stable, on the south side of Front Street, just east of Boardman Avenue.

For the first 15 years, the tiny village was completely isolated from the outside world except by boat and Indian trail—and not even by boat in winter. Perry Hannah, elected to the Michigan legislature in 1854, had to make the trip to Lansing that winter on snowshoes, accompanied by an Indian guide. It took them ten days.

The first road south, the Northport-Newaygo State, was opened in 1864, closely following the old Indian trail. That helped some, but Traverse City's first big "breakout" was the coming of the first railroad, Grand Rapids & Indiana, on November 15, 1872. Whistles blew and church bells rang and people danced in the street. "Out of the Woods at Last" trumpeted the Grand Traverse Herald in banner headlines.

Henry D. Campbell, who had established the first stagecoach lines in the 1860's, built Traverse City's first big hotel, The Park Place, in 1873. The city became a railroad center with the coming of the Chicago and West Michigan (1890) and the Manistee & Northeastern (1892). It was incorporated as a village in 1881, and as a city in 1895, Perry Hannah elected president of both. (Even during his lifetime, Hannah was called the "Father of Traverse City.") City water, electricity and gas lines were established by H.D. Campbell in the late 1880 and 1890's. The population reached almost 10,000 in 1900—a ten year gain of 116%.

But dark clouds had already begun to gather on the horizon. Pine timber was depleted by 1895, and by 1915 so were the hardwoods. Also gone were Traverse City's mainstay industries based on wood and wood products. Its largest employer, Oval Wood Dish Company, for example, pulled up stakes in 1917 and moved to Tupper Lake, NY, taking with it some 200 worker families and plunging the area into an economic decline that lasted until World War II, when the town seemed empty with all its young men gone — some of whom died in battle and were gone forever.

Traverse City actually lost population in the 1920's and stagnated in the 1930's. The city was partly sustained during this period by the Northern Michigan Asylum (later called Traverse City State Hospital), which opened in 1881 under its legendary first superintendent Dr. James Decker Munson. Over the course of the next 70 years the hospital employed an average of 1,000 people while caring for an estimated 50,000 patients.

But the seeds of resurgence had been sown as early as the 1890's, when the first commercial fruit farms were established and summer people began to spend their vacations at resorts on Grand Bay and the inland lakes. Tourism and fruit farming led the way to Traverse City's phenomenal growth and development during the past 40 years, making it the "World's Cherry Capital," with its annual National Cherry Festival, and one of the nation's prime tourist attractions.

Over time, Traverse City has also become northern Michigan's center for medical care, communications, banking, insurance, government and legal services, shopping and travel, which, along with its great natural beauty, have made it one of the most desirable places in the country to live.

Now, faced with an accelerated pace of growth and development, it has become the primary task of its people to ensure the quality of life in Traverse City remains high.

"Thanks, Mrs. Towne, for helping us give readers a good look back at Traverse City through the years."—C.L.

Neva Towne
By Anne Brasie

On December 9, 1900, Neva Elsie Marie Lindquist Towne was born to Peter and Emma Lindquist, Swedish immigrants living in Greilickville. William McKinley was President of the United States, the Packard Motorcar was first introduced and a good breakfast cost only 15 cents.

Now ninety-five years young, Neva has seen a lot of changes in her lifetime and so has Traverse City. At the turn of the century, most of the city's sidewalks were still made of wood planking. Fires were doused, usually unsuccessfully, by firemen manning horse drawn fire equipment. Very few households owned a telephone. In the first few years of Neva's life, Front Street was paved between Union and Cass; the first moving picture was shown at the Steinberg Opera House; and Traverse City founding father, Perry Hannah, died.

"All of a sudden things have grown so rapidly," she muses when asked about the changes she has seen. "Sometimes it seems that progress has gone too far. Back when I was a kid, you knew all your neighbors - now we only know the people right next door."

But, progress has brought good things too, Neva agrees. "I like all the inventions - like radio and television!"

Neva is an identical twin. As she tells it, after she was born her father had to chase after the doctor to get him to come back and help his wife deliver the second baby, Neva's sister. "Hey, come back", he cried. "I think there's another one coming!"

There is a lovely framed, hand-painted photo of Neva and her sister, Neta Ellen Martha, hanging in the stairway of the Towne home. It shows two pretty girls in white dresses and beribboned hair gazing out shyly from an era long past. The resemblance between the two girls is truly remarkable. Neta died young, at age fifteen, of pernicious anemia. 80 years later, Neva still feels the loss. "She died so young - and there was really nothing that could be done - we didn't have the medicine that we do now."

Another photo depicts the two sisters when they were about six years old standing in front of a large

Steinbergs owned the Steinberg Opera House, one of the two opera houses that once graced Front Street. The Steinberg was located on Front Street, next to the current location of the State Theater.

Neva remembers that only one of the neighbors had a phone. Her family did not own a car or a carriage when she was young. Friends took them places or they occasionally rented a carriage and horses from the stables that were on Front Street near where the Record Eagle now exists. "I do remember surreys with fringe", says Neva. "And the first car I saw was a Ford owned by friends from Suttons Bay."

Shopping was a little different back then and so were the prices. The family shopped at a number of different markets, including a downtown meat market run by the Sleder family. Farmers from the Old Mission Peninsula delivered milk and eggs to folks

Christmas tree, adorned with candles, both proudly showing off their new dolls and doll carriages. "We did decorate our trees with real candles," says Neva. "Of course, someone always had to be in the room when they were lit."

Like many towns of that era, Traverse City had its fair share of catastrophic fires, including one that burned down a large portion of Front Street in 1900. "Fires were big entertainment", remembers Neva. "No matter what time of night people would get up, get dressed and go watch." She remembers the night when the Steinberg's house, which was a few blocks from their own, burned down. The

in town. Sugar cost four cents a pound, butter was ten cents a pound and eggs were fourteen cents a dozen.

When the circus came to town, people flocked to Front Street to watch the parade as the performers and animals arrived. Neva and Neta's first circus parade was a frightening experience for Neta. Along with the many strange new things she saw, Neta, who was standing on the wooden sidewalk, was brushed right under her chin by a large elephant's swinging trunk. While the event was certainly an accident as far as the elephant was concerned, it was hard to convince the terrified Neta of this.

The twins would go downtown to buy penny candy when they had a few spare coins. Neta remembers the sense of frustration she felt from a peculiar problem inherent in wooden sidewalks. "All of our clothes had big pockets in them so we could carry things around," she recalls. "When I had a penny or two I would go down to the store for some candy or other sweets and it always seemed like just before I got to the store I would reach in to get my penny and it would slip between my fingers as I fumbled to get it out of my deep pockets. And, the penny always went through the crack in the sidewalk planking!"

Neva's father was a manager at the Oval Wood Dish Company, a prosperous manufacturing company at the time. Mr. Lindquist made about $3 a day, a paltry sum by today's standards. But, Peter somehow managed to build a comfortable home for his family at 827 State Street on those wages. A house on that street today can cost $75,000-100,000.

The Oval Wood Dish Company was owned by Henry Hull, one of the scions of Traverse City. The large Victorian home he built at 229 Wellington, at the corner of State, is one of most magnificent homes from that era. His son built the wonderful neo-Classical, pillared home directly across the street.

According to Neva, there was a real disparity between the haves and the have nots in Traverse City. There were wealthy people, like the Hulls, the Hannahs and the Morgans, but most of the area's residents were pretty strapped. "We used to watch the rich people play," laughs Neva. "There was a tennis court where we sometimes sat and watched, and a lot of the wealthier people played croquet. I think they played at the Park Place." Neva remembers the influx of wealthy people from Chicago and other cities that would come for the summer to escape the heat. They stayed in the Park Place, and other resort hotels or in private summer homes. Most of the old hotels are long gone, but the migration of people to the area in the summer has remained a tradition.

Much of Traverse City's waterfront and downtown looked a lot different back in the early 1900's. Most of the streets were still dirt, or mud depending on

Neva met her future husband, Howard Roswell Towne through her friendship with the Shriver family. She was at the Shriver's for dinner one evening when she answered the door and there stood Howard. He had come to ask that Mr. Shriver join his choir. She remembers thinking, "Oh, it's that young squirt of a minister who's working at the Congregational Church." Neva was 26 and Howard was 25 when they met. He asked her to go tobogganing for their first date - they went to the hills south of town off Cass, a popular place for winter activities.

Neva and Howard courted for a number of years. Times were hard in Tra-verse City. It was the early years of the Great Depression and "We were too poor to get married," says Neva. "The church didn't even have a parsonage."

They married at Howard's church, the First Congrega-tional Church on Park Street behind the Park Place on June 10, 1934. It was rainy the day of the ceremony, Neva recalls, and they held their wedding dinner at the Park Place. She remembers there was a fountain behind the hotel at that time. The newlyweds embarked on a six week honeymoon which included a trip to Yellowstone and Niagara Falls.

Their first home was across the street from the town high school, which is now the site of the Central Grade School. The school burned to the ground the year they were married and the current, brown brick structure was built to replace it. They moved to their current home at 521 Webster and rented it for six years before they bought it. They have lived in the house ever since.

Neva was born as the lumber baron days were waning and a new era in Traverse City was emerging. Agriculture became the more dominant industry and a growing population supported a greater variety of service businesses. The city has gone through many changes since the turn of the century and Neva was witness to every one of them. The stories she tells of her childhood describe a life that was in many ways simpler, but also much harsher than what most enjoy today. Many of the conveniences of our time did not exist - but you get the sense that maybe amidst the day to day effort to survive, people may have enjoyed the simple pleasures more.

the season. A railroad station was located near the water at the foot of Park Street. There were several docks and a lot of commercial activity on and near the water. If you look at pictures from that era, you will also notice there weren't as many trees. One photograph shows a house under construction several doors west of the Perry Hannah home and there is barely a tree in sight to the west and north of the house all the way to the lake.

Neva remembers the large dock owned by the Oval Wood Dish Company. It was a popular spot for Sunday strolls. "I'm sure many a young man proposed out there on the dock - it was really very lovely," she says. Excursions by boat out to the dance Pavilion on Bassett Island (a small island next to what is now known as Power Island) were also a welcome diversion.

When Neva was a young woman, she began working at Hamilton's Haberdashery, owned by Mr. Shriver. Once known as Hamilton Milliken and Company, the original partnership was dissolved in the early 1900's and the store was known simply as "Hamilton's" by the time Neva started working there. The store remained at its original location just east of Milliken's on Front and Cass and was run by Mr. Shriver's grandson, Pete Strom, up until just a few years ago.

Housing & Real Estate

Chapter 14

Housing & Real Estate

Judith Wood Lindenau

Association Executive
Traverse Area Association of Realtors

Any discussion of housing and real estate in the Grand Traverse area needs to start with the definition of trends unique to our area. First, it must be recognized that in any discussion of property values, particularly in the area of residential property, the Grand Traverse waterfront and its breathtaking views play an important part in the valuation of any property in the vicinity. Secondly, because of the recognized quality of life of this region, growth pressures are strong — particularly as telecommuting becomes an acceptable arrangement in many professional careers.

Because of these two key factors, the demand for residential properties and resultant impact on available inventory and property valuation is strong and secure. The average selling price of a home in this area is approximately $107,000, a figure which probably will not include direct ownership of waterfront property. On the other hand, moderate and low income housing is at a premium and extremely difficult to find during the summer months, when there is a dramatic increase of visitors and laborers to our area. Add to that the pressure of an increasing number of students attending Northwestern Michigan College, and many retirees and older citizens who remain in the area in close proximity to excellent medical care facilities and other leisure activities, and the demand on housing in the below-$80,000 range and in rental housing forces cost-of-living factors to continue to rise.

A wide variety of housing styles can be found in this region. There are many elaborate homes, retreats, and family compounds; there are old summer "cottages" which have been in families for generations; there are the stately Victorian homes in the central neighborhood historic district; there are luxury condominiums with boat slips and golf courses; and there are typical ranch homes and vacation hideaways. People who live here take their lifestyles seriously, and their housing accommodations indicate their versatility.

For those planning to move to the area, a complete range of support services exists for buying or selling real estate, and planning to buy, redecorate, or build a home. Both the Homebuilders Association and the Traverse Area Association of Realtors have strong organizations which encompass much of the real estate community. A computerized Multiple Listing System is available, complete with photos.

The Traverse Area Association of Realtors is also working on the Internet. Along with a sampling of available real estate offerings for the Traverse City area, you will also find the current newsletters, a listing of affiliate members, our Code of Ethics, legal updates, and even the Traverse City weather. Our Internet address is: <<http://www.taar.com>>

Many newcomers to the area consider a real estate career. The Traverse Area Association of Realtors has approximately 450 members, and is a good starting point to begin your investigation of this field as a potential job opportunity. There are approximately 90 offices from which to choose, with a wide range in size from the small and specialized operation to the larger real estate office. In Michigan, all licensees must take a 40 hour pre-licensing class and successfully pass an examination offered by the state—a letter or telephone call to the Realtors Association can provide you with further information.

Finally, a word about homebuying: Michigan has adopted laws which require sellers' disclosure statements in most transactions. Environmental regulations are also a very important part of the Northern Michigan lifestyle, and each unit of government has zoning and development laws as well. We suggest that a competent real estate professional can guide you smoothly through the processes of property acquisition in northern Michigan.

Please don't hesitate to call the Traverse Area Association of Realtors at 947-2050 for assistance and direction.

Hope

VILLAGE

Senior Apartments and Assisted Living Center

"This will be the finest facility of its kind in Northern Michigan. Opening date is August 1996."—P.O.

Hope Village is a retirement community designed to fit senior life-styles through a variety of living options and social opportunities.

Independent living in one and two bedroom apartments with full kitchens and many conveniences is available. For those who like to eat out, a noon dinner is provided at no extra cost in the apartment facility's community dining area.

Hope Village also offers an assisted living facility on its beautifully landscaped campus. This building is perfect for seniors who need increased personal care but do not require the services of a skilled nursing home.

Each facility is designed to provide social opportunities, safety and a fulfilling quality of life for seniors. Each facility offers opportunities for personal growth through recreation, spiritual expression and learning. Hope Village is located on the east side of Grand Traverse Bay, just north of Traverse City. It is owned and operated by Lutheran Social Services of Michigan. For more than half a century, LSSM has been known for its tradition of providing quality living for seniors. The comforts of home, the warmth of family and the freedom to live a satisfying life combine to create the setting of Hope Village.

Models are open for viewing and occupancy is expected by August, 1996.

> 4354 Mt. Hope Road
> Williamsburg, MI 49690
> Phone: 938-HOPE

Kids

Chapter 15

Kids

Lissa Edwards
Traverse, Northern Michigan's Magazine

The happiest moments of my childhood took place during the many summers my family spent in Northern Michigan. Events like tumbling down the Sleeping Bear Sand Dunes, swimming in Lake Michigan, Petoskey-stone hunting and canoeing on the Crystal River are etched into my memory like faded, much-loved photographs.

Looking back, I see that what links all these memories is a connection with the natural world, something that was lacking in the East Coast suburbs where I was raised. When it came time to raise my own family, that connection drew me to Northern Michigan.

Raising our two daughters here has been a wonderful adventure for my husband and me. To my delight, I have found that all four seasons are packed with so many family-oriented, outdoor activities, we have to struggle to work everything in.

One of the great benefits of writing the Families Up North (F.U.N.) sections for Traverse, Northern Michigan's Magazine is that I get to share the joy of these experiences with other families. Conversely, through my F.U.N research I've learned that there's no end to the family fun in Northern Michigan.

It would take volumes to share it all, but here are some seasonal highlights I've gathered from F.U.N. and from my own family's experiences.

SPRING

Spring in Northern Michigan begins when the sap flows. Usher in the season by taking your family to a sugar shack—where they turn maple sap into maple syrup. Better yet, learn to make the syrup yourself. For information on maple sugaring call the Roscommon Cooperative Extension Service District (they take care of sugaring all over the North): 517-275-4670. The folks at Hide-Away Antiques and Sugar Bush in Mesick are also gallons of help on the subject. 616-269-3473.

Around the end of April, morel mushrooms start to pop their heads through the forest soil. Our kids have been moreling since they were old enough to carry in backpacks. Along the way, they've gained a love of hiking—not to mention a taste for this expensive fungus. State and federal land where these mushrooms are free for the taking abound in the Traverse area. The 2,300-acre Sand Lakes Quiet Area east of Traverse City is a great place to begin a morel search. You'll find a parking area by taking Broomhead Road off U.S. 31 to Sand Lakes Road. Before you head out, pack along a net bag for bringing back your treasures. The netting will allow your morels to spread their spores—and plant next year's harvest. Morels are easy to identify. For a picture, check out a book on mushrooms at the Traverse Area Public Library. If you have doubts about what you've picked, most local chefs are authorities on morels.

From the woods, it's a short jump into the river this

time of year. The slow moving, shallow Boardman, Platte and Crystal Rivers make for wonderful family paddles. You can rent a canoe and paddle the Boardman at Ranch Rudolf: 616-947-9529. To paddle the Platte rent canoes at Riverside Canoes in Honor. 616-325-5622. The Glen Arbor Shell Station rents canoes for the Crystal. 616-334-3831.

SUMMER

I know that summer is really in gear when my kids decorate our car for the Glen Arbor Fourth of July parade. This casual parade looks like it wound its way out of a Norman Rockwell painting. After the parade, we spread our blanket on Glen Arbor's Lake Michigan beach for fireworks. You'll find similar annual events in virtually every small town around Traverse City. The following week the National Cherry Festival arrives with its colorful parades, air show and fire works. The folks at Cherry Festival headquarters will happily fill you in on the details: 616-947-4230.

Between all this fun you'll want to get the kids wet. Great public beaches in Traverse City range from West End and Clinch Park off Grandview Parkway to East Bay Park at the foot of Eighth Street. Another quieter, Lake Michigan spot is Sayler Park off U.S. 31, north of Traverse City in Yuba.

The summer always winds up with a visit to the Northwestern Michigan Fair, where the farm animals and products always make me feel autumn in the air: 616-943-4150.

FALL

Autumn in Northern Michigan is like a big red apple: it's so beautiful and smells so good you want to take a bite. You can do just that at the area's many farm markets where the counters are crammed with apples—caramel, candy, fresh and made into cider—this time of year. You'll also find pumpkins, Indian corn, baked goods and baskets full of everything else that gives the season its color.

For a cider experience you won't forget, stop by the Hitch Point Cider Mill in Williamsburg where owners Carol and Michael Maten power their antique cider press with two Norwegian Fjord ponies. At break time, a miniature horse entertains guests by

jumping hurdles. The fun at Hitch Point peaks the first weekend of October during the Matens' Norwegian Pumpkin Rolling contest. The Matens invented Norwegian pumpkin rolling—and a whole lot of other fun events for their festival.

A couple of farm market stops will probably leave everyone needing to burn off a few calories. Biking is a natural exercise this time of year. Traverse City cyclists love to tour the Old Mission Peninsula. Another great choice—especially for kids—is the Traverse Area Recreational Trail (TART) that winds through Traverse City. It's easy to pick up the trail along Grandview Parkway. Mountain bikers will want to try their wheels on the VASA trail. The VASA trailhead is on Bunker Hill Road in Acme.

In the past few years, the bright colors of soccer jerseys have become as synonymous with fall in the Traverse area as flame-colored leaves. Teams for kids from kindergarten through sixth grade are organized by the Grand Traverse Bay YMCA: 616-947-5880. Teams for older children are organized by Traverse Bay Area Youth Soccer: 616-933-8229.

WINTER

If you do winter right in the Traverse area, kids and parents alike won't mind if spring never comes. One must is to get the family involved in an outdoor sport like skiing or skating.

Countless Traverse City kids have grown up learning to ski at the city-owned Hickory Hills ski area. It's all rope tows and not much fluff, but Hickory turns out some great skiers and ski racers—Hickory is home to the Grand Traverse Ski Club. You can find out more about Hickory by calling the Traverse City Department of Recreation. 616-922-4910.

If they don't go to Hickory, Traverse City kids flock to Holiday Hills, where there are a fully-equipped day lodge and chair lifts: 616-938-2500.

Within easy drives of Traverse City are Sugar Loaf Resort in Cedar, The Homestead in Glen Arbor, Shanty Creek in Bellaire and Crystal Mountain in Thompsonville. All three resorts offer state-of-the art ski programs. The phone numbers are: Sugar Loaf 616-228-5461; Crystal Mountain 946-3585; Shanty Creek 800-678-4111. Cross-country skiing family-style starts at Jellystone Park on Hammond Road. Jellystone has a big lodge with a crackling fire in the fireplace and treats for sale, miles of groomed cross-country trails (a portion of the trails are lit for night skiing) and an instructional program: 616-947-2770.

The Howe Arena operated by the Grand Traverse Civic Center is the hub of all organized skating programs in the area: 616-922-4818.

For disorganized—but nonetheless fun—skating, head to one of the two city-owned outdoor rinks either on 14th Street next to the State Police Station, or on Rose Street next to Traverse Heights Elementary School. For information call the Department of Recreation: 616-922-4910.

Children's Services

SOME TRAVERSE CITY CHILD CARE FACILITIES

Alphabet Soup Pre-School & Daycare Center
222 East 14th Street
Traverse City, MI 49684
941-1330
Pamela Yeager

Children's Discovery Center, The
164 High Street
Northport, MI 49670
386-7700
Michol Tanner

Community Nursery School
First Congregational Church
6105 Center Road
Traverse City, MI 49686
947-1650

Country Lane Daycare
3100 Country Lane
Traverse City, MI 49684
941-7282

Leelanau Children's Center
111 N. Fifth Street
P.O. Box 317
Leland, MI 49654
256-7841

Little Ones Child Care Center
2555 Garfield Road, North
Traverse City, MI 49686
947-1988 or 947-6520

Montessori
979 Elm Street
Suttons Bay, MI 49682
271-3291
Colleen Christensen

Montessori
6105 Center Road
Traverse City, MI 49686
946-5720
Colleen Christensen

Small World Nursery School
701 Westminster
Traverse City, MI 49684
947-7117
Bev Granger

Traverse City Co-Op Pre-School
720 S. Elmwood
Traverse City, MI 49684
929-3323
Dana Entz

Traverse Learning Center
601 E. 8th Street
Traverse City, MI 49684
946-4141

Trinity Lutheran Preschool
1003 S. Maple Street
Traverse City, MI 49684
946-2721

SOME STORYTIME IDEAS FOR KIDS

Stories for Kids

10:30 a.m. Saturdays
for children 4 and older
Traverse Area District Library
Children's Department
322 Sixth Street, Traverse City
922-4822 or 922-4843

Wiggler's Programs

9:30 & 11:00 a.m. Wednesdays & Thursdays
for children 2-4, 30 minutes
Traverse Area District Library
Children's Department
322 Sixth Street, Traverse City
922-4822 or 922-4843

The Children's Hour

2:00 p.m Sundays
Horizon Books
243 E. Front Street, Traverse City
946-7290

Storytime

10:00 a.m. Mondays
Celebrities read outstanding children's literature
Channel 46, Traverse City
WCMW-TC Channel 21 Manistee
WCMV-TV Channel 27 Cadillac
Channel 69 Leland

Story Time Treasure

7:30-8:00 p.m. Tuesdays
for 3 to 8 year olds
channel 2 and 56
sponsored by: TCAPS Elementary Libraries, REMC 2
and Northwest Michigan Reading Council

Children's Stories

10:00 a.m. Wednesdays
for children ages 4 to 9
Elk Rapids District Library
300 Noble Street, Elk Rapids
264-9979

Story Stew

11:00 a.m. Thursdays in February
for pre-school children (registration requested)
Peninsula Community Library
2735 Island View Road, Traverse City
223-7700

East Bay Branch of the Traverse City Library

1:30 p.m. Saturdays
all ages welcome
1989 Three Mile Road, Traverse City
922-2085

Suttons Bay Public Library

416 Front Street, Suttons Bay
271-3512

Manufacturing

Manufacturing

Steve Anderson, President
Alcotec Wire Company

We moved Alcotec Wire Company to Traverse City in the mid-1980's. We manufacture aluminum welding metallizing and mechanical wire and ship to markets around the world. I'd like to share with you some ideas with you about the things we have  discovered about manufacturing in the Grand Traverse Area.

LABOR MARKET

When we arrived, we found an excellent labor market. Dedicated people with good work ethics were relatively easy to find and employ. In the mid-1990's, we find it far more difficult to get good, well-qualified people to meet our increased business needs. We are not alone in this, since we have heard the same complaint from other manufacturers in the area.

EDUCATIONAL OPPORTUNITIES

The quality of the K-12 education in this area is very good. The opportunity for a college degree and post graduate work is good and getting better.

In September, 1995, the University Center opened at NMC and is providing 45 programs from 12 Michigan universities and colleges. The center consists of 19 classrooms with interactive TV connections to the professor and his/her campus. The opportunities for education and training with this facility are tremendous. We have had six of our employees earn degrees while working: three MBA's, a BS and two associates degrees.

QUALITY OF LIFE

Quality of life has become more important, in part, because of the deterioration of quality of life in many of our major cities and manufacturing centers. Traverse City is not only quite safe, but it also has exceptional recreational opportunities. Further, it has many and varied cultural opportunities especially at the Interlochen Center for the Arts. At Interlochen, you can hear and see some of the most talented young people in the world along with internationally famous entertainers. A love of music and the arts pervades the community which has nationally-recognized school music programs and boasts strong community support for the Traverse Symphony Orchestra.

SUPPORTING INDUSTRIES

Many manufacturing businesses, including ours, need supporting industries within a 50-mile radius. These might include such types of companies as tool and die shops, heat treating companies, industrial supply companies, printing, construction contractors and employment services. We have found an excellent supply of such qualified companies in the local area.

LOCAL BUILDING CODES AND ENVIRONMENTAL REGULATIONS

Every community has its own building codes. Traverse City has been a recreational area for many decades and has only recently begun to deal with large manufacturing firms. We have found Traverse City's building codes and inspectors to be unfamiliar with generally accepted large industry practices and procedures. Because of this, it is important to take extra precautions to ensure that all plans and processes are carefully reviewed with the city in advance.

The Grand Traverse area has exceptional natural resources and we are very sensitive about the environment, as we should be. It is important to know the prior use and environmental history of prospective sites and what lies both up gradient and down gradient from them. This could save the potential investing manufacturer many future headaches.

FINANCING

We found the financial community quite friendly toward our local industry. The lending institutions are familiar with industry and willing to provide funds at competitive rates.

SHIPPING

Because of the long distance to our primary markets, we thought locating our plant in Traverse City would incur proportionately higher shipping costs.

This has simply not been a problem for us. The Grand Traverse area is a four-season area. Trucks arrive filled with food products, clothing, recreational equipment, etc. and leave empty or with our light loads. We have found that we can exploit this opportunity and negotiate good shipping rates for our products leaving the area.

Traverse City Airport has about forty flights per day for air freight shipping of materials or samples. Federal Express has its own planes that fly daily in and out of Cherry Capital Airport.

SUMMARY

Traverse City is a good place for the right kind of business. The area lends itself to high tech manufacturing, where a well-educated and reliable work force is important. The area has well developed support industries and services. Additionally, the area has a strong pull for specialists who need to be recruited from elsewhere.

CAPTAINS OF INDUSTRY

The Chamber of Commerce maintains a listing of all manufacturers in the area under the name of "Captains of Industry." It is very complete and manufacturers are listed by SIC code. This report is available for sale through the Chamber office for a nominal fee. If you would like a copy of this report, contact Charles Blankenship: 947-5075.

SOME LOCAL MANUFACTURERS

United Technologies
1567 South Airport Road., P.O. Box 1049
Traverse City, MI 49685-1049
Phone/Fax: 947-3000/947-3037
Parent Company: United Technologies Automotive
Top Local Executive: Dick Green
Products: Automotive electronics and mechanical devices

United Technologies
1110 Woodmere Ave.
Traverse City, MI 49684
Phone/Fax: 947-0160/947-4337
Parent Company: United Technologies Automotive
Top Local Executive: Jim Wainright
Products: Automotive electronics and mechanical devices

Masco Tech Stamping Technologies Inc.
1974 Cass-Hartman Court, 280 Hughes Drive
Traverse City, MI 49684
Phone/Fax: 946-2520/946-2493
Parent Company: Masco Corporation
Top Local Executive: Bill Schulz
Products: Metal stamping, thread rolling

Burwood Products Inc.
807 Airport Access Road
Traverse City, MI 49685
Phone/Fax: 946-4950/941-3211
Top Local Executive: Bill Kemner
Products: Decorative clocks

Cone Drive Operations Inc.
240 E. 12th Street
Traverse City, MI 49685
Phone/Fax: 946-8410/946-0235
Parent Company: Textron Inc.
Top Local Executive: John Melvin
Products: Gears and speed reducers.

Century Inc.
2410 Aero Park Court
Traverse City, MI 49686
Phone/Fax: 946-7500/947-4456
Top Local Executive: William Janis
Products: Specialized tooling

Carpenter Enterprises Ltd.
1867 Cass-Hartman Court
Traverse City, MI 49685
Phone/Fax: 946-7964/946-6671
Top Local Executive: John O'Toole
Products: Machined motor vehicle parts

National Cherry Festival

Chapter 17

National Cherry Festival

Tom Kern

Executive Director,
National Cherry Festival

Welcome to Traverse City from the office of the National Cherry Festival. As one of the nation's top ten festivals, our annual celebration of the cherry harvest is an integral part of life in northern Michigan.

Michigan produces both sweet and tart cherries, and leads the country in production of the latter. The fruit trees thrive on the shores of Lake Michigan where good air, adequate drainage, relatively high elevation and a medium sandy soil help ensure a successful harvest. Indeed, the western shoreline of Michigan's Lower Peninsula boasts the greatest cherry-producing area in the United States, making Traverse City the "Cherry Capital of the World."

The first cherry festival in Traverse City-officially known as the Blessing of the Blossoms—was held on Friday, May 22, 1926, at a time of year when the Old Mission peninsula bursts with acres of blossoming cherry trees. Activities centered around a parade and selection of the Cherry Blossom Queen by drawing from a hat filled with the names of 72 local "photogenic" young women. The actual blessing of the blossoms was held the following Sunday on Center Road at the highest point of Old Mission Peninsula.

Today, the National Cherry Festival honors its humble beginnings even as it cultivates its current identity as a major agricultural festival. Held the first full week after the Fourth of July, the Festival now hosts over 150 activities, including three parades, sporting events, big-name entertainment, band competitions, children's events, midway rides, an air show and cherry promotion events.

With few exceptions, these activities are available free of charge to the Festival-goer, thanks to both corporate and community sponsorships. Entertainment at the 1995 Festival included free performances by dozens of artists, including rock legends The Guess Who and flutist Alexander Zonjic, as well as ticketed concerts by Clint Black and Ringo Starr. The 1996 event will continue the tradition of bringing top-notch contemporary and country artists to the Grand Traverse area.

Since 1926, the mission of the National Cherry Festival has remained consistent: to promote the cherry industry; to encourage tourism and community involvement; and to cultivate the business, entertainment and cultural interests of the Grand Traverse region. Each year the Festival works to implement this mission by returning financial resources to local civic, service and charitable groups; by honoring a cherry industry person of the year; by attracting visitor investment; by organizing a canned food drive to benefit locally needy individuals and families; by providing scholarships to deserving students through the Taste of Cherries event, the Queen Program and the National Cherry Festival Commemorative Print; and by facilitating the production of homes for low-income families through Habitat for Humanity.

These activities, as well as a commitment to make the Festival an exceptional experience for everyone and to contribute positively to the quality of life in Northern Michigan, help define both the National Cherry Festival and the experience of living and working in Traverse City. Over 700 volunteers contribute significant time and energy to ensure that the Festival realizes its mission, and it is this that makes the National Cherry Festival a successful entertainment event and a productive community experience. We hope that you will take advantage of all that the festival offers and consider becoming a part of the National Cherry Festival family of volunteers.

CHERRY AMBASSADOR PROGRAM

If you would like to join over 700 other Area residents and become a Cherry Ambassador, call the National Cherry Festival office and have them send you an application. It is a great way to meet new people in town, help out the festival, and have some fun. There are three big parties each year: a sign-up party in May, a Festival Kickoff Party just before the festival and a post-festival party. The small fee covers the costs and is a real bargain. Call the office: 947-4230.

National Cherry Festival 1996 Schedule of Events

This schedule of events was submitted several months in advance of the 1996 National Cherry Festival, and is presented here as an example of a typical annual National Cherry Festival. For more current information, refer to the Traverse City Record-Eagle during the festival, or call the NCF offices at 947-4230 or (800) 968-3380.

Saturday, July 6 Opening Day
Festival Air Show/U.S. Navy Blue Angels
Big Wheel Race
Taste of Cherries
Mountain Bike Race
Beach Volleyball Tournament

Sunday, July 7
Festival Air Show/U.S. Navy Blue Angels
In-line Skating Race
Bike Tour
Arts & Crafts Fair
Traverse Symphony Orchestra
Beach Volleyball Tournament

Monday, July 8 Cherry Day
"Putt'n Pizza"
Cherry Pie Eating Contest
Turtle Races

Tuesday, July 9 Heritage Day
Native American Exhibits
Pet Show
Ice Cream Social
Bed Race
Heritage Parade - 7:00 pm

Wednesday, July 10 Special Kids Day
Bike Rodeo
Cherry Pie Eating Contest
Royal Pageant of Fashion
Streetside Teen Dance

Thursday, July 11 Kids' Day
Cherry Pie Eating Contest
Junior Royale Parade-7pm

Friday, July 12 Seniors' Day
Sand Sculpture Contest
Cherry Pie Eating Contest
Very Cherry Luncheon
Fun Run & Walk

Saturday, July 13
Festival of Races
Golden Mile Race
Wheelchair Mile Race
Cherry Royale Parade
Hole-In-One Final Shoot Out
Queen Coronation
Commemorative Pin Drawing
Milk Carton Boat Regatta
Fireworks Grand Finale

EVERY DAY
Cherry Connection
Hole-In-One Golf Contest
Free Entertainment Stage
Cherry Farm Market
Arnold's Amusement Rides
Bingo

Major concerts all week long

Nature & Environment

Nature & Environment

New Designs For Growth

*Linking Community, Economy, and Land
in Northwest Michigan*

By Keith Schneider
Michigan Land Use Institute

A coalition of business, government and environmental organizations, responding to surging population growth and unchecked development in rural Northwest Michigan,, has established a novel planning project to prevent damage to natural resources and strengthen the regional economy.

Led by the Traverse City Area Chamber of Commerce, New Designs For Growth is providing public education and land use planning services to townships in five counties along the coast of Lake Michigan. In partnership with builders and business executives, New Designs For Growth also is establishing a new regulatory framework for development that uses incentives to reduce costs and encourage resource conservation.

The principal services offered by New Designs For Growth are:

Organizing public meetings to inform township leaders and residents about modern conservation land planning principles. The curriculum of the meetings will include an extensive analysis of modern regulatory tools that safeguard natural resources and encourage orderly development.

Holding workshops and conducting personalized planning review sessions for builders, developers, and large property owners that emphasize new approaches to rural land division which enhance economic returns, protect cultural heritage, and preserve natural features.

Sending a team of technical experts to assess a township's land use plan and then provide professional advice, at a shared cost, about how it could be strengthened. Conceived as a thorough "zoning check up," the assessments will assist townships in fashioning new planning approaches and putting them into effect.

Providing technical assistance to community leaders for constructing new tax, zoning, and permitting provisions. The rules will be designed to save money and provide economic incentives for protecting small towns and natural resources. The intent is to create new policy initiatives so that Northwest Michigan's built environment of the 21st century does not undermine the region's principal attributes: new economic opportunities and a healthy natural environment.

THE NEED IS APPARENT

For most of the 20th century, the essential images of Northwest Michigan have been its inviting forests, peaceable orchards, and sparkling blue lakes. These treasured attributes are threatened as the next century approaches, since the entire region has been swept up in a powerful economic restructuring.

Traverse City is now an influential regional center of information-age industries. Jobs are being generated in record numbers, spurring fast-paced growth in nearly every township and village within 40 miles. If current trends hold, by 2020 the population of the five-county area surrounding Traverse City will reach 190,000, a 41% increase from today. As forests fall to subdivisions, and meadows are turned into malls, unsettling new regional symbols are emerging: traffic jams, chaotic strip developments, an explosion of steel and concrete.

Most residents are of two minds about the growth. A century after the natural frontier was settled, a new economic frontier based on banking, construction, education, medical care, professional services, recreation, telecommunications, transportation, and energy development is providing welcome business and career opportunities in Northwest Michigan. But throughout the Grand Traverse area, residents also are becoming more politically restive about the unpleasant and discomfiting consequences of loosely organized growth: a quickening pace of life, rising taxes, frayed community spirit, and a disfigured landscape.

The most important issue now facing Northwest Michigan is: Will the region succumb to the same old sprawl that has ruined countless beautiful places before? Or will developers and communities work together to establish innovative land use plans that provide room to grow while safeguarding the clean rivers, inviting lakes and green forests that make the region one of the truly stirring rural landscapes in the United States?

The groups involved in New Designs For Growth believe there is a deep political resolve in Northwest Michigan to blaze a new path to improve the region's economy, preserve its small towns, and sustain its clean environment. Putting ideas into effect to realize this goal means years of persistent, thoughtful work. "We see growth as desireable for this region," said Keith Charters, the retired restaurant owner hired by the Chamber of Commerce to oversee the project. "What is not desireable is how we are growing. Growth needs to be managed. This project is about trying to build the will in the region to do that."

In order for communities to protect their land and their culture, they will need to:

Amass a more extensive data base on economic policy and land use management.

Establish a much more inclusive public education program to bring in residents, business leaders and public officials.

Gain access to teams of technically-qualified professionals to help them understand the distinctive growth challenges they face and come up with sensible regulatory responses that work.

New Designs For Growth intends to provide for all of these needs by sustaining Northwest Michigan's vibrant economy and safeguarding its wondrous natural heritage.

PROJECT HISTORY

New Designs For Growth is the latest stage of a community planning effort that began in 1992 with publication of the Grand Traverse Bay Region Development Guidebook. Underwritten by a broad-based coalition of business and government planning officials, and prepared by a prominent Lansing-based planning consultant, the guidebook is a compendium of model development practices. It employs simple drawings to compare inadequate and superior uses of land. In its 128 pages, readers take a visual tour of practical development techniques that minimize clutter, improve appearance, and preserve natural features.

One of only a dozen illustrated regional planning documents in the country, the Guidebook won the Michigan Chapter of the American Planning Association's top award in 1993. Produced at a cost of $110,000, the Guidebook's planning principles were incorporated in the general plans of many of northern Michigan's townships and municipalities.Leelanau County, for example, borrowed heavily from the Guidebook's principles for its general plan. It also prompted the Grand Traverse County Planning Commission to establish separate awards for developers and communities that followed the Guidebook's principles.

The initial surge of interest in the Guidebook gradually faded. "When it first came out, it was seen as an educational tool, and provided a catalyst for thinking about these issues," said Marsha Smith, the executive director of the Grand Traverse Regional Community Foundation. "It's concepts were endorsed by every governmental unit in Grand Traverse County. But when it came to translate the guidelines into ordinances, everybody found out how time consuming, how difficult that is especially at the same time they were reviewing so many new development projects."

In 1994, the Traverse City Area Chamber of Commerce, one of the Guidebook's principal sponsors, decided that its major goal for the year would be to revive the innovative planning ideas and instill as many as possible in the Traverse City metropolitan area, and in the region's rural townships. Mr. Bergsma and Ms. Smith were named co-chairmen of the project. In May, 1995, Mr. Charters, a member of the Natural Resources Commission appointed by Gov. John Engler, was asked to coordinate the work. Three months later, Mr. Charters and Ms. Smith formed a steering committee composed of business, governmental, educational and environmental organizations to held design the project's overall structure.

By October, 1995 the steering committee had laid out a course of action. The Guidebook would serve as the central text in a public education effort aimed at providing communities with innovative tools to respond to change. One of the project's central goals is to broaden the civic discussion about growth by improving the public's understanding of land use planning. Another goal, at least as important, is to convince local officials and residents of the high stakes for the environment, the economy, and Northwest Michigan's superior quality of lfe if new land use management tools are not used.

A PROMISING START

New Designs for Growth began on March 12, 1996 with a regional conference attended by more than 300 local leaders and featuring as the keynote speaker Henry Richmond, the founder of 1,000 Friends of Oregon and one of the nation's foremost land use planning authorities.

During the conference, townships submitted applications for the planning services provided by New Designs for Growth. According to Mr. Richmond, New Designs For Growth is among the most comprehensive planning programs ever proposed by a rural community. It is one of the very few sponsored by business groups and taking shape outside the purview of local or state government.

The total cost of the five-year project is estimated at more than $150,000 per year. The Traverse City Area Chamber of Commerce has set aside $65,000 to finance the project in 1996. The Traverse City Convention and Visitors Bureau and its members have committed $30,000, and Rotary Charities of Traverse City contributed $30,000. The New

Designs for Growth steering committee is seeking additional financing from prominent regional and national foundations.

Indeed, what makes New Designs for Growth unique is its pedigree. The heart of the community's business and political leadership have expressed enthusiastic support. Business leaders in turn looked to the region's governmental, educational, and environmental organizations for help. Such a broad coalition is precisely what's needed to tackle one of the most politically and economically complex issues of our time. As Ms. Smith has said, the key is to build relationships with township and county leaders in order to court their help and avoid the turf issues that could delay or even derail the project. If such barriers are overcome, the result is likely to be a prize cherished by generations that follow: a matchless natural landscape of green hills and blue water, and a handsome, prosperous community like none other.

PROJECT PARTNERS

Traverse City Area Chamber Foundation
Grand Traverse Regional Community Foundation
Northwest Michigan Resource Conservation and Development Council
Grand Traverse Regional Land Conservancy
Landscape Architects & Planners, Inc.
Elk Rapids Village Council and Planning
Antrim County Planning Department
Traverse City Transportation and Land Use Study
Peninsula Township Planning Commission
Whitewater Township Planning Commission
Leelanau Conservancy
Michigan Land Use Institute
Grand Traverse County Planning Department
Home Builders Association of the Grand Traverse Area
Environmental Solutions, Inc.
Environmental Consultants & Services, Inc.
Michigan State University Extension
Northwest Michigan Council of Governments
Grand Traverse Bay Watershed Initiative

> For more information please write or call:
>
> New Designs For Growth
> P.O. Box 5316
> Traverse City, Michigan 49686
> 947-7566

MICHIGAN LAND USE INSTITUTE

The Michigan Land Use Institute is a nonprofit economic and environmental policy research organization dedicated to fostering a new approach to development that respects the land, the communities that inhabit the land, and the inherent process of change. The Institute's philosophy is to look well beyond the conventional jobs versus environment debate. Our goal is to promote economic opportunity, while respecting the value of open land, and clean air and water.

We value the integrity of local economic self-reliance. The gap between rich and poor in rural America is widening, causing polarization and diminishing communication between classes. Economic hardship puts pressure on political leaders to accept, indiscriminately, any kind of development. Failing to solve this problem means that we end up with sprawl, junk architecture, and hollowed out town centers.

The Michigan Land Use Institute seeks to develop a new framework for shaping a community's future by encouraging much broader participation. We seek to engage the whole of the community in a unified effort to take control of our own destiny, and in so doing, create a joyful place to live and work, an optimum human habitat.

The Institute focuses its research and policy work on agriculture, energy efficiency, forestry, land use planning, state and federal tax policy, rural economic development, and transportation

The Institute has a nine member board from four Northwest Michigan counties and Washington, D.C. The Institute's executive director is Keith Schneider, a former national environmental correspondent with the New York Times and a member of the Springdale Township Planning Commission in Manistee County.

The Institute carries out its work by offering the following services to the community:

A professional research and consulting staff, with technically qualified specialists, to assist grass roots groups, businesses, farmers, and government bodies.

Research on land use planning and policy in order to create new concepts that communities can apply to the problem of integrating economic development into working rural and urban landscapes.

A library that communities can tap to more quickly understand the complexities of economic and environmental issues.

Through communications in its two newsletters, The Great Lakes Bulletin and the MCLUC Reporter, and through pamphlets, reports, newspaper and magazine articles, and in video, audio and multi-media presentations.

PROGRAMS AND ACCOMPLISHMENTS

The Institute designed a series of land use management and planning studies for Benzie County. The project, Benzie County: At the Precipice will provide a more solid foundation for a community wide discussion on how to harness economic opportunity while safeguarding the county's environment and rural way of life.

The Institute is working with a coalition of business, government and other conservation groups in a five-year project to improve land use planning in the Grand Traverse region. The project, New Designs for Growth, is sponsored by the Grand Traverse Area Chamber of Commerce and is meant to provide public education and land use planning services to townships in five counties.

With the aid of several other prominent environmental organizations, the Institute launched the Michigan Energy Reform Coalition in May, 1995. The statewide Coalition, which now has ten environmental groups and three local governments as partners, is building a highly influential campaign at the grass roots to formulate new public policy and dramatically increase oversight of the oil and gas industry.

The Institute is designing a public education program for the trans2 Corporation, a Livonia, Michigan-based designer and manufacturer of personal electric vehicles. Use of the small, affordable, recyclable, lightweight and versatile vehicle promotes compact village centers, reduces need for more expensive roads and parking lots, and aims to encourage a new economic and social vitality based on appropriate use of new technology.

Keith Schneider is the Executive Director. For the past ten years Keith was a national correspondent with the New York Times, specializing in environment, agriculture, energy, and land use issues. As chairman of the Michigan Communities Land Use Coalition, he helped build an effective statewide campaign to increase citizen involvement in the development of Antrim Shale natural gas. Keith is the environmental columnist for Traverse maga-zine and writes for several other national and regional publications. He is secretary of the Springdale Township Planning Commission in Manistee County.

For more information, please write or call:
Michigan Land Use Institute,
P.O. Box 228,
Benzonia, Michigan 49616,
882-4723

"You will be impressed with his knowledge of organic gardening and his commitment to protecting our environment."—P.O.

Erick Takayama
Grand Traverse Organic

I moved my family to this area two years ago, after vacationing here all my life — remembering the clean air, forests and lakes — with a desire for a quieter and more satisfying lifestyle. My father was a member of the committee that designed the Leelanau County General Plan that received recognition from Lansing for foresight and planning. His influence must have rubbed off on me, since I felt it was time to start my own business and do something positive for the region I have admired all my life.

The rate of growth and development in Traverse City and the surrounding area has made us more conscious of the region's beauty and natural resources. This is an environmentally sensitive area, geographically, due to the natural watershed and runoff of the hillsides into our streams, lakes and bay. It is inevitable that some of the chemicals used in lawn, orchard and garden care end up in our waterways. To be cost-effective in agriculture, chemical controls are unavoidable; however, there are other alternatives for lawn and garden care.

**3845 Kennedy Place
Williamsburg, MI 49690
Phone: 938-2626**

These facts and our concern for natural resource conservation are what have inspired us. Grand Traverse Organic is a garden care and consulting company, specializing in organic and natural enhancement of the environment for the benefit of the entire community. We do organic lawn treatments for residential and commercial properties and consult and assist people who like to do their own yard work, yet would like to switch to safer alternatives.

We also do wildflower and bulb naturalizing and improve on open space preserves for those wishing to attract native wildlife or birds. We set up composting programs to turn yard and kitchen waste into useful organic fertilizer for yards and gardens, helping to reduce the demand on area landfills. Our local trash companies already refuse yard waste and recommend composting as a solution, but very few people know how to do this. I'd like to think of GTO as an environmental care company for the 21st century.

My suggestions for those making the move to this area are to support small business in your community and do whatever you can to preserve the beauty of the area for future generations.

"This is the place to go for all your birding needs. A fun store to browse with lots of nature related items."—C.L.

Judy Barrett
Wild Birds Unlimited

Traverse City and Wild Birds Unlimited are a natural!

Ten years ago, I left my job teaching Suzuki violin in Kalamazoo and came to Traverse City to open a birdfeeding specialty store. I lived in the State Park that summer as we transformed an abandoned gas station on the river (across from WTCM) into my first store. Start-up capital came from a banker who went out on a limb because he believed in me. He was a birder.

Fast forward ten years of personal and business growth; a husband and a wonderful set of twin girls came along. The business grew out of two locations, and in 1995, we moved into our present site across from the Civic Center. We carry a full range of supplies and equipment for the birding enthusiast. This includes feeders, feed, birdhouses, binoculars, books and other bird-related products. My staff grew to its present twelve members. All are informed and intelligent and they are loyal birders and naturalists, as well as animal and environmental activists. I run the business and continually learn from them about birds and the natural world.

I knew I would personally be happy in Traverse City for many reasons - Interlochen, WIAA, NMC and even a good symphony orchestra to play viola in. These are all rich and unusual resources for a community of this size.

This area attracts many people because of its natural beauty. I am honored to be here and to have a business that helps people live in harmony with the birds and nature surrounding us.

> 1213 E. Front Street
> Traverse City, MI 49686
> Phone: 946-0431

"Our grandchildren will be thanking them for their efforts in preserving out beautiful region. They need our support."—C.L.

Grand Traverse Regional Land Conservancy

Glen Chown, Executive Director

Founded by a start-up grant from Rotary Charities in 1991, the Grand Traverse Regional Land Conservancy's mission is to protect significant natural, agricultural and scenic areas in Antrim, Benzie, Grand Traverse and Kalkaska Counties and to advance land stewardship - now and for future generations. Since its beginning, the Conservancy has established thirteen nature preserves, completed 33 conservation easements and successfully protected over 2,400 acres of land including more than nine miles of shoreline.

A non-profit, membership supported organization, the Conservancy is endorsed by a broad coalition of citizens - neighbors, business people, farmers, friends and summer residents. Our philosophy of voluntary, common sense land conservation is a key to our success. Land is a resource that is owned by individuals, but enjoyed by many. When it is overdeveloped or misused, we all suffer. Our land conservation goals are achieved through the donation of land, conservation easements, watershed protection programs, stewardship and education.

624 Third Street
Traverse City, MI 49684
Phone: 929-7911

As more people discover the beauty of Northern Michigan, increasing population and urban development threaten our region's natural resources. The Conservancy works to balance this area's growth with corresponding efforts to protect significant natural lands. Quality of life and a stable Northern Michigan economy are directly related to a healthy natural environment.

Land conservation is best achieved at the local level. I feel doubly blessed to be able to pursue my professional life's work in the midst of such spectacular and diverse natural beauty and in a business climate in which the goals of the Conservancy have been embraced by the region. The cooperation of Rotary Charities, the Chamber of Commerce and the Grand Traverse Convention and Visitors Bureau in supporting the goals of the Conservancy has been a key ingredient in our early success.

A case in point is the "New Designs for Growth Project" for which the Grand Traverse Chamber of Commerce is taking the lead in educating local governments and in promoting conservation-minded development approaches in our region. The Conservancy is working hand-in-hand to provide technical assistance, utilizing tools such as conservation easements.

THE GRAND TRAVERSE AUDUBON CLUB

President, Molly Harrigan, 269-3113
Vice President for Conservation, Bob Carstens, 946-3234
Membership, Harry Zeeryp, 946-6259

Meetings

The Grand Traverse Audubon Club meetings are usually held on the fourth Thursday of each month, except in November and December, when meetings are on the third Thursday of the month. No meetings are held in June July and August. The club meets at the Oleson Center dining room on the campus of Northwestern Michigan College. A brief business meeting begins at 7:30 pm, followed by an informative and entertaining program at 8:00 pm. For more information, contact President Molly Harrigan.

Field Trips

All interested persons are encouraged to attend field trips. Participants should dress for the weather. Remember that some trips may involve physical exertion and/or require special equipment. If you plan to attend, please contact the trip leader or President Molly Harrigan. For a schedule of field trips, contact Molly Harrigan.

Membership

If you would like to become a member of the Grand Traverse Audubon Club, please send your name, address and phone number to:
Harry Zeeryp
324 Fairlane Drive
Traverse City, MI 49684

Annual dues are: $12 per family, $10 for and individual and $5 for students.

DIRECTORY OF ENVIRONMENTAL GROUPS

Grand Traverse Regional Land Conservancy
624 Third Street
Traverse City, MI 49684
929-7911
Executive Director, Glen Chown

Leelanau Conservancy
105 N First Street
Leland, MI 49654
256-9665
Executive Director, Brian Price

Old Mission Conservancy
PO Box 88
Old Mission, MI 49673
929-7911
Coordinator, Rob Manigold

Michigan Land Use Institute
845 Michigan Avenue
Benzonia, MI 49616
882-4723
Executive Director, Keith Schneider

Grand Traverse Bay Watershed Initiative
1102 Cass St, Suite B
Traverse City, MI 49684
935-1514
Director, Chris Wright

Little Traverse Conservancy
3264 Powell Road
Harbor Springs, MI 49740
347-0991
Executive Director, Tom Bailey

Inland Seas Education Association
101 Dame Street, P.O. Box 218
Suttons Bay, MI 49682
271-3077
Executive Director, Tom Kelly

**Northwest Michigan Resource
Conservation & Development Council**
3193 Logan Valley Road
Traverse City, MI 49686
946-6817
Executive Director, Jim Haveman

Tip of the Mitt Watershed Council
P.O. Box 300
Conway, MI 49722
347-1181
Executive Director, Gail Gruenwald

Friends of the Jordan River
106 Depot Street, Complex 2
Bellaire, MI 49615
533-8363
Director, John Hummer

Grass River Natural Area
P.O. Box 231
Bellaire, MI 49615
533- 8314
Director, Mark Randolph

**Northern Michigan Environmental
Action Council**
P.O. Box 1166
Traverse City, MI 49685
946-6931
Co-Chairs, Kima Kraimer and Tim Young

Antrim Conservation District
Depot Street
Bellaire, MI 49615
533-8363
Coordinator, Janet Person

**Grand Traverse Soil & Water
Conservation District**
1222 Veterans Drive
Traverse City, MI 49684
941-0960
Administrator, Lew Coulter

**Leelanau Soil & Water
Conservation District**
Bunek Building, 208 W. Main
P.O. Box 205
Lake Leelanau, MI 49653
256-9783
Administrator, Judy Egeler

Benzie Soil & Water Conservation District
207 Benzie Blvd.
Beulah, MI 49617
882-4391
Administrator, Jean Kadlec

**Charlevoix Soil and Water
Conservation District**
5-K West Main Street
Boyne City, MI 49712
582-6193
Coordinator, Kelly Repputin

New Designs For Growth
P.O. Box 5316
Traverse City, Michigan 49686
947-7566
Director, Keith Charters

Odds & Ends & Free Stuff

Chapter 19

.

Odds & Ends & Free Stuff

This chapter is a collection of discoveries made over the years and is as close to a "catch all" as we have in this book. As you find more of these, pass them along to us. While we have made an effort to assure accuracy here, you should check these out individually, since things like this have a way of changing.

AMOCO Station
Front Street at Boardman: Free car wash with fill-up

Apache Trout Grill
Punch a lunch—10 punches gives 1 free lunch

Bartlings:
Downtown, has a frequent buyer program. Spend $500 and get a $50 certificate good toward another purchase.

Baskin-Robbins
Free ice cream cone on your birthday

Bayview
Buy a punch card and get 2-for-1 meals.

Blarney Castle Gas Stations
Fill up 15 times and get $5 off your next fill-up.

Blue Photo
Double prints at no extra charge on certain days.

Broadway Bagel
University Plaza on Front Street and on 14th Street: Discount coupons offering things like a free half-dozen with purchase of a full dozen on certain days.

Camera Shop, The
Downtown, offers deals on film processing. Process 5 rolls, get the next one developed free. Also, they offer a quick picture postcard-type birth announcement that is kind of unique.

Celebrations Store
On Lake Avenue, between Cass and Union Great source for party supplies, balloons, etc. They deliver and offer a discount punch card with grad-

uated discounts that begin at 10% and go up to 25% discount.

DTCA
Free Christmas ornament upon presentation of $200 in receipts from downtown merchants

Family Video
Rent one $1.00 video and get the second one free

GKC Theaters
Frequent movie-goer card—8 stamps entitle you to free admission, 14 stamps will get you 2 free admissions

Good Harbor Coffee Shop
Front Street and Union: Frequent User Card — buy 10 coffees, get one free

Grand Traverse Soil Conservation District
Offers free seedlings in the spring. Watch the Record-Eagle for details in the spring.

Heavenly Ham
Frequent buyer's card.

Holiday Gas Station
Gas discount card. Buy a certain amount and get some money off your next fill-up.

Horizon Books
A purchased $10 discount club card gives 10% discount on many items in the store.

Horizon Video
One free video rental on your birthday

Kids on the Move
This unique transportation service has an appeal to a lot of people with kids. You will see their well-marked vans around town.

Mabel's Restaurant
Free dessert on your birthday

Marathon Gas Stations
Discount card gives you 2 cents off a gallon.

Marifil's Cafe, Downtown
10% discount for downtown employees

Martinizing (One Hour) Dry Cleaning
Get a 20% discount card

Master Cleaners
VIP shirt service gives you a free laundry bag and shirt drop-off service

Maxbauer's Market
Free carryout service to your car.

McGough's
Lake Avenue, south of Eighth Street—Punch Card for free pet food after eight purchases of the same item.

Muffin Tin
Frequent Customer Card—1 free item after 7 visits

My Favorite Things and Peppercorn
Downtown—twenty $10 punches on card gives you a free $10 gift certificate.

Munson Hospital
Baby car seats for rent, really cheap. A $35 deposit and you get $32 back when you return the seat up to six months later.

Northwest Michigan College Library
Open to the public

Oleson's Markets
Free carryout service to your car.

Oryana
Show your Oryana membership card at Edson Farms and at other food co-ops around the state and get a 10% discount.

Pasta Company
Downtown—free dessert on your birthday

Pizzarama
South Airport Road—a good low-key local place for kids' birthday parties. They set tables, do the balloons, etc. You bring the kids and the presents. There is a small video area and a couple small rides. Call for reservations, since they only do one party at a time.

Prescription Shoppe
14th Street—a 10% discount on prescriptions for children under age 6.

Prevo's Markets
Free carry-out service from the store to your car.

Prevo's Markets
Accepts styrofoam, phone books, and plastic bags for recycling. These may not be recyclable elsewhere.

Reflections Restaurant
Free dessert on your birthday

Sara Lee Store
Frequent buyer punch card for $5 off on a $50 purchase

Spring Clean-Up Week
TC Sanitation crews collect nearly anything you put at the curb, free of charge in early May. Watch the Record-Eagle for details.

Subway
Sandwich Card—buy 24 subs and get one free

TC Hunan (Chinese Restaurant)
Free delivery within a three-mile radius of their South Airport location

TC Library
For $1, they'll gladly search for any book in print and borrow it from another library

TC Power and Light and Record-Eagle
Free conifer seedling on Earth Day

Tom's Markets
Free half gallon ice cream on your birthday with a pre-registration card they send you after you sign up

Tom's Markets and Meijer's
Each of these has a "drive up" service and they will help load groceries in your car.

Tom's Market
Valued Customer Card. It offers savings on different advertised items each week. You only get the savings if you have the card.

Wild Birds Unlimited
Seed sale. When you buy bulk birdseed at discount, they will store it for you until you need it.

Woodland Oil (Total) Gas Stations
Fill up 15 times and get $5 off your next fill-up.

Yarn Quest
$50 gift certificate when you spend $500.

YMCA
They sell a discount book as a fundraiser that offers many savings on local goods and services.

Pets

Chapter 20

Pets

Mike Cherry
Executive Director
Cherryland Humane Society

Pets and people are a natural combination. It is not surprising then, that many facets of living in the Grand Traverse area are en-joyed mutually by humans and their furry companions. It is not un-common to witness pets accompanying their families on scenic auto excursions or leisurely boat rides. The region's many trails serve hikers, joggers, runners, or cross country skiers, some of whom would not think of leaving their pets at home. Certainly, the area's abundant lakes, rivers, and streams are as much a source of refreshment and recreation to many pets as they are to their families. The spirit of enjoyment involved in living in the Grand Traverse region is tremendously enhanced when our pets are included.

Our pets are the beneficiaries of a wide array of area services. An outstanding group of veterinarians provide up-to -date medical assistance. Professional groomers keep our animal companions looking their best. Boarding facilities and pet sitters are abundantly available to care for our pets while we are away. We are also blessed with a variety of businesses that offer pet food and supplies essential to providing proper nourishment and care for our pets. For those who enjoy well-behaved animal companions, several area pet training services are available.

I moved to Traverse City permanently in 1968, after having spent many summers in the area while growing up. Little did I realize at that time that I could combine my desire to work for causes and my love for pets into a vocation. It has been a privilege to serve as the Executive Director of the Cherryland Humane Society since March of 1989.

Founded in July of 1956, the CHS celebrates its fortieth anniversary of service to pets, people, and communities in 1996. The CHS is a non-profit organization dependent upon donations for its existence. It is an independent shelter, not affiliated with any other humane society, organization, nor government entity. The CHS is conservative in nature and is not involved with political issues, nor is it activist in nature. It does not deal with wildlife, nor wildlife issues. The purpose of the CHS is to take in unwanted and homeless pets, mainly previously owned puppies and dogs (stray puppies and dogs are, by law, the responsibility of county animal control agencies) and previously owned and stray kittens and cats. In addition, it is the purpose of the CHS to adopt such animals out to humane, compassionate and caring homes. It is also the objective of the society to promote spaying and neutering and responsible and humane care of pets through public education and awareness programs.

The CHS works to provide a bright and positive future for all pets. That slogan is imperative to the focus of the work of the society, because the future is not bright for the majority of pets. This is sometimes difficult to believe, because most of us are accustomed to having healthy and happy pets in our own homes and seeing such pets in the homes of our friends and relatives. Those pets, however are in the minority. Consider that 70,000 puppies and kittens are born each day in the USA, compared with only 10,000 daily human births. The problem is that there are not nearly enough homes for them all. The tragedy is that, because of the overpopulation problem, 50,000 pets have to be euthanized each day in shelters throughout our nation. Locally, between 25 and 30 pets must be euthanized each week. It is also sad to note that less than 20% of pets that do find homes will end up in their original residences. The remainder are sold, given away, abandoned, or taken to shelters where many are eventually euthanized. It is because of the plight of our animal companions that the CHS has a vision of one day realizing a time when there will be a responsible, loving caring, and permanent home for all pets and a heightened public awareness of the benefit of pets to mankind. It is toward that end that the society works with diligence and purpose.

In 1990, the CHS adopted a ten year plan called Plan for Animal Welfare Success 2000 (P.A.W.S. 2000). The purpose of the plan is to end the pet overpopulation problem in the area and thereby end the need for euthanasia, as well as to realize the above-mentioned vision of the CHS. A number of programs have been implemented which have helped reduce the shelter population on an annual basis and which have helped raise the adoption rate significantly. Much remains to be done, however. An expanded educational program is currently being developed and is a key to the attainment of a better life for all of our local pets. An enhanced volunteer program is also vital. Volunteers are needed for direct in-shelter animal care, fund raising activities, educational and public awareness programs, program development, and clerical duties, as well as for other miscellaneous responsibilities. We believe that the sum total of our effectiveness on behalf of homeless animals has a direct correlation to the strength of our volunteer effort.

The shelter is located at 3200 N. Keystone Road in Traverse City, directly behind United Technologies, just off of South Airport Road. The shelter is open from 11 AM until 5 PM, Monday through Friday, and from 11 AM until 3 PM on Saturdays. There is no fee for bringing an animal to the shelter, but a donation of one's choosing is suggested. There is a $20.00 adoption fee for kittens and cats and a $30.00 adoption fee for puppies and dogs. In addition, a minimum of $20.00 is required as a spay/neuter deposit for animals not altered. The deposit is refunded once the animal is spayed or neutered. Participating veterinarians provide a free well-health checkup for each animal adopted from the CHS, plus reduced spay/neuter fees. The adoption procedure requires a questionnaire to be completed and a contract to be signed. Each animal entering the shelter receives an initial distemper shot and initial worming medication. Animals that are adopted receive a free identification tag that is registered with the CHS.

Financial support for the work of the CHS comes mainly in the form of donations, memberships, memorials, wills and fund raising activities. The work of the society is carried out by an outstanding volunteer board of directors and a small, but caring, staff as well as concerned and committed volunteers serving in various capacities.

Our animal companions give us joy, companionship, loyalty and unconditional love. In turn, they deserve the best that we can give them. Proper nutrition, plenty of water, and exercise, socialization, grooming, medical attention, shelter and love are but a few of the considerations our pets deserve. To remain a permanent part of our lives pets, including cats, should wear collars with identification tags. If pets become lost, timely notification should be given to county animal control agencies and local humane societies. It is important to remember that all dogs six months of age and older must be licensed in the county in which they reside. Proof of a current rabies vaccination must accompany the license application. Because of the extreme temperature variations in northern Michigan, it is vital that proper shelter from the elements be provided for our pets. Finally, we can all be good neighbors by keeping our furry friends properly confined.

It is readily apparent that the Grand Traverse region is a unique and wonderful place in which to live, work and recreate. Our pets help our lifestyles to become even more enriched. As we sometimes pause to reflect upon the blessings of our lives, it is apparent that a special note of thanks and tribute goes to our animal companions for helping to make life so special for each of us.

PET GROOMING

Acme Creek Kennels
5311 Bunker Hill Road, Acme
938-9518

Bokhara Pet Care Centers
606 W. Front Street
946-7333

Canine Clipper Mobile Dog Grooming
Buckley
946-7387

Clipper Dog Grooming The
441 E. Front Street, 947-6894

Nancy's Pet Salon
390 Four Mile South, 947-2318

Pets & Things
318 S. Cedar, Kalkaska, 258-5115

Tulamar Kennel Boarding & Grooming
6281 Barney Road, 947-4494

PET SHOPS

House of Pets Inc.
839 S. Garfield Avenue, 941-0470

Ovaitt's Pets & RC Speed Shop
744 Munson, 947-6670

Petland
3200 S. Airport Road West, Grand Traverse Mall, 929-3244

Pets & Things
318 S. Cedar, Kalkaska, 258-5115

PET SITTING SERVICE

Christi's Critter Sitting
7792 Cook, Williamsburg, 267-5151, 922-0703

PET SUPPLIES & FOODS - RETAIL

Acme Creek Kennels
5311 Bunker Hill, Acme, 938-9518

Clipper Dog Grooming The
441 E. Front Street, 947-6894

Collar Clinic The
3189 Logan Valley, 497-2010

House of Pets Inc.
839 S. Garfield Avenue, 941-0470

McGough's Inc.
501 Lake Avenue, 947-5900

Pet Supplies Plus
1185 S. Airport Road West, 935-1661

Square Deal Country Store
900 Woodmere, 946-5030

Tulamar Kennel Boarding & Grooming
6281 Barney Road, 947-4494

Westbay Akitas
3535 Three Mile Road, N., 929-3223

KENNELS

Acme Creek Kennels
5311 Bunker Hill, Acme, 938-9518

Bokhara Pet Care Centers
606 W. Front Street, 946-7333

Christi's Critter Sitting
922-0703

Diana's Personal Touch
2716 Hammond Road, E., 946-5630

Gray's Kennels
County Road 611 Mayfield, Kingsley, 263-5643

Leelanau Boarding Kennels
8761 E. Kovarik Road, Northport, 386-7340

Limberlost Kennel
M-88 Highway, Bellaire, 533-8475

Northwood Animal Hospital
7966 U.S. 31 South, Grawn, 276-6361

Paradise Veterinary Clinic PC
10349 Blackman Road, Kingsley, 263-5116

Pet Nanny of Traverse City
Maple City, 228-7387

Tulamar Kennel Boarding & Grooming
6281 Barney Road, 947-4494

KENNELS-EQUIPMENT, SUPPLIES

Invisible Fence of Northwest Michigan
Lake Leelanau, 256-8891

Publications & Broadcasting

Chapter 21

Publications and Broadcasting

Here is a list of some of the media in the Traverse City area: print, television and radio.

PRINT MEDIA

Advisor Community Weekly
POB 797, Beulah 49617
882-9615

Antrim County News
P.O. Box 337, Bellaire 49615
533-8523

Benzie County Record Patriot
POB 673, Frankfort 49635
352-9659

Dick E Bird News
POB 377, Acme 49610-0377
267-5630

Entertainment Guide
3054 Cass, TC 49684
946-7650

The Gazette
POB 885, Elk Rapids 49629
264-6800

Leader & Kalkaskan
318 N Cedar, Kalkaska 49646
258-4600

Leelanau Enterprise
POB 527, Leland 49654
256-9827

Northern Express
POB 209, TC 49685-0209
947-8787

Penny Stretcher
POB 647, Mancelona 49659
587-8471

Preview Community Weekly
3054 Cass Rd., TC 49684
946-7650

Prime Time News
733 E 8th St STE B9, TC 49684
929-7919

Stewardship Quarterly,
PO 885, Elk Rapids 49629
264-6890

The Town Meeting,
PO 33, Elk Rapids 49629
264-9711

TC Record Eagle
POB 632, TC 49685-0632
946-2000

Traverse, Northern Michigan's Magazine
121 S Union, TC 49684
941-8391

TELEVISION

FOX 33 — WGKI
7400 S 45 Rd, Cadillac 49601
775-9813

TV 29 & 8 (ABC) — WGTU/WGTQ
201 E Front St, TC 49684
946-2900

TV 7 & 4 (NBC) — WPBN/WTUM
POB 546, TC 49685
947-7770

TV 9 & 10 (CBS) — WWTV/WWUP
22320 130th Ave, Tustin 49688
775-3478

RADIO

WTCM AM & FM
314 E Front, TVC 49684
103.5 FM — Country, 580 AM — Newstalk
947-7675

WIAA Interlochen Public Radio
1 Lyon St, Inter. 49643
88.7 FM— Classical Music, News
276-6171

WNMC
1701 E Front St, TVC 49686
90.9 FM — Jazz, Diverse
922-1091

WAIR/WIAR
322 Bay Street, Petoskey 49770
92.5 FM, 94.3 FM — Oldies
348-2000

WBNZ
1532 Forrester Road, Frankfort 49635
99.3 FM — Adult Contemporary
352-9603

WCCW
121 E Front St, TVC 49684
107.5 FM — Oldies, 1310 AM — Big Band
946-0000

WGFM
232 E Front St, TVC 49684
105.1, 98.1 FM — Classic Rock
922-0981

WLDR
118 South Union, TVC 49684
101.9 FM — Adult Contemporary
947-3220

WKHQ
120 W State, TVC 49684
105.9 FM — Adult Contemporary
941-0963

WKLT
745 South Garfield, TVC 49686
97.5, 98.9 FM — Classic Rock
947-0003

WLJN
POB 1400, TVC 49685
89.9 FM, 1400 AM — Christian Talk
946-1400

WJML
2175 Click Rd, Petoskey 49770
1100 AM — News/Talk/Sports/Weather
347-9565

WJKF
314 E Front, TVC 49684
92.9 FM, 1370 AM — Country, News Talk
947-7675

WKPK,
PO 190, Gaylord 49735
106.7 FM — Contemporary
732-2474

LITE
120 W State St, TVC 49684
96.3, 96.7 FM — Soft Adult
941-0963

Regional Growth & Economic Data

Chapter 22

Regional Growth & Economic Data

Paul Oppliger & Nancy Hayward

The population growth being experienced by this area is part of a larger migration pattern in Michigan and around the country. We are seeing a flight from the problems of larger cities such as Detroit, Lansing, Flint, Saginaw, etc. to counties north and west. There is also flight from Chicago, Ft. Wayne, etc., especially to the west coast of Michigan.

The counties with 8% or greater growth from 4/90 to 7/94 are shown here.

Figure 2
Michigan Counties With Growth Rate Greater Than 8% (from 4/90 to 7/94)

County	Number	Percent
Alger	847	9.4
Benzie	1,064	8.7
Clare	2,638	10.6
Crawford	1,127	9.2
Emmet	1,994	8.0
Gladwin	2,042	9.3
Grand Traverse	5,310	8.3
Keweenaw	179	10.5
Leelanau	1,595	9.7
Livingston	13,438	11.6
Newaygo	4,533	11.9
Ogemaw	1,570	8.4
Ottawa	17,570	9.4
Michigan	201,268	2.2

Source: Office of the State of Michigan Demographer 10/5/95

T he Grand Traverse area has experienced substantial growth for the last 25 years. The rate of population growth in the 1980's, and so far in the 1990's, appears to be running at about 17-18% per decade, which is down from the 30-40% in the 1970's. Growth is generally good, unless it is too fast or is the wrong kind.

POPULATION GROWTH

Figure 1

County	1970	1980	%inc.	1990	%inc.	1994	%inc.
Grand Traverse	39, 175	54,890	40.1	64,273	17.1	69,583	8.3
Leelanau	10,872	14,007	29.8	16,527	18.0	18,122	9.7

The two counties with the largest population growth in numbers are Ottawa and Livingston. They represent an extension of suburbia — the attempt to get a piece of land or a small farm while commuting to a well-paid job in the city. The third largest population growth is in Grand Traverse County and this represents more of a a "pulling up stakes" and moving to a new job, new community, new friends, new churches and a new lifestyle.

Who are these people who migrate to the Greater Grand Traverse area? While we cannot examine the migrant cohort by itself, we can examine the influence the migrant cohort has on the total population.

AGE

Any analysis of the age of a population group must take into account the "baby boomers". By now, we know that the leading edge of boomers are turning 50 in 1996, while the trailing edge turns 34 in 1996. As this wave moves through the U.S. economy, it will produce both large opportunities and problems.

Figures 3 and 4 clearly show the wave of boomers in Grand Traverse and Leelanau Counties. Note the increase of people 75 and over in 1990.

Figure 3

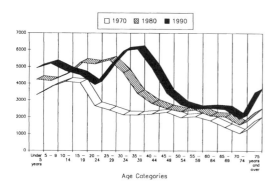

Population by Age
Grand Traverse County

Figure 4

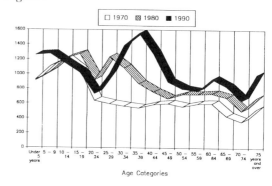

Population by Age, Leelanau County

WAGES

There is an old saying around here: "A view of the bay is worth half the pay." That has an element of truth and there are two reasons. The quality of life has a strong attraction to people, resulting in a condition where there are always more people than jobs, or at least good jobs: therefore, lower wages. There are virtually no labor unions in the area to artificially raise wages.

Figures 5 and 6 compare wages paid in Grand Traverse and Leelanau Counties to wages paid in Michigan. It is interesting to note how differently job sectors in Grand Traverse and Leelanau County compare to the state average.

Figure 5

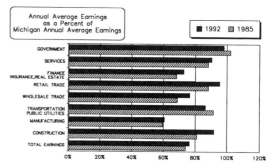

Grand Traverse County Wages
and Michigan Wages

Figure 6

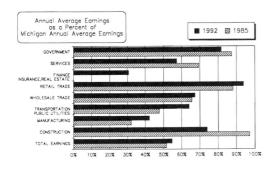

Leelanau County Wages
and Michigan Wages

Figure 8

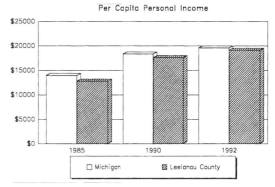

Per Capita Income: Michigan
and Leelanau County

Professional jobs are also paid at lower rates than the state average. The best estimate is that they are about 15% lower than state-wide salaries.

INCOME

Income can come from many sources, including wages, investments, inheritance, pensions, royalties, social security, etc.

Figures 7 and 8 compare Personal Income per capita in the two counties with state-wide averages. Both counties were almost on a par with the rest of Michigan in 1992. The difference between wages and income reflects the impact of a significant number of people who move here after retirement.

Figure 7

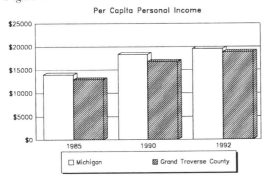

Per Capita Income: Michigan and
Grand Traverse County

source: US Department of Commerce, Bureau of Economic Analysis

EDUCATION

The level of education of a community generally reflects on income, cultural activities, participation in government and in the community. Educated parents expect a good educational system for their children.

In both education categories, 12 years plus and 16 years plus, Grand Traverse and Leelanau Counties are significantly ahead of the Michigan average. See Figure 9.

Figure 9

Years of Education, Age 25 and Over

	1980		1990	
	12 Yrs+	16 Yrs+	12 Yrs+	16 Yrs
G. Traverse	77.2%	19.1%	84.9%	22.1%
Leelanau	76.8%	19.4%	85.1%	24.1%
Michigan	68.0%	14.3%	76.8%	17.4%

Source: US Bureau of the Census

SUMMARY

GROWTH

The population growth in the greater Grand Traverse Area for the past 15 years appears to have stabilized at an increase of 2% per year. This rate is down from the frantic rate of 3.5% to 4.0% per year in the 1970's.

AGE

The median age of the greater Grand Traverse area is increasing

1970	28.6 years
1980	29.4 years
1990	33.9 years

WAGES AND INCOME

Wages are about 80% of the state average. The lower rate also applies to professional jobs. Per capita income of the area is very close to the state average.

EDUCATION

Grand Traverse and Leelanau Counties both have citizens who are significantly better educated than the state average.

Religion

Religion

Dr. Homer E. Nye
The Presbyterian Church

Rev. Edwin Frederick "Father Fred"
The Father Fred Foundation

Nestled between two bays of clear water lies the gorgeous region of Traverse City, an area whose spiritual tradition spans 10,000 years. Ancient cultures were guided by practices which supported the well-being of their community. Belief was inseparable from daily life given the people's constant attention to the spiritual nature of all things. Modern descendants, the Ottawa, Chippewa, Potowatami, and others claim and continue to practice those religious rites handed down through the millennia. Christianity was introduced to the area in 1839 with the arrival of Peter Daugherty and John Fleming. The two men had been sent by the Presbyterian Board of Foreign Missions to assist the

Rev. Ferry who had established a mission on Mackinac Island. Finding that project well supported, Daugherty and Fleming set out in their canoe down the waters of Lake Michigan. They landed near Yuba Park and began their work among the Native Americans, establishing the first mission and school on what is now known as Old Mission Peninsula. Due to a land dispute with the federal government, Daugherty and Chief Aghosa, who converted to Christianity, chose to move the tribe to a new mission site in Omena. There, another school and church were established. The Omena Presbyterian Church continues as a worshipping congregation today.

Following Daugherty's efforts, and with the growth of the Grand Traverse Region, many other Christian traditions began to develop. The Congregational, Baptist, Methodist and Episcopal Churches were among the first. Today, there are over eighty Protestant congregations in the area, representing nearly every tradition. Independently and ecumenically, these active and involved churches have supported several Christian schools. In 1996, over 700 students were involved in these educational programs.

The Roman Catholic tradition began in 1855, when Father Mrak began his work in Peshawbestown. He was succeeded by the Reverend Father A. Herbstreet through whose efforts the first Catholic church, St. Francis, was begun in 1870. Grand Traverse County now encompass five parishes. Over the years, these vital congregations have united in the cause of education, resulting in the Grand Traverse Area Catholic School System. From nursery through high school, over 1100 students are enrolled.

While Jewish settlers were among the first to settle in the Grand Traverse Area, a synagogue was not completed until 1886. It is still used by the congregation, Temple Beth El, making it the oldest continuously used synagogue in Michigan. Temple Beth El, reflecting several Jewish traditions, continues to be a valuable part of the spiritual community. In addition to regular worship services, a religious school is run by the congregation.

More recently, other spiritual traditions, such as the Unitarian Universalist, Mormon, Bahai, and Unity have added their presence to the religious community. As the community grows, others will be included, providing a spectrum of spiritual expression for the residents and visitors in this area.

Over the years, these diverse traditions, recognizing their differences, but coming together for the common good of others and the community have addressed the needs of the area. Common efforts have included work among migrant workers, the homeless and the hungry. With such a spirit of cooperation, the long tradition of spiritual presence will continue for years to come. It will also continue the ancient affirmation that belief is inseparable from daily life. In the light of that tradition and belief, the Grand Traverse spiritual community welcomes all who live or visit among us.

> Church services are listed each in the Traverse City Record-Eagle. Information on services is also in the Yellow Pages.

Area Churches

We thank the Kiwanis Club of Traverse City for sharing this listing of religious organizations in the Grand Traverse area. It is provided by the Kiwanis Club as a service to the residents and visitors of the Grand Traverse Area. The listings are subject to change. For changes in listings, please notify:

Kiwanis Club of Traverse City
P.O. Box 864
Traverse City, MI 49685-0864

ASSEMBLY OF GOD

Faith Assembly of God
3050 S. Airport Road
947-4530

BAPTIST

(American Baptist)
First Baptist Church
244 Washington Street
946-4727 or 947-0014

(Conservative Baptist Association)
Bethany Baptist Church
302 Washington Street
947-5761 or 946-4961

(General Association of Regular Baptist)
Immanuel Baptist Church
1027 McRae Hill Road
946-6938 or 943-4897

Kingsley Baptist Church
107 Blair, Kingsley
263-5650 or 263 5433

(Independent Baptist)
Bible Baptist Church
1915 Cass Road
947-0660 or 947-1028

Liberty Baptist Church
4875 West Blair Townhall Road
943-8827

Riverside Baptist Church
1895 Keystone Road
Home of Riverside Christian School
946-0710

Inland Baptist Church
US 31 South, Interlochen
275-6323 or 275-7417

(Southern Baptist Church)
Cherryland Baptist Church
4050 Barnes Road
P.O. Box 168
946-5337

BIBLE

Bible Methodist Church
7640 South US 31, Grawn
276-9316

CHRISTIAN (DISCIPLES OF CHRIST)

First Christian Church
3686 West Townhall Road
946-4074

CHRISTIAN REFORMED

Fellowship Christian Reformed
2555 Garfield Road, North
947-6520

CHRISTIAN SCIENCE

First Church of Christ Scientist
Glen Arbor
334-4961

First Church of Christ Scientist
320 Sixth Street
Reading Room, 118 S. Union Street

CHURCH OF CHRIST

Church of Christ
225 West 14th Street
946-9670

Church of Christ
3250 Rennie
946-9252

Grand Traverse Church of Christ
748 East State Street
947-5240

The Church of Christ
S. Airport Road West (One block west of Cass)
946-9252

CHURCH OF GOD

(Cleveland, Tennessee)
Church of God * Lighthouse
2770 LaFranier Road
947-7965

(Anderson, Indiana)
Pinegrove Church of God
790 Indian Trail
946-8720

CHURCH OF JESUS CHRIST OF LATTER DAY SAINTS

The Church of Jesus Christ of Latter Day Saints
3746 Veterans Drive
947-6500 or 946-9149

REORGANIZED CHURCH OF JESUS CHRIST OF LATTER DAY SAINTS

Reorganized Church of Jesus Christ of Latter Day Saints
813 Parsons Road
947-0600

CONGREGATIONAL

First Congregational Church
(United Church of Christ)
8106 Center Road
947-8696

Suttons Bay Congregational Church
Lincoln and Madison, Suttons Bay
271-6036

Old Mission Congregational Church
(United Church of Christ)
in the village of Old Mission
929-1014

Trinity United Church of Christ
Warren & Nagonaba Streets, Northport
386-5801

EPISCOPAL

Grace Episcopal Church
349 Washington Street
P.O. Box 1001
947-2330

St. Paul's Episcopal Church
403 Traverse Street, Elk Rapids
264-8871 or 264-9625

EVANGELICAL COVENANT

Northport Evangelical Covenant Church
409 Shabwasung Street, Northport
386-7362

West Bay Covenant Church
12720 West Bayshore Road
946-7947

FREE METHODIST

Free Methodist Church
Kingsley
263-5630

HOLINESS

Pilgrim Bible Holiness Church
7144 North Long Lake Road
947-2649

SOCIETY OF FRIENDS

Long Lake Friends Church
4172 Church Rd. at N. Long Lake Rd.
946-5289

Friends of the Light/Pleasant Grove Friends
corner of 5th and Oak Streets

INDEPENDENT FUNDAMENTALIST OF AMERICA

East Bay Calvary Church
2368 Holiday Hills Road
938-1966 or 938-1160

Forest Lake Bible Church
4331 Spider Lake Road
946-2118

Interlochen Bible Church
M-137 South, Interlochen
276-6401

JEHOVAH'S WITNESSES

Kingdom Hall of Jehovah's Witnesses
3819 Four Mile Road
938-2180

JEWISH SYNAGOGUE

Congregation Beth-El
311 S. Park Street
946-1913 or 949-8868

LUTHERAN

(ELCA)
Bethany Lutheran Church
220 W. Nagonaba, Northport
386-5037 or 271-6946

Calvary Lutheran Church
10180 N. Elk Lake Road, off U.S. 31
P.O. Box 149, ElkRapids
264-8841

Immanuel Lutheran Church
203 Lincoln St., Suttons Bay
271-6946

Feast of Victory Lutheran Church
4400 Mt. Hope Road, Acme
938-1070

Bethlehem Lutheran Church
1050 Peninsula Drive at Garfield
947-9880 or 947-9888

(Missouri Synod)
First Lutheran Church, Sutton's Bay
271-3271

Grace Lutheran Church
508 Elm Street at 1st St., Elk Rapids
264-5312

Bethlehem Lutheran Church
Lake Street, one block south of M-22, Glen Arbor
334-4180 or 228-7209

Redeemer Lutheran Church
US 31 at Rogers Road, Interlochen
276-6372 or 943-9623

St. Johanne's Lutheran Church
Summit City Rd., 1 mi.E. & _ mi.S.of Kingsley
263-5110

St. Michael's Lutheran Church
1030 Centre St. at Garfield
947-5293

St. Paul's Lutheran Church
7 miles S.of Leland on M-22 near Sugar Loaf, Good Harbor
228-6888

Trinity Lutheran Church
13th and Maple Streets
946-2720

Immanuel Lutheran Church
Pearl and Grand, Leland
256-7271

(Wisconsin Evangelical Lutheran Synod)
Prince of Peace Lutheran Church
1776 High Lake Road
941-7812 or 941-4975

MENNONITE

Mennonite Church
915 Carver Street
947-8103

MISSIONARY CHURCH

Bates Missionary Church
6517 Bates Road, Williamsburg
267-5543

NAZARENE

First Church of the Nazarene
1023 Division St.
947-5446 or 947-4115

Mayfield Chapel
Mayfield

NON-DENOMINATIONAL

Church of the Living God
Church of the Living God School
1514 Birmley
947-7645

Christ's Ecumenical Church
4276 Ridgemoor Drive
946-2541
Meets at the T.C. West Junior High Little Theatre

Leelanau Community Church
_-mile South of M-204 on County Road 641
Lake Leelanau

Maple City Community Church
89 Church Street, Maple City
228-5275

New Hope Community Church
US -31, three miles north of Acme
935-3885

Oak Park Evangelical Free Church
400 Fair St. (SE corner of Civic Cntr.)
946-1347

NON DENOMINATIONAL MINISTRIES

Gideons International—Traverse City Camp
For information, call: 947-1138 or 946-2011

Northwestern Michigan College
Ecumenical Campus Ministries
922-1499

Youth For Christ
P.O. Box 854
947-5574

REFORMED IN AMERICA

Faith Reformed Church
1139 E. Front Street
947-7082 or 947-8039

Glen Lake Community Reformed Church
4902 County Rd. 616 West, Glen Arbor
334-4563 or 334-4571

ROMAN CATHOLIC

Carmelite Monastery
3505 Silver Lake Road
946-4960

Christ the King Church
3801 Shore Road, Acme
938-9214

Holy Rosary Church
228 Route 1-A, Cedar
226-5429

Immaculate Conception Church
720 Second Street
946-4211

Immaculate Conception Church
Peshawbestown, Suttons Bay
271-6651

St. Francis Church
1015 S. Union St.
947-4620, 947-4621, or 947-0590

St. Gertrude's Church
701 Warren Street, Northport
386-5221

St. Joseph – Mapleton
13400 Center Road
223-4303

St. Mary's Church
411 St. Mary's St., Lake Leelanau
271-3574

St. Mary's Hannah
M-113, Kingsley
263-5640

St. Patrick's Parish
630 W. Silver Lake Road
943-4633

St. Philip Neri Church
8707 Hill Street, Maple City
326-5255

St. Rita / St. Joseph Parish
8707 Hill Street, Maple City
228-5823

St. Wenceslaus Church
Corner of County Rd. 637 & 626,
Gill's Pier, 271-3574

SALVATION ARMY

Salvation Army
1239 Barlow
946-4644, 946-4641 After hours

SEVENTH DAY ADVENTISTS

Seventh Day Adventist Church
Seventh & Oak Streets
947-8111

UNITARIAN

Unitarian Universalist Fellowship
of Grand Traverse
6726 Center Road
947-3117

UNITED METHODIST

Asbury United Methodist Church
1200 Bay Street at Ramsdell
946-5323

Central United Methodist Church
222 Cass Street
946-5191 or 946-5750

Christ United Methodist Church
Three Mile and Hammond Roads
946-3048

Elk Rapids United Methodist Church
Traverse & Pine Streets, Elk Rapids
264-8134

Emmanuel United Methodist Church
402 W. Ninth St.
946-4930 ro 946-7524

Empire United Methodist Church
Empire
326-5510

Grant United Methodist Church
County Rd.137, Interlochen
Corner of Ramsay and Karlin Roads

Grawn United Methodist Church
1280 W. Silver Lake Rd. S
943-8353 or 943-8353

Kewadin United Methodist Church
Kewadin
264-9640

Keswick United Methodist Church
S.on County Rd. 633, Suttons Bay
271-3755

Northport Indian Mission
8626 N. Manitou Trail, Northport
386-7702

Ogdensburg United Methodist Church
16426 Center Road
223-4393 or 223-7643

Lake Ann United Methodist Church
Lake Ann
275-7236

Leland Community Methodist Church
Leland
256-9161

Kingsley United Methodist Church
Spring & Blair, Kingsley
263-5999, 263-5278

Williamsburg United Methodist Church
Church St. & Williamsburg Rd., Williamsburg
267-5792

UNITED PRESBYTERIAN

The Presbyterian Church
701 Westminster at Airport Access Road
946-5680 or 947-8648

First Presbyterian Church
404 Spruce St., Elk Rapids
264-5680 or 264-5680

Omena Presbyterian Church
(designated National Historic Site) Omena
724 S. Joseph, Suttons Bay
271-3008

UNITY

Unity Church of Traverse City
3600 5 Mile Road
938-9587

WESLEYAN

Bayview Wesleyan Church
Corner Wayne, Cedar & Bay Streets
947-3792 or 946-5588

College Terrace Wesleyan Church
2825 S. Airport Road
946-9665 or 946-4217

Restaurants

Restaurants

Howard Schelde
Chairman, Schelde Enterprises, Inc.

The first time I saw Bowers Harbor Inn was during a raging snow storm in the winter of 1973. Even then, it had a charm that I couldn't resist. My partner, Bob Kowalewski, and I had just begun construction on a new restaurant in Traverse City on Munson Avenue. We thought Bowers Harbor Inn would provide a great opportunity for another Schelde Enterprise restaurant. Yet, we didn't think the bankers would go along with the purchase of an old place that had always failed to make it as a dining spot. We made our presentation, and to our surprise they went along with the idea. We were then faced with the job of opening two restaurants in the spring of 1974. I spent the spring and summer in Traverse City getting the two of them up and running. In the process, I also fell in love with the Grand Traverse area. Since then, our business, like the Grand Traverse area, has grown. We have properties in Grand Rapids, Holland, Petoskey and Ann Arbor, along with four restaurants in Traverse City.

As the Grand Traverse area has grown, it has seen the arrival of a variety of dining establishments to meet every taste and budget. The options for dining in Traverse City are indeed diverse. If you need a quick meal on the go, all the fast food chains are ready and waiting. For family dining, a variety of eateries exist where the menus offer many choices at moderate prices. The area also boasts several exceptional fine and ethnic dining establishments. For the diner who is looking for a true dining experience, you have come to the gastronomic center of the Midwest.

There is a term that has become very popular among chefs of the world. That term is "Regional Cuisine." The Grand Traverse area is very fortunate to have some food products to call its own. Whitefish is caught from local waters, and many area chefs have their own special way of preparing this fresh-water delicacy. Morel mushrooms are also found locally, growing in abundance in the hardwood forests that surround us. Morels are featured on many local menus accompanying chicken, veal and steak entrees. The region is also one of the world's premier fruit growing areas. As a result, chefs use these products to create interesting entrees, salads and desserts.

The Grand Traverse area is also an excellent grape producing region. In the last several years, vineyards have begun to pop up all around the area. The territory is located on the 45th parallel, as are the wine regions of Germany and France. The vineyards have been a grand experiment that seems to be paying off with some very nice wines that stand up to some of the best in the world.

So, what is on the menu in the Grand Traverse area? - Outstanding "Regional Cuisine," accompanied by some wonderful local wines, served in a setting that is as lovely as it gets!

"When we want a special intimate dinner, we go to Hattie's. It's an enjoyable ride to Sutton's Bay and we're never disappointed."—P.L.

Jim Milliman
Hattie's Restaurant

There are days when I feel that I am not really in the restaurant business, but rather in the dishwashing business. Suffice it to say the work appears glamorous, but with all professions there are those moments!

I opened Hattie's in June of 1987. It was the end of a dream that had begun three years prior while I was employed at The Rowe Inn, one of the area's first real "gourmet" dining restaurants. Previous to my experience at the Rowe Inn, I, too, had lived downstate and was a partner in a bar and restaurant in downtown Detroit.

Hattie's has provided a way for me to pursue my

111 St. Joseph
Suttons Bay, MI 49682
271-6222

true interest in creating great food and dining experiences. As a chef, great food doesn't necessarily involve the most expensive ingredients, but rather is defined by great ingredients prepared impeccably well! Food has to taste good, and I strive to make every bite truly memorable.

Moving to the area was certainly a challenge. As fall approached, gone were the warm beaches and gentle breezes. Summer stopped on Labor Day. All the friends we had were now 250 miles away and stopping by was not convenient. Boy, some friends!! But the commitment to live here eventually prevailed. And over time, my wife, Mary Beth, and I have acquired two dishwashers (kids of our own), a dog and our own retreat "up north." As for the business, the seasonality in this area is a difficult challenge, but one of the few trade-offs in having an address with the words "Traverse City" in it.

"Dan's restaurants are great places to meet your friends — relaxing, with varied menus. Next stop: All aboard The Dinner Train."—P.L.

Dan Kelly
Kelly's Restaurants

I opened D. J. Kelly's in the winter of 1986. After graduating from Michigan State University, I ran restaurants in California, Arizona and Colorado. Then, the desire to move back home became a reality. My wife and I decided to move back to Traverse City, our hometown. In fact, the Kellys have been in Traverse City for five generations.

The restaurant had gone through many owners, but I was confident that if we developed a menu unique in nature, using only the finest ingredients and coupling that with great service, we should do just fine. We have.

Two years after the opening, we opened Kelly's Roadhouse Cafe on Old Mission Peninsula. Using the same philosophies, it became an instant success. During the next eight years, we have steadily grown in the area of catering. We are now one of the largest off-premise catering companies in the region. We continue to stick to the same philosophy — specializing in customized menus and excellent service.

After ten years of operation, we are now starting our next venture, The Grand Traverse Dinner Train. This totally restored 1956 train, seats 224 guests. It will leave from the depot at Railroad Place, near Eighth and Woodmere, to travel along the Boardman River Valley while a five-course dinner or lunch is served.

I have lived in many areas of this great nation of ours, but I rank Traverse City as one of the finest. I find it to be supportive of good, honest, hard-working, service-oriented people who have a love for the area's God-given beauty.

D. J. Kelly's, 120 Park
941-4550
Kelly's Roadhouse Cafe, 14091 Center Road
223-7200
Catering by D. J. Kelly, 120 Park
941-4550
Grand Traverse Dinner Train, Railroad Place
93-DEPOT

Some Area Restaurants

We present you with this list of restaurants, taken from the Dining Guide in TRAVERSE, Northern Michigan's Magazine. For a more comprehensive and up-to-date listing, refer to a current issue of the magazine. We thank the publisher for letting us share this list with you.

EMPIRE

CAFE LA RUE, M-22, 326-5551. Gourmet dining, fresh fish, beef tenderloin, lamb, specials. B, L, D, Δ, RR, $$$, MC, V.

CLIPPER GALLEY PIZZERIA & DELI, Front St., 326-5222. Soups, subs, baked goods. B, L, D, $, ✓.

EMPIRE VILLAGE INN, M-22, 326-5101. Sandwiches, pizza, soups/chili. L, D, Δ, $, ✓.

JOE'S FRIENDLY TAVERN, Front St., 326-5506. Burgers, chili & soup. B, L, D, Δ, $-$$, ✓.

THE MANITOU, M-22 between Empire and Frankfort, 882-4761. Whitefish, seafood, steaks, ribs. D, RR, beer/wine, $$, ✓, MC, V.

GLEN LAKE

ART'S TAVERN, M-22, Glen Arbor, 334-3754. Burgers, whitefish, steaks, Mexican. B, L, D, Δ, $, ✓.

BOONE DOCK'S, 5454 Manitou, Glen Arbor, 334-6444. Shrimp, burgers, steaks. L, D, Δ, $-$$, ✓, MC, V.

GLEN LAKE DAIRY BAR, C-616 on M-22 at the Narrows, 334-4145. Burgers, sandwiches, breakfast all day. Ice cream treats. B, L, D, $, ✓, CC.

GLEN LAKE INN, C-616, Burdickville, 334-3587. German & regional menu in a country setting. D, Δ, RR, $$-$$$, ✓, MC, V.

GOOD HARBOR GRILLE, M-109, 334-3555. Vegetarian, whitefish, steaks. B, L, D, $$, ✓, CC.

THE HOMESTEAD, M-22, 334-5000. THE INN: Dining in classic setting overlooking Sleeping Bear Bay. D, RR, $-$$$. WHISKERS: Pizza, burgers. D, $. NONNA'S RISTORANTE DELLA FAMIGLIA: Italian. Children's menu. B, D, RR, $-$$. ALL RESTAURANTS: Δ, ✓, CC.

JOHNNIE SALAMI'S RIVERFRONT PIZZA, M-22, Glen Arbor, 334-3876. Salads, sandwiches. L, D, $-$$, ✓.

LA BECASSE, C-675 & C-616, Burdickville, 334-3944. French cuisine. Full menu including vegetarian selections. D, Δ, RR, $$$, ✓, CC.

LE BEAR LANDING, Lake St., Glen Arbor, on Sleeping Bear Bay, 334-4640. Family, late-nite dining. Deck, private

THE KEY TO THIS GUIDE

B - Breakfast, L - Lunch, D - Dinner, Δ - Cocktails, ✓ - Checks accepted (L) - local
RR - Reservations recommended

DINNER ENTREE PRICE RANGES:
$=under $10; $$=$10 to $20; $$$=above $20

CREDIT CARDS: AE - AMERICAN EXPRESS DIS - DISCOVER MC - MASTERCARD V - VISA, CC - most major cards accepted

USING THE LISTINGS: The headings are arranged by geographical location from southwest at the beginning of the guide to northeast at the end. Restaurants are listed alphabetically under each geographical heading.

MANY RESTAURANTS ARE SEASONAL. ALWAYS CALL TO VERIFY HOURS.

UNLESS OTHERWISE NOTED, ALL PHONE NUMBERS USE THE 616 AREA CODE.

parties. B, L, D, RR, Δ (L), $-$$, ✓, CC.

SAVORIES AT THE FOOTHILLS, 7097 S. Dunn's Farm Rd., Burdickville, 334-4466. International cuisine with vegetarian meals. B, L, D, $$, ✓.

WESTERN AVENUE GRILL, M-22, Glen Arbor, 334-3362. Pasta, seafood, whitefish. B, L, D, Δ, $-$$, ✓, CC.

CEDAR/MAPLE CITY

BENJAMIN'S CAFE, C-667, Maple City, 228-6692. Pizza, prime rib, shrimp. Fish fry Fri. L, D, Δ, $$, ✓.

CEDAR TAVERN, 9039 Kasson, Cedar, 228-7445. Sandwiches, steaks, seafood. L, D, Δ, $, ✓, MC, V.

EDDIE G'S ROADHOUSE, C-651, Cedar, 228-6266. Complete dinners, pizza. B, L, D, $-$$, ✓ (L).

LEELANAU COUNTRY INN, M-22, S. of Leland, 228-5060. Pasta, seafood, steaks. D, Δ, $$, ✓, CC.

SUGARFOOT SALOON, C-651 and Bodus Rd., Cedar, 228-6166. Mexican and American. BBQ rib night Tue., walleye night Thu. L, D, Δ, $, ✓.

SUGAR LOAF RESORT, Sugar Loaf Mtn. Rd., Cedar, 228-5461, 800-748-0117. CAFETERIA & DELI: Open during the ski season, B, D. FOUR SEASONS DINING ROOM: Year-round. Sun. brunch. B, L, D, RR, Δ, $-$$, ✓, CC.

LELAND

THE BLUEBIRD, River St., 256-9081. Family eatery. Famous for cinnamon rolls. Whitefish, seafood, steaks. Sun. brunch. L, D, Δ, RR, $$, ✓, MC, V.

THE COVE, River St., 256-9834. Overlooking Fishtown. Outdoor deck. L, D, Δ, $$, ✓, CC.

EARLY BIRD, Main St., 256-9656. Breakfast all day. Lunch counter: soups, sandwiches, burgers. $, ✓.

LELAND LODGE, 565 E. Pearl, 256-9848. American menu, L, D, Δ, $$, ✓, CC.

RIVERSIDE INN, River St., 256-9971. Eclectic cuisine, overlooking the Leland River. B, L, D, Δ, $$, ✓, CC.

SUNSET SQUARE CAFE, 106 N. Lake St., 256-7500. Seasonal. Pizza, deli sandwiches, burgers, yogurt, daily specials. B, L, D, $, ✓.

LAKE LEELANAU

DICK'S POUR HOUSE, M-204, 256-9912. Homemade soups & sandwiches, burgers. L, D, Δ, $, ✓.

MR. B's, M-204, 256-8880. Pizzas, subs, dinners. L, D, $, ✓.

POWERHOUSE TAVERN, 104 Main, 256-7372. Burgers, pasta, whitefish, entertainment. D, Δ, $, ✓.

NORTHPORT

BEECH TREE, Main & Waukazoo St., 386-5200. Outdoor cafe. Sandwiches, salads, soups, desserts. Espresso and cappuccino. L, $, ✓, MC, V.

THE CLUB RESTAURANT AT MATHESON GREENS, C-633 at Matheson Rd., 386-5172. Sandwiches, snacks, soup. L, D, Δ, $$, ✓, CC.

FISCHER'S HAPPY HOUR, M-22 between Northport and Leland, 386-9923. Family-style roadhouse known for burgers and soups. L, D, Δ, $, ✓ (L).

HARBOR BAR, M-22, Omena, 386-5388. Ground round, soups. L, D, Δ, $, ✓, CC.

SHIP'S GALLEY, 110 Nagonaba, 386-5701. Pizza, burgers, sandwiches, ice cream. L, D, $, ✓ (L).

STUBB'S, 115 Waukazoo, 386-7611. Regional American cuisine like Parmesan-crusted whitefish and vodka penne. B (weekends), L, D, Δ, $$, ✓, CC.

WILLOWBROOK, 201 Mill St., 386-5617. Ice cream parlor & grill. L, D, $, ✓ (L), CC.

WOODY'S, 116 Waukazoo, 386-9933. Steaks, seafood, cherry-smoked chicken. L, D, Δ, $$, ✓, CC.

SUTTONS BAY

BOONE'S PRIME TIME PUB, 102 St. Joseph St., 271-6688. Seafood, burgers, steaks. L, D, Δ, $-$$, ✓, MC, V.

CAFE BLISS, 420 St. Joseph St., 271-5000. Vegetarian and ethnic foods. B, L, D, $$, ✓, CC.

CAPPUCCINO'S, 102 N. Broadway, 271-2233. European pastries, Italian pastas, gourmet breakfast and lunch. B, L, D, $$, ✓, DIS, MC, V.

EDDIE'S VILLAGE INN, 201 St. Joseph St., 271-3300. Complete dinners, burgers. Neighborhood bar. B, L, D, $, ✓ (L), CC.

EAGLE'S RIDGE FINE DINING, at the Leelanau Sands Casino, M-22 Peshawbestown, 271-4101. Gourmet buffet. Native American cuisine. B, L, D, Δ, $-$$, ✓.

HATTIE'S, 111 St. Joseph St., 271-6222. Elegantly prepared food. D, Δ, RR, $$$, ✓, CC.

HOSE HOUSE DELI, 303 St. Joseph St., 271-6303. Soups, salads, pizza, Greek. B, L, D, $, ✓, MC, V.

SILVER SWAN, 1381 M-22, 271-4100. German-American eatery. B, L, D, Δ, $$, ✓, MC, V.

INTERLOCHEN AREA

BOB AND JO'S, 2480 M-137 S., 276-6351. Roast pork, steaks, seafood. Real mashed potatoes. Everything homemade. D, Δ, $-$$, ✓, CC.

CICERO'S PIZZA PARLOR, 2506 M-137 S., 276-6324. Salads, subs, ice cream. D, $, ✓, MC, V.

FIREPLACE INN, 5954 Karlin Rd., 276-9696. Casual dining, full menu. Fish and chips. D, Δ, $, ✓.

GIOVANNI'S, US-31 and M-137 S., 276-6244. Italian, closed Mondays. L, D, Δ, $, ✓ (L), CC.

KARLIN INN, M-137 S. of Interlochen, 263-7995. Dinners, steaks, fish-fry Fri. and Sat. L, D, $, ✓.

L.A. CAFE, downtown Lake Ann, 275-7082. Burgers to specialty dinners, jazz events, deck seating available, non-smoking. B, L, D, beer & wine, ✓, CC.

PUNZEL SCANDINAVIAN, C-633, north of Buckley, 263-7427. Soups, imported foods, ethnic entrees, desserts. L, RR, $, ✓, MC, V.

THE RESTAURANT AT MISTWOOD, 7568 Sweet Lake Rd., Lake Ann, 275-5500. Regional and ethnic cuisine. L, D, Δ, RR, $$, CC.

TRAVERSE CITY-WEST

APACHE TROUT GRILL, 13641 M-22, 947-7079. Ribs, steak, pasta. L, D, Δ, $$, ✓, MC, V.

BIG BOY, 3828 US-31 S., 941-7430. B, L, D, $, ✓, MC, V.

BROADWAY BAGELS, 502 W. 14th St., 935-4548. Bagels, sandwiches, coffee. B, L, D, $, ✓.

FLAP JACK FAMILY RESTAURANT, 3890 US-31 S., 941-1890. B, L, D, $, ✓ (L), CC.

GREAT LAKES SUBMARINE CO., 13164 S.W. Bay Shore, 947-3231. Subs, pizza, salad, calzone. Takeout. L, D, $, ✓ (L).

GROUND ROUNDER, 1407 US-31 S., 947-6200. Steak, seafood, Tex-Mex. L, D, Δ,$, ✓, CC.

HAYLOFT INN, 5100 W. M-72, 941-0832. Steaks, Tex-Mex, fish, chicken. Weekend entertainment. L, D, Δ,

$$, ✓ (L), MC, V.

MARIFIL'S BAKERY, 537 W. 14th St. 933-0099. Soups, sandwiches, salads. Hearth-baked breads and chocolate-raspberry cakes are specialties. (L), $, ✓, MC, V.

SCOTT'S HARBOR GRILL, 12719 S.W. Bay Shore, 922-2114. Waterfront dining. Whitefish, burgers. L, D, △, $$, ✓ (L), CC.

SLEDER'S FAMILY TAVERN, 717 Randolph St., 947-9213. Burgers, ribs, chicken. One of Michigan's oldest saloons. Dining room. L, D, △, $-$$, ✓ (L), CC.

SWEITZER'S BY THE BAY, 13890 West Bay Shore Dr., 941-3463. Dinners, sandwiches, soup and salad bar. Healthy-choice menu. B, L, D, △, $-$$, ✓, CC.

THAI SPICY, 3650 US-31 S., 947-2803. Thai and Chinese cuisines. L, D, $, ✓, MC, V.

UNDERGROUND CHEESECAKE CO., 824 W. Front St., 929-4418. Desserts served all day. $-$$, MC, V.

WINDOWS, M-22 , 7 miles N. of Traverse City, 941-0100. Extensive menu of seafood, lamb, duck. Imaginative appetizers, homemade desserts. View of West Bay. D, RR, △, $$-$$$, ✓, MC, V.

TRAVERSE CITY-DOWNTOWN

BIG BOY, 161 E. Front St., 941-2020. B, L, D, $, ✓ (L), MC, V.

BON APPETIT, 810 E. Front St., 947-2634. French cuisine, nightly specials, homemade soups, salads. Homemade desserts. B, L, D, $-$$, ✓,CC.

CATHIE'S TOTE AND DINE, Cass & Front Sts., 929-4771. Subs, salads, burgers, soup, cheesecake. Deli, carryout, indoor/outdoor seating. L, D, $, ✓ (L).

CHEF'S IN, 519 W. Front, 941-1144. Sandwiches, salad bar, soups. L, D, $, ✓ (L), MC, V.

COUSIN JENNY'S CORNISH PASTIES, 129 S. Union, 941-7821. Pasties, soups, salads. B, L, D, $, ✓.

D.J. KELLY'S, 120 Park, 941-4550. Seafood, steaks and veal, pasta. L, D, △, RR (weekends), $$, ✓ (L), CC.

DILLON'S, 153 E. Front St., 941-1616. Homemade ice cream, yogurt, sorbet. B, L, $, ✓, MC, V.

DILL'S OLDE TOWNE SALOON, 423 S. Union, 947-7534. Ribs, fish, burgers. L, D, △, $-$$, ✓ (L), CC.

DILLINGER'S PUB, 121 S. Union St., 941-2276. Appetizers, salads, sandwiches, luncheon specials. L, D, △, $, ✓ (L), MC, V.

FOLGARELLI'S MARKET, 424 W. Front St., 941-7651. Italian and imported foods, deli sandwiches, home-baked goods. L, D, $, ✓.

HOLIDAY INN, 615 E. Front St., 947-3700. CYGNET ROOM: L, D, △, $, ✓, CC. PORTAGE DINING ROOM: Fri. seafood buffet, Sat. steak buffet, Sun. brunch. $$. △, ✓, CC.

J&S HAMBURG, 302 W. Front St., 947-6409. Burgers, fries, shakes & malts. B, L, D, $, ✓.

KUCH'S DELI, 542 W. Front St., 947-6779. Soups, salads, sandwiches, homecooking. L, D, $, ✓.

LA CUISINE AMICAL, 229 E. Front St., 941-8888. Bistro dining, beer and wine, year-round patio dining. B, L, D, $, ✓(L), CC.

LEFT BANK CAFE, 439 E. Front St., 929-9060. Salads, sandwiches, soups. Salmon patties, horseradish mashed potatoes, banana cream pie. L, $, ✓.

LITTLE BO'S BAR AND GRILLE, 540 W. Front St., 946-6925. Burgers. L, D, $, △, ✓ (L).

MARIFIL'S BAKERY, 149 E. Front, 946-1516. Soups, sandwiches, salads. Hearth-baked breads and chocolate-raspberry cakes are specialties. (L), $, ✓, MC, V.

MARY'S KITCHEN PORT, 539 W. Front St., 941-0525. Gourmet carryout. L, D, $, ✓, MC, V.

MILLIKEN'S TEA ROOM, 204 E. Front St., 947-5140. Homemade fare and breads. Salads, sandwiches, desserts. L, D, $, ✓, CC.

MODE'S BUM STEER, 125 E. State, 947-9832. Steak, seafood, ribs, soup, sandwiches. L, D, △, $$, CC.

MUFFIN TIN, 115 Wellington, 929-7915. Muffins, scones, cookies, bagels. Carryout. B, L, $, ✓, CC.

OMELETTE SHOPPE, 124 Cass, 946-0912, and Campus Plaza, 1209 E. Front St., 946-0590. Extensive breakfast menu, homemade breads and pastries, soup and sandwiches. B, L, $, ✓, MC, V.

PARK PLACE HOTEL, 300 E. State St., 946-5000. TOP OF THE PARK: Gourmet rooftop dining with a panoramic view. L, D, RR, $$-$$$. THE PARLOUR: Casual family meals, salad bar, sandwiches. Sun. brunch, outdoor dining. B, L, D, $-$$. BOTH RESTAURANTS: △, ✓, CC.

PAESANO'S, 447 E. Front St., 941-5740. Pizza, sandwiches, salads. L, D, $, ✓ (L), MC, V.

PEPPER'S GRILLE, 626 E. Front St., 947-6260. Steaks, seafood, fajitas. B, L, D, △, $$, CC, ✓ (L).

POPPYCOCK'S, 128 E. Front St., 941-7632. Sandwiches, pasta, salads. L, D, △, $, ✓, MC, V.

THE S&J PASTA COMPANY, 221 E. State St., 922-7732. Pizza, calzone. L, D, $-$$, ✓, CC.

SLOPPY JOE'S, 704 E. Front St., 946-1470. Sandwiches. L, D, △, $, ✓.

STONE SOUP II, 115 E. Front St., 941-1190. Soups, salads, sandwiches, muffins. B, L, $, ✓ (L).

T.C. ATHLETIC CLUB, 428 E. Front St., 929-7247. Sports bar. L, D, △, $, ✓ (L), CC.

U & I LOUNGE, 214 E. Front St., 946-8932. Gyros, Greek salad, pizza. L, D, △, $, ✓, CC.

UNION STREET STATION, 117 S. Union St., 941-1930. Sandwiches, soups, salads, burgers, nachos. L, D, $, △, ✓ (L), CC.

THE UPPER CRUST, 720 W. Front St., 946-5252. Pizza and salads. Outdoor dining. L, D, $-$$, ✓(L).

TRAVERSE CITY-SOUTH

AUNTIE PASTA'S ITALIAN CAFE, 2030 S. Airport Rd., 941-8147. Casual dining overlooking the Boardman River. Pastas, veal, chicken, salads. PIZZA PUB: Pizza, sandwiches, pastas, salads. BOTH RESTAURANTS: L, D, Δ, $-$$, ✓, CC.

BLONDIE'S DINER, 933 US-31 S., 943-8019. Ribs, soup, salad, B, L, D, Δ, $, ✓, MC, V.

BOONE'S LONG LAKE INN, 7208 Secor Rd., 946-3991. Steaks a specialty, ample portions, seafood, daily specials, Sun. prime rib. D, Δ, $-$$, ✓, MC, V.

CATHIE'S TOTE AND DINE, 42nd St. Plaza, S. Airport Rd., 947-0300. Subs, salads, burgers, soup, cheesecake. L, D, $, ✓ (L).

CHINA FAIR, 1357 S. Airport Rd., 941-5844. Chinese-American food. L, D, Δ, $$, ✓ (L), CC.

CHUMLEY'S, 1057 US-31 S., 943-8089. Burgers, sandwiches, home-cooked meals. B, L, D, Δ, $, ✓.

GRAND TRAVERSE DINNER TRAIN, 8th and Woodmere, 933-3768. Four-course lunches, five-course dinners. L, D, Δ, RR, $$$, ✓ (L), CC.

J&S HAMBURG, 1083 S. Airport Rd., 941-8844. Burgers, fries, shakes & malts. B, L, D, $, ✓.

JONATHON B. PUB, 3200 S. Airport Rd. in Grand Traverse Mall, 935-4441. Pastas, seafood, Black Angus steaks, sandwiches, burgers. L, D, Δ, $-$$, ✓ (L), CC.

MAIN STREET SAMPLER, in Cherryland Mall, 946-2442. Omelets, soups, sandwiches. B, L, D, $, ✓.

MANCINO'S, 841 US-31 S, 943-4844. Pizza, grinders, salads, dessert pizza. L, D, $, ✓.

PANDA NORTH, Logan's Landing, 929-9722. Chinese. $, RR, ✓ (L), CC.

TC HUNAN, 1425 S. Airport Rd., 947-1388. Chinese, Sun. buffet. L, D, $-$$, ✓ (L), CC.

TC TRADER'S, 1769 S. Garfield, 929-9885. A classic steakhouse & seafood restaurant in a nautical setting. L, D, Δ, $$, ✓, CC.

WILLIE'S EATERY, 1315 S. Airport, 946-4342. Soups & sandwiches. B, L, $, ✓.

TRAVERSE CITY-EAST

BAY WINDS, 1265 US-31 N., 929-1044. Overlooking East Bay beach. Veal, whitefish. Full menu on outdoor deck. L, D, Sun. brunch, Δ, $$, ✓, CC.

BOB EVANS, 1964 US-31 N., 938-1005. Full menu. B, L, D, $, ✓ (L).

THE CLOCK, 1500 US-31 N., 938-2338. Meals, soup &

salad bar. Open 24 hrs. Δ, $, ✓, MC, V.

COTTAGE CAFE, 420 Munson Ave., 947-9261. Sandwiches, dinners, weekend breakfast buffets. B, L, D, $, ✓ (L), MC, V.

THE DINER, 1103 S. Garfield, 946-0789. Soups, salads and sandwiches. B, L, $, ✓.

DON'S DRIVE-IN, 2030 US-31 N., 938-1860. An American classic, straight from the '50s. Burgers, fries and shakes. Jukebox. L, D, $, ✓ (L), MC, V, D.

GOLDEN CHOPSTICKS, 1752 US-31 N., 938-1960. Chinese. L, D, $$, ✓, CC.

GORDIE HOWE'S, 851 S. Garfield, 929-4693. Family pub featuring burgers, sandwiches, pizzas and hockey memorabilia. Smoke-free. L, D, Δ, $, ✓, CC.

GRAND TRAVERSE RESORT, US-31 N., Acme. 938-2100. TRILLIUM: Regional cuisine in a 16th-floor setting with an East Bay view. Music, dancing. L, D, Sun. brunch, $-$$$, RR. ORCHARD ROOM: Coffee shop with soup and salad bar. B, L, D, $-$$. PAPARAZZI: Northern Italian. D, RR, $-$$. SANDTRAP: M-72. Steaks, seafood, pizza. Shuttle service available. L, D, $. ALL RESTAURANTS: Δ, ✓, CC.

GREAT LAKES SUBMARINE CO., 920 US-31 N., 947-2011. Subs, pizza, salad, calzone. L, D, $, ✓ (L).

HEAVENLY HAM, 815 S. Garfield, 935-4267. Box lunches, soups, salads, sandwiches. L, Δ, $, CC.

LA SENORITA, 1245 S. Garfield, 947-8820. Mexican and American dining. L, D, Δ, $, ✓ (L), CC.

MABEL'S, 472 Munson, 947-0252. Dinners, vegetarian entrees, bakery. B, L, D, $-$$, ✓ (L), CC.

MANCINO'S, 5872 US-31 N., Acme, 938-1442. Pizza, grinders, salads, dessert pizza. L, D, $, ✓.

MOUNTAIN JACK'S, 5555 US-31 N., Acme, 938-1300. Steaks, chops, chicken and fish with a bay view. L, D, Δ, $$, ✓ (L), CC.

PEEGEO'S, 525 High Lake Rd., 941-0313. Tex-Mex, pizza. Outdoor dining. L, D, $-$$, Δ, ✓, CC.

PAPA ROMANO'S, 703 S. Garfield, 941-7272. Pizza, pasta, chicken and ribs. (L),D, Δ, $-$$, ✓, CC.

RANCH RUDOLF, 6841 Brown Bridge Rd., 947-9529. Ribs. Ranch-style dining. B, L, D, Δ, $, ✓, MC, V.

REFLECTIONS, 2061 US-31 N., 938-2321. Atop the Waterfront Inn, overlooking East Bay. Fresh seafood. Sun. brunch. B, L, D, RR, Δ, $$, ✓, CC.

ROMA ITALIAN, 118 Munson, 946-6710. Pizza, homemade soups & breads. D, $, ✓ (L).

ROUND'S, 1033 E. 8th St., 941-4124. Neighborhood diner. Full menu, homemade pies. B, L, $-$$, ✓ (L).

SCHELDE'S, 714 Munson, 946-0981. Steaks, seafood, soup, salad. Breakfast buffet. B, L, D, Δ, $$, ✓, CC.

SUNCATCHER, Cherry Capital Airport, 941-0192. Small

bar with sandwiches. B, L, D, $, Δ, ✓.

THAT'SA PIZZA, 5130 US-31 N., Acme, 938-2836. Gourmet pizza, subs, salads. L, D, $, ✓.

OLD MISSION PENINSULA

THE BOATHOUSE AT BOWERS HARBOR, 14039 Peninsula Dr., 223-4030. Popovers, bouillabaisse, chicken Wellington. B, L, D, Δ, $$, ✓(L), CC.

BOWERS HARBOR INN, 13512 Peninsula Dr., 223-4222. Regional cuisine served in an elegant old bayfront mansion. Outdoor cocktail deck. Extensive wine list. D, RR, Δ, $$-$$$, ✓ (L), CC.

THE BOWERY, 13512 Peninsula Dr., Bowers Harbor, 223-4333. Ribs, burgers, fish. D, Δ, $$, ✓ (L), CC.

KELLY'S ROADHOUSE CAFE, 14091 Center Rd., 223-7200. Pasta, steak, subs, homemade soups. Smoked fish and meats. L, D, Δ, $$, ✓ (L), CC.

OLD MISSION TAVERN, 17015 Center Rd, 223-7280. Restaurant/art gallery in country-house setting. Dinners, soups, sandwiches. L, D, $$, Δ, ✓, CC.

ELK RAPIDS

CHEF CHARLES', 147 River St., 264-8901. Pizza, sandwiches, soups. L, D, $-$$, ✓, MC, V.

ELK HARBOR, 714 US-31, 264-9201. Breakfast all day, Fri. fish fry, Sun. all-you-can-eat chicken, daily specials. B, L, D, $, ✓ (L), CC.

ELK RIVER INN, US-31 at the bridge, 264-5655. Seafood, steaks. L, D, Δ, $$, ✓, CC.

HACIENDA VASQUEZ', US-31 N., 264-5892. Mexican, American. L, D, Δ, $, ✓ (L), CC.

HARBOR CAFE, 129 River St., 264-8700. Breakfast, burgers, sandwiches. B, L, $, ✓(L).

OASIS RED BULL TAVERN, 7204 Cairn Hwy., Kewadin, 264-5821. Burgers, BBQ, finger food, chili. Outdoor dining. L, D, Δ, $, ✓ (L), MC, V.

HARBOR CAFE, 129 River St., 264-8700. Breakfast, burgers, sandwiches. Takeout available. B, L, $, ✓(L).

PACIFIC COFFEE HOUSE, 139 River St., 264-7241 Espresso bar, bagels, scones. B, L, D, $, ✓.

RIVER VIEW CAFE, 212 River St., 264-9186. Deli sandwiches, salads, gourmet pizzas, Belgian waffles, daily lunch specials. B, L, $, ✓, MC, V.

T.J. CHARLIE'S, 135 River St., 264-8819. Family dining, soup, salads, sandwiches. B, L, D, $, ✓ (L).

VILLAGE INN PIZZA, River St., 264-6150. Italian dishes, delivery, all-you-can-eat soup, salad & pizza buffet. L, D, $, ✓ (L).

ALDEN

PETE & KATHY'S KOUNTRY KITCHEN, 5069 Helena Rd., 331-6777. Sausage gravy & biscuits, soups, outside patio, fish-fry Fri. B, L, D, $, ✓ (L).

POMA'S PIZZA, 11921 S.E. Torch Lake Dr., 331-6262. Pizza, chicken, subs, salads, homemade cheesebread. Eat in or takeout. D, $, ✓.

SPENCER CREEK, 9166 Helena St., 331-6147. Country French dining in a Victorian home on the shores of Torch Lake. D, Δ, RR, $$$, ✓ (L), CC.

SPENCER CREEK CAFE & MARKET, 9160 Helena St., 331-4171. Appetizers, light meals, pastas. L, D, Δ, $, ✓ (L), CC.

TORCH RIVIERA, 12899 Cherry Ave., Torch River, 322-4100. Sandwiches, appetizers, shrimp, steak, pizza. L, D, $-$$, ✓, MC, V.

CENTRAL LAKE/ELLSWORTH

BROWNWOOD FARM HOUSE RESTAURANT, 2474 N.E. Torch Lake Dr., Central Lake, 544-5811. Home-style American fare. D, Δ, $$, CC.

THE CLUB, 2443 Main, Central Lake, 544-9800. Chili, burritos, chicken, shrimp. L, D, Δ, $, ✓ (L).

J.P.'S RESTAURANT, 9247 Main St., Ellsworth, 588-2025. Country-style cooking and breakfast any time. B, L, D, $, ✓.

THE LAMPLIGHT INN, M-88 Central Lake, 544-6443. Seafood, steaks, prime rib. D, Δ, $-$$$, ✓ (L), CC.

MARY LOU'S TEA ROOM & CAFE, E. Torch Lake Dr., Central Lake, 544-3910. Soups, steaks, seafood, chicken, fish, pasta. L, D, $-$$, ✓, CC.

ROWE INN, East Jordan Rd., Ellsworth, 588-7351. Michigan regional cuisine. Specialties: pecan-stuffed morels, rack of lamb, venison scaloppini. Most extensive wine list in state. D, RR, Δ, $$$, ✓, CC.

TAPAWINGO, 9520 Lake St., Ellsworth, 588-7971. Modern American cuisine—a blend of Thai, Southwestern and French. Award-winning pastry chef. D, RR, Δ, $$$, ✓, MC, V.

THAT'SA PIZZA, 2420 N. Main, Central Lake, 544-6727. Lunches, dinners, pizza. L, D, $, ✓.

Services, Business

Chapter 25

"A.J. and her family are committed to quality printing services. More than we'd expected in a quick print shop."—P.L.

Alyce J. ("AJ") Lorenzen
American Speedy Printing

American Speedy Printing opened for business in December, 1980. My parents and brother moved from Rochester, Michigan, to fulfill a life-long dream of changing their status from summer to year-round residents. In 1985, my new husband, Terre, and I purchased the business. Terre and I received have numerous sales and operation excellence awards and have ranked among the top five percent in the American Speedy system for the past eleven years.

The printing industry has dramatically changed due to advances in technology. Today, we offer first quality high speed copying and full state of-the-art printing services. Our designers are highly talented and well-versed in computer desktop publishing.

We have grown from two employees in 1985 to twelve in 1996, including my brother, David, and two of my five children. We are the only franchise printing/copying business in the Traverse City area. This affords us the opportunity to network with over 600 centers to share technical knowledge and state-of-the-art equipment to best serve our customer's needs. We provide a winning combination of small, family-run business friendliness with high-tech ability. We cater to small business owners and individuals who require helpful assistance and quality product at reasonable prices.

I like being in a business climate where growth is abundant. The energy, the new opportunities, being part of developing a safe, dynamic community in this beautiful area are a real draw. I moved away from the overdevelopment of the city and don't miss it a bit. I support and admire those working hard in Traverse City to maintain the natural beauty of the area. Living and working with people dedicated to preserving quality of life is the most important reason to be here.

In 1994, Terre passed away suddenly. We miss his endearing smile but have wonderful memories of his strong leadership, commitment to the community, our business, family and his golf game. Each day brings the opportunity to make a difference. By living the Golden Rule and using my talents and resources to best serve others and God, I will make a difference. We're all in this together — we may as well make the best of it!

1425-C South Airport Road
42nd Street Plaza
Traverse City, MI 49686
Phone: 941-5770

"They make buying office supplies easy. Their in-town delivery service makes it really handy."—C.L.

Professional Office Supply

Chuck Jaqua

Professional Office Supply opened for business in 1982 with six employees. The company grew rapidly and, in 1984, we purchased Union Office Supply. This gave the company two locations downtown. In 1988, the main store was remodeled into a state-of-the-art retail operation. In 1989, we purchased Commercial Office Supply and moved into the Professional Office Supply building. Near the end of 1991, we purchased Burek Office Products in Petoskey and, in 1992, we opened a new store there. During 1993, Union Office Supply was closed while the building was remodeled, and Professional Office Furniture opened in its place. At the furniture store, we offer better lines of furniture, systems furniture, and space planning for our commercial customers. The company now employs 30 people, with additional expansion and remodeling plans scheduled for 1996.

There is one thing that makes Professional Office unique and therefore so successful. It is our ability to combine the personal one-on-one service and advice that people in a small town like and want, with the low prices and fast service they were accustomed to in the big city. By being a member of an international group of independent dealers, we have been able to keep our prices down and maintain a large selection of the latest products.

Traverse City is a great place to live and do business. While the obvious advantage to Traverse City is the scenic beauty, the real advantage is the people who live here. They are a positive thinking, proactive group who, for the most part, have given up a life somewhere to be here. They realize what they have here and are willing to work hard to keep Traverse City a great place to work and live.

If you are moving to Traverse City, you should understand that when you live in a large city you may be a spectator at a sporting event; here you are more likely to participate in sports. While you may prefer watching or listening to fine arts performances, here you can also participate in them if you choose. If politics is your game, you might want to run for city commission or township board. New comers are welcome here. You will never be locked out because you were not born and raised here. So come on in and become proactive in your future.

148 E. Front Street
Traverse City, MI 49684
Phone: 946-5727

"John does it all, from portrait work to commercial – studio and lab work. You can tell he loves dealing with people."—P.L.

John Robert Williams

John Robert Williams Commercial Photography, Inc.

Welcome to Traverse City! Being a professional here, one can easily become a big fish in a small fish bowl. This is a small town and we live here because we like it small. However, pursuing a career in commercial photography, an occupation generally practiced in large metropolitan areas, is a special challenge. I operate one of the largest private photo operations in the state.

Rural areas, without large bases of manufacturing and marketing, don't have the need or the resources to keep a studio this size in business. Early on, I started reaching out across the country to build a client base in need of our services. Because of the volume of work we produce and the lack of professional processing available locally, I have added a complete custom photographic lab on site. This addition allows me to provide almost immediate turn-around on jobs, brings all quality control in-house and provides anyone in the community with local access to professional, custom processing usually found only in large city photo labs.

I make photographic illustrations for many different types of businesses. It is one of my personal joys to light something and make it dazzle (and hopefully sell!). Through my sixteen years in operation here in town, my business continues to see steady growth. I depend on repeat customers satisfied with our blend of creative imaging, speed of turn-around, quality craftsmanship and a friendly atmosphere.

My love for this area spreads across many different volunteer activities. I am very active in development of non-motorized recreation trails, many charitable entities, local land use planning and zoning and the arts. I believe that one "has to pay rent" for the privilege of living in such a wonderful area, by giving a lot of themselves to the needs of the community.

227 E. State Street
Traverse City, MI 49684
Phone: 941-4020

"You can count on this team for good computer support and education. They're doing it right!"—P.L.

Tim and Diane Heger
SOFTEK

We moved to Traverse City from Cincinnati in May, 1995. Tim had worked in sales management for a Fortune 300 company for five years. When the company asked us to move to New York City, we said, "No thanks." We wanted to move to a place where we could start our own business that was also a good place to raise our two children. We chose Traverse City.

Tim has always been drawn to computers and has been involved with them in one way or another, from high school until now. Diane's background as a Computer Systems Engineer with EDS, and Tim's natural interest in computers made opening SOFTEK Computers a perfect fit.

At SOFTEK we believe in a superior level of customer service. Uncompromising quality in our computers and being there when customers need us has made SOFTEK the place for users at all levels of experience. We offer state-of-the-art computers systems, service on all makes and models of PC's, training, networks, software and all the fun stuff that makes computers so interesting. Each of our computer systems is hand-built for the user, to their exact specifications.

SOFTEK is a 14 year old computer company started in Columbia South Carolina. We are independently owned and operated, but work with the other SOFTEK stores to bring you the very best in products and pricing. Stop by and see why we enjoy living and working in Traverse City.

3311 S. Airport Road
Traverse City, MI 49684
Phone: 933-5393

Local Business Service Sources

SOME OFFICE SUPPLY RESOURCES

Professional Office Supply
148 E. Front Street
Traverse City, MI 49684
Phone/Fax: 946-5727/946-2017

Lloyd Business Machines Co.
3074 N. U.S. 31 S.
Traverse City, MI 49684
Phone/Fax: 946-4396/946-5491

Modern Interiors Inc.
P.O. Box 4045
Traverse City, MI 49685
Phone/Fax: 935-1555/935-4460

Hovinga Business Systems
1132 S. Garfield
Traverse City, MI 49686
Phone/Fax: 941-4464/941-4350

Hughes Systems Inc.
413 N. Division Street
Traverse City, MI 49684
Phone/Fax: 946-7750/946-7767

Microage Computer Center
10850 Traverse Hwy. #1104
Traverse City, MI 49684
Phone/Fax: 946-8808/946-0719

Acme Business Machines Inc.
6100 U.S. 31 N.
Acme, MI 49610
Phone/Fax: 938-2834/938-1129

Kopy Sales Inc.
821 Robinwood Court
Traverse City, MI 49686
Phone/Fax: 946-3020/946-3666

The Computer Haus
813 S. Garfield Ave.
Traverse City, MI 49686
Phone/Fax: 946-1045/946-5125

Great Lakes Business Systems Inc.
733 Woodmere
Traverse City, MI 49686
Phone/Fax: 946-1446/941-4329

**Inacomp Computer Center
Pointe of Sales Inc.**
1323 S. Airport Road
Traverse City, MI 49686
Phone/Fax: 929-2990/929-4265

Syscom Corporation
3409 Veterans Drive
Traverse City, MI 49684
Phone/Fax: 946-1411/946-1560

B.E.C. Office Furniture
3025 Cass Road
Traverse City, MI 49684
Phone/Fax: 947-8990/947-6132

Bay Area Office Supply Inc.
834 Hastings Street
Traverse City, MI 49686
Phone/Fax: 947-1603/947-1427

Commercial Office Interiors Inc.
1454 S. Airport W.
Traverse City, MI 49686
Phone/Fax: 946-2200/946-1937

The Computer Supplies Co.
710 Centre Street
Traverse City, MI 49684
Phone: 929-7989

Fidelity Computers
1721 Park Drive
Traverse City, MI 49686
Phone: 929-1443

Image Makers-Xerox Sales Agent
3301 Veterans Drive, Suite 102
Traverse City, MI 49684
Phone: 947-1588

Laser Printer Technologies
425 S. Airport Road, Suite 1
Traverse City, MI 49686
Phone: 941-LASER

Michigan Computer Consultants
160 E. State Street
Traverse City, MI 49684
Phone: 929-1233

Paper Plus
425 S. Airport Road, West
Traverse City, MI 49686
Phone: 929-1221

The Pinery Inc.
955 S. Airport Road
Traverse City, MI 49686
Phone: 947-7363

SOFTEK
3311 S. Airport Road
Traverse City, MI 49684
Phone: 933-5393

The Software Shop
1320 S. Airport Road, West
Traverse City, MI 49686
Phone: 929-3660

TC Computers
413 E. Eighth Street
Traverse City, MI 49684
Phone: 946-6347

Tech Office Equipment
710 Centre Street
Traverse City, MI 49686
Phone: 941-8818

Terrapin Computer Co.
1128 E. Eighth Street
Traverse City, MI 49686
Phone: 941-1966

Traverse Cash Register
710 West Front
Traverse City, MI 49684
Phone: 922-5900

SOME LOCAL ADVERTISING SOURCES

Anderson Gordon Associates
P.O. Box 724
Traverse City, MI 49685
Phone/Fax: 947-0180/946-1854

CB Marketing Services
1250 Lindale Drive
Traverse City, MI 49686
Phone/Fax: 223-4090/223-4095

CML Associates
NBD Building, Suite 420
Traverse City, MI 49684
Phone/Fax: 922-6782/922-7162

Deb Anton Design Studio
2668 Shenandoah
Traverse City, MI 49684
Phone/Fax: 935-4226/935-4226

Fox Design
432-A West Welch Court
Traverse City, MI 49686
Phone/Fax: 947-1820/947-2406

Knorr Marketing
160 E. State Street
Traverse City, MI 49684
Phone/Fax: 947-9707/947-3608

McConnell & Associates
541 W. Front Street
Traverse City, MI 49684
Phone/Fax: 947-3787/947-7328

McPhail Advertising Associates
P.O. Box 5312
Traverse City, MI 49685
Phone/Fax: 946-3787/946-4870

Morse Advertising & Communications
3920 N. U.S. 31 S.
Traverse City, MI 49684
Phone/Fax: 946-4800/946-4855

Mueller & Associates Inc.
12719 S.W. Bay Shore Drive, Suite 1
Traverse City, MI 49684
Phone/Fax: 941-9112/941-1447

O.C.I. Corp.
3691 Cass Road
Traverse City, MI 49684
Phone/Fax: 946-9000/941-9113

Photo Communication Service, Inc.
6055 Robert Drive
Traverse City, MI 49684-8645
Phone/Fax: 943-8800/none

Profile, The
P.O. Box 10322 Cedar Run Road
Traverse City, MI 49684
Phone/Fax: 941-9661/none

Saxon Design
10666 Watkoski
Traverse City, MI 49684
Phone/Fax: 929-0979/929-4889

Watson/Swope Advertising & Design
102 1/2 E. Front Street
Traverse City, MI 49684
Phone/Fax: 947-7550/947-8138

Zernow Advertising
P.O. Box 912
Traverse City, MI 49685
Phone: 941-1434/941-6578

SOME LOCAL DESIGN RESOURCES

Brauer Productions
530 S. Union
Traverse City, MI 49684
Phone/Fax: 941-0850/941-0947

Byte Productions
733 E. 8th Street
Traverse City, MI 49686
Phone/Fax: 946-2983/none

Corbin Design
109 E. Front Street, Suite 304
Traverse City, MI 49684
Phone/Fax: 947-1236/947-1477

Design Direction
P.O. Box 201
Elk Rapids, MI 49629
Phone/Fax: 264-8104/none

Design Ink
2243 Timberlane
Traverse City, MI 49686
Phone/Fax: 941-0815/941-7352

Dick Forton Graphic Arts
2648 N. U.S. 31 S.
Traverse City, MI 49684
Phone/Fax: 941-1652/941-2249

Huffman Fisher Design Corp.
13685 S.W. Bay Shore Drive, Suite 116
Traverse City, MI 49684
Phone/Fax: 929-2667/929-4349

Nielsen Design Group Inc.
114 E. Front Street, Suite 205
Traverse City, MI 49684
Phone/Fax: 946-0925/946-2363

Petersen Productions Inc.
283 Garfield Road, S.
Traverse City, MI 49686
Phone/Fax: 947-2568/947-2579

Red Horse Productions
408 W. 10th Street
Traverse City, MI 49684
Phone: 941-9493/941-5313

Services, Home

Chapter 26

"Experts in helping you light your home or business. Wide in-store selection and custom orders."—C.L.

Julie Falconer
Lighting Center

In 1988, Julie and Bruce Falconer became the owners of Lighting Center, a lighting fixture store that was started in 1980. They wanted to become involved in a business that would offer them growth potential and the opportunity to stay in Traverse City. The business is expanding and will soon move to a new location, giving them more room to display their sizable selection of fixtures in a more pleasing way. This location also affords them the ability to create "cloud" displays. Rather than having all the fixtures directly overhead so the customer must be looking upward constantly, these new displays will stagger the fixtures at various heights. This is in keeping with Julie's desire to have her showroom be a pleasant environment and to make it possible to carry a large inventory in the store. "When people are spending a considerable amount to customize a home, I want them to be able to see the quality of the fixture as often as possible rather than having to order from a picture," she explains.

The Lighting Center's display, the largest in Northern Michigan, has something for every budget. The staff is well-trained and is always willing to give the time and attention needed to solve each customer's lighting problems. A new conference area will allow for consultation with customers and the many builders, architects and designers who depend upon the Lighting Center's expertise. This room will be used to demonstrate various types of lighting so customers can see the lighting effects before completing their purchases.

Julie is most excited about the store's ability to offer unique fixtures. She also will be expanding into home accessories with a casual northern Michigan look.

Julie says her family enjoys many of the things that bring people to the area. They love the natural beauty, the pleasant people and the many services Traverse City offers by being the hub for the small villages in the areas. For newcomers, she advises finding your niche in the community — then the adjustment will be minimal.

144 Hall Street
Traverse City, MI 49684
Phone: 941-5414

"Don't let the relaxed and casual atmosphere fool you. Laura is all business when it comes to customer satisfaction."—P.L.

Laura Keenan
Room Settings Furniture

In an area like Traverse City, with tremendous growth and the appeal of a small town, it is not unusual to find uniquely talented retailers from many geographic areas offering a wide variety of designs and styles. We consider our showroom to be a reflection of the casual lifestyles of Northern Michigan.

Our store's presentation is truly enhanced by the variety of vendors we house. Being a single entity in the franchise world allows our true colors to shine through. We always strive to further define an image, so our resources are limitless. As the store evolves, the most important component remains: 100% customer satisfaction.

While you are in the area, if you have not had a chance to visit our new showroom, please treat yourself with a visit. We are happy to share our talents, whether it be in design consultation, making a statement with accessories, or steering you to a good restaurant! We hope to see you soon.

831 South Garfield
Traverse City, MI 49686
Phone: - 941-4076

"You'll have to meet these people to believe their energy. They are committed to quality with a personal involvement in every job."—P.L.

Jill Little & Brian Riggs
Mighty Maid Cleaning Service/Home Care Specialists

We operate a personalized cleaning service, specializing in custom residential homes. We also provide office and post-construction cleaning. We are owner-operated, with direct hands-on supervision of all our work.

I relocated to Traverse City from Florida to be closer to my relatives in the state where I was raised. Mighty Maid was formed in Traverse City, in 1989, from a vision I had. I wanted to create a system to provide consistent quality cleaning and guaranteed customer satisfaction.

I worked in the business myself for the first few years. I developed a system that would be trainable to others. In 1992, I married Brian, whose family has resided in the Traverse City area for over 100 years. We became business partners, expanding into post-construction cleaning and home-care maintenance. Mighty Maid continues to grow, mostly by referrals. We employ four cleaning professionals and expand each year. Even though we want to grow, we don't want to lose our personal touch with our staff and our clients.

We are a detailed cleaning service, catering to our clients' needs. Our trained cleaning technicians are knowledgeable in the care of wood, tile, marble and brass fixtures. Mighty Maid offers guidance to our clients on total home care by offering a referral service for any home maintenance need.

Traverse City offers unique breathtaking beauty and a peaceful atmosphere. The smaller community allows for word-of-mouth referrals. The move to Traverse City enriched my life with happiness, security and opportunity. It gave us the chance to grow with this outstanding community and to be in business for ourselves.

We believe that we should "Do more than expected, willingly and be thankful in life."

1421 E 8th Street
Traverse City, MI 49686
Phone: 941-4270

"Herb has built quite a company and you won't find anyone more active in community activities. THE place for windows and carpet cleaning."—P.L.

Herb Lemcool
C & H Maintenance Service, Inc.

As President of C & H Maintenance Service, Inc., I welcome you to Traverse City. Having lived here all my life, I know you will enjoy all our area has to offer. C&H Maintenance Service, Inc., has been serving the residents of the Grand Traverse region since 1958 and has grown from a one-person operation to almost 100 employees.

C & H Maintenance Service, Inc., specializes in residential window and carpet cleaning with expert and friendly technicians. After initial cleaning we offer a carpet maintenance program which entitles you to cleaning of all traffic patterns, entrance ways after six months, free spotting and a complete carpet cleaning at the end of one year for a low monthly fee. C & H technicians are also certified in furniture and upholstery cleaning.

We have doubled our customer base in the last five years and are very proud of our certified technicians who serve you in your home. We use environmentally safe products, the latest in cleaning equipment and we guarantee the work of our employees. Our employees are also bonded and covered under workers compensation and liability insurance for the protection of our customers. C&H Maintenance Service, Inc. is the residential carpet and window cleaners of choice in the Grand Traverse area - just ask your neighbors - they know who we are.

2810 North Garfield
Traverse City, MI 49685-0877
Phone: 947-9286

"This is the place we always go for special framing. A unique and diverse frame selection and great artwork in the gallery."—C.L.

Steve Loveless
State of the Art

State of the Art is the largest custom frame shop in the Grand Traverse area. We offer many of the finest materials and products available to the picture framing industry, and we provide services and techniques not found everywhere. We also offer a gallery of original art by many of the region's finest artists. Supplementing this is a wide selection of nationally-known prints and posters along with works by local artists.

I am a native of Traverse City. Living here has given me a sense of pride in the area and an understanding of the region. I began picture framing in 1974 as an after school job. After working in and managing frame shops for eleven years, I knew it was possible to offer expanding services and products in picture framing. I was also working part-time as an artist producing serigraphs when I recognized the need for an outlet for myself and other area artists.

State of the Art opened in May, 1985, near the Cherryland Mall and prospered there for ten years. Our growth was steady and in 1995, we relocated to our current location. We have a 1200 square foot gallery and a sales area that features some of the best known regional artists. We represent Charles Murphy, David Grath, James Gartner, Sue Brightheart, Bonnie Rhoads and myself, to name a few. We have works in watercolor, oil, acrylic, pastel, blown glass, porcelain, color photography and silk-screen. Our selection of framing materials is second to none. We search extensively for a wide range of moldings and matting materials exclusive to the region. We specialize in frames with unique styles, finishes and colors.

I feel the Grand Traverse Region offers a lot in its natural beauty and lifestyle. My goal is for State of the Art to help you enhance the beauty and appreciation of the area through the art and picture framing that we offer.

430 West 14th Street
Traverse City, MI 49684
Phone: 947-5456

"Experts in sound systems and home theatre. Their service and installation staff are well-trained, courteous and capable."—P.L.

Bob LaMontagne & Greg Walton
The Sound Room

Two young entrepreneurs, Bob Lamontagne and Greg Walton, started their unique fine home audio/video products business seven years ago and have already expanded twice. Although the business has grown in scope, as well as in physical size, they continue to maintain strong personal contact with the customer. It is the largest local facility displaying the full operation of custom sound and home theater equipment. The highly-trained associates are certified in many areas and help you figure out what you need to meet your audio/video needs. Numerous active speakers and systems in the store allow you to test the equipment.

Since everyone's needs and budgets are different, Sound Room staffers help identify the right system. Many customers who are building or remodeling have The Sound Room plan the audio/visual system before construction begins. Working directly from the blueprints, they decide where speakers should go, what walls would be best for controls, etc. It's a very personal process and by the time you're done, they've taught you everything about using your system, right down to using your remote.

Another great feature of this business is their music collection. Headphones allow the customer to listen to CD's before purchase. You don't have to get home and realize you don't care for the CD you just purchased.

Bob and Greg feel there are many positives to living and working in the area. They have been delighted with the personal care and attention they receive from builders and subcontractors. They know that, often, things are done more slowly here than in a large city, but they see that as positive, since there is often more time and care in the work done. Both men love the diversity of the area and are involved in many outdoor activities: hiking, fishing, and water sports. They are happy with the educational opportunities and safety their families enjoy. Their primary business goal is to continue to maintain the consistency of service which has afforded them such a loyal clientele.

3275 South Airport Road
Traverse City, MI 49684
Phone: 947-4710

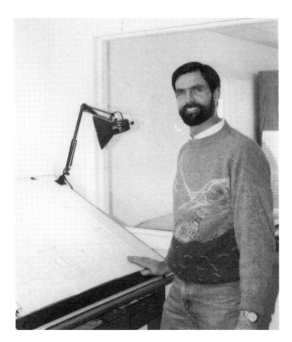

"We can give a strong personal endorsement. Commitment to quality is outstanding . We would recommend Bill to anyone!"—C.L.

Bill O'Mara
O'Mara Construction

I knew I wanted to build homes since I was a kid. It started with a building-trades course I took as a high school junior and a student co-op during my senior year. I got my builder's license when I was 18. I was accepted as journeyman carpenter at 19. My field experience has proven to be invaluable since at that time we did everything on the job.

We're general contractors, specializing in upper-end custom homes. There are two things that make us unique. First, about 75% of our projects are design/build projects. Secondly, we maintain our own staff. All our projects are pre-sold and consist of various design themes.

I operate directly with the client on each project. I want to make sure people are treated fairly, get value for what they receive, and that our working relationship is good - clear communication is critical.

Working from home, I started the company in 1982. Today, we have five office staff and a field crew of about 20 employees. We have even designed our own estimating software and have integrated it with our job costing and accounting.

Many positive things are happening here in Traverse City. The area is unique because of the high quality people who truly care about the community, the environment around them, their lives and their relationships. People don't just exist here - they thrive. The citizens take ownership of the community.

My wife and I have six children and as the company grows, I can see that there might be an opportunity for some of them to join the business. Who knows? Maybe one will join as an architect, accountant, computer specialist or engineer, or work in the field as a journeyman carpenter. These are all options in a viable company.

852 Robinwood Court
Traverse City, MI 49686
Phone: 947-1982

"John and his company are ready to do your electrical work, no matter how big or small. They're available 7 days a week."—C.L.

John Findley
Alpine Electric

Alpine Electric is a very service-oriented company that has served the needs of the Grand Traverse area since 1968. Our business has evolved from the days when three employees did mostly residential and light commercial work. Today, we have sixty to seventy employees performing a wide range of electrical contracting services in areas such as residential, commercial, industrial, institutional, oil field and automation.

We think that what sets Alpine Electric apart from others in this field is our emphasis on service and our commitment to our employees and to our customers' satisfaction.

The benefits of living in this area are many. It does not take long to become aware of he area's natural beauty. We have wonderful access to lakes, parks and recreational areas, ski resorts and state forests. There are all kinds of outdoor activities here. Doing business in Traverse City is enjoyable because we have a skilled work force and a good supply/distribution network.

We at Alpine Electric believe that a customer should be served as quickly and efficiently as possible. We encourage our employees to treat the customer as well as they would like to be treated, themselves. We also believe the job should be done properly in an honest, professional manner.

1670 Barlow
Traverse City, MI 49685-1065
Phone: 947-3600

"The wide selection of posters is always fun to view. Framing is well-done, reasonable and finished quickly. You can even do your own framing here."—C.L.

Tim Simonelli
The Great Frame Up

The Great Frame Up, owned and operated by Tim Simonelli, has been in downtown Traverse City since 1981. This full-service shop offers a wide variety of frames. The first things you notice about the store are the distinctive wood front and large windows. When you peek in, you'll see a wide range of framed posters and local art work. The aerial photos of the Grand Traverse region have become a real feature of the gallery. Posters are available in the gallery but an extensive number can also be ordered through catalogs.

This is a busy place and it's fun to come in to watch the activity. You'll notice the vertical work areas, where you can place your artwork in an upright position, just like you'd see it on your wall. Magnets hold it up while various mats and frames are tried. The staff, along with Tim and Leon, the manager, are readily available to work with customers to create the proper framing. The work is custom - all moldings and mats are cut on site.

Benches along the walls are for assembly. Most of the framing is left to be done at the store, but customers have the option of doing the framing themselves on site. It's really an enjoyable process because the staff is right there to help. The Great Frame Up offers many alternatives to fit different budgets and also offers archival framing.

Tim has lived in the Traverse City area since 1981. Having access to the water on a daily basis is important to him since he loves boating and skiing. He enjoys getting to know his customers and he appreciates the feeling of safety in doing business in the downtown area.

145 E. Front Street
Traverse City, MI 49684
Phone: 946-9302

"They do some of the best tile work in the area. The shop grew from customers' needs to select from a wide selection of products."—C.L.

Dale and Mary Jo Censer
TileCraft

At TileCraft, our focus is on the design and quality of workmanship of ceramic tile, natural stone and glass block applications throughout the home. I established TileCraft in 1986, and have been installing tile for fourteen years in the Traverse City area.

Over the past ten years, TileCraft has seen steady growth within a competitive market. This growth has enabled us to service our customers' needs more effectively using a design-oriented showroom and a professional design and sales staff. It has also allowed us to employ and train some of Northern Michigan's best artisans and tile setters.

The history of tile goes back thousands of years, and many in the tile industry have a great respect for the time-honored tradition of tile. TileCraft believes in the proven traditional method of mud-set installation, while at the same time keeping abreast of the most modern technology the industry has to offer. What makes TileCraft unique is quality and service, from selection and design to the installation by a TileCraft professional.

The people we meet and the relationships we build during a job make doing business in Traverse City so much fun. Working in a variety of homes and assisting in the selection of tile to suit each separate residence represent two specific challenges in our business. Challenges we look forward to.

It is our goal to sell and install quality ceramic and natural stone surfaces at competitive prices. We treat each and every customer with respect and understanding for their individual job needs.

We at TileCraft will always consider quality installation to be the cornerstone of our business.

2748 N. Garfield Road - Unit 13
Traverse City, MI 49685-2004
Phone: 929-720

"TC is blessed with some excellent builders - Andy is one of them. His homes are known for attention to quality and detail."—C.L

Andy Valdmanis
Seven Hills Custom Homes

Seven Hills is a general contracting firm operating in the Traverse City area since 1981. My construction experience and work ethic developed early in life. I was born into a family building a new life in a new country and no pair of hands went idle. My family immigrated to the United States from Latvia. I was born in 1952, in the Grand Rapids area, and have been around building projects ever since. My family and other immigrant families pulled together to get things done at our homes, church or community center. Our church was built with 'hands-on labor' with carpenters, cabinet makers, masons and painters. I have worked with all of them since I was a young child.

Besides hands-on experience, I have pursued formal education as well. My teaching degree and Masters Degree in Personnel and Guidance are tremendous assets in dealing with the often challenging experience of building. I have also been awarded the "Master Builder" designation by the National Association of Home Builders, which required 10 years of management experience, a battery of classes and tremendous commitment.

Selecting a builder can be very difficult for either a long-time resident or someone new to the area. I feel that experience, integrity, a capability to provide full service and an intimate knowledge of the community are the key qualities of a successful building firm. We are committed to Northern Michigan and we have the experience and staff to provide custom building projects whether newly constructed, remodeled or renovated.

Homes built by Seven Hills Incorporated are intended to be individual expressions of beauty, comfort and utility. Designing and building a personalized project should be a rewarding and pleasing experience and our firm will take pride in being part of your project. To the experienced eye, the pride and caring with which a Seven Hills project has been constructed is readily apparent.

13795 Seven Hills Road
Traverse City, MI 49686
Phone: 223-9222

"One of TC's oldest businesses. It's fun to shop here and get a glimpse of the past."—C.L.

Tim Lampton
McGough's

McGough's is a business that's not easy to describe, and that's what makes it so much fun to shop here. You'll find all kinds of items that relate to your garden, from grass seed to fertilizers and garden tools. Walk a few steps and there's a full supply of pet products and wild bird seed. Our business has evolved with the times and has been in operation for more than a hundred years.

The original business was the H. J. McGough Company, started sometime in the 1890's, and we still operate in part of the original building. The business was originally geared toward the agricultural community providing hay and feed. We also supplied coal to local residents. Obviously, things have changed over the years and we needed to shift our emphasis to keep up with the changing market.

I started at McGough's in 1978. I was hired to do the books, but that never happened. Instead, I started learning the business, and today am part owner. McGough's now does less than 20% of its business in the agricultural area, although we still have a number of commercial dairy farmers who rely on our services.

Wholesale remains an important part of our business, but I see the growth for us now in addressing the needs of what I call the "gentleman farmer." So many people are interested in gardening and lawn care and we offer the expertise and products to help them. I attend classes frequently at MSU to stay current with new product development so I can help our customers with their questions. We will continue to evolve into more niche markets, such as bulk mulches, erosion blankets and landscape plants. We also repair small engines on snow blowers, lawnmowers, etc. Our in-town location makes us easily accessible.

I really enjoy the relaxed pace of things in Traverse City. My children have never known any other life, so I won't be surprised if they feel a need to get away and explore, someday. But also, I won't be surprised if they come back.

501 Lake Avenue
Traverse City, MI 49684
Phone: 947-5900

"Not only are they ready for any glass project, but their management style is unique in a company this size and their success shows it."—P.L.

Mark Bowie & Dick Corey
Twin Bay Glass

When my wife and I moved from the big city twenty years ago, we wanted to start a business, start a family and raise our kids in this place I had grown to love. I had spent many summers on Glen Lake and simply fell in love with the area. My feeling for this area is still the driving force behind Twin Bay Glass.

Running a locally-owned business, we find ourselves working with friends and neighbors. We try extra hard to treat them right.

My partner, Dick Corey, and I had a lot of experience in the glass business. However, we had to learn to make adjustments in our way of doing business in a smaller market. One way was to provide a wide variety of products and services. In addition to auto glass, we handle shower glass work, curved glass for china cabinets, sand blasting artwork on glass, store front glass and table top glass. We also handle installation and bending of plexi-glass.

In 1983, we opened our facility in Charlevoix. We have fourteen full-time employees who operate in a casual atmosphere of cooperation and trust. Our offices are fully computerized, allowing us to rapidly respond to our customer needs.

Many of our customers have vacation homes in the area but live downstate, and our people occasionally work in these homes during the day when no one is home. This arrangement represents a trust given us by our customers and we must continually respect and honor that trust.

Since the successful introduction of the wild turkey in northern Michigan ten or fifteen years ago, damaged windshields from wild turkeys has increased at an alarming rate. We hope the turkeys find a way to reverse this trend.

My philosophy of business is the Golden Rule: "Treat others as you would like to be treated." It may sound a little corny, but it is true, and we plan to continue with that philosophy for as long as Dick and I are at the helm.

418 E. Eighth Street
Traverse City, MI 49684
Phone: 941-7112

Home Service Resources

GARDEN CENTERS

Barker Creek Nursery and Landscape
7048 M-72 NW, Williamsburg, MI
267-5972

Dan's Market and Garden Center
2415 Garfield Rd.
946-8685

Garden Goods
3510 N. US 31 S.
933-4769

Grand Traverse Nursery Sales
4715 US 31 S.
943-4060

Halls Green House
10461 Carter Rd.
946-1585

Manitou Gardens
12066 S. West Bay Shore Drive
947-5639

McGough's Inc.
501 Lake
947-5900

Plant Masters of Suttons Bay
M-22 near Suttons Bay
271-4769

Saundra's Garden
5363 North Long Lake Rd.
929-9791

Tom's Garden Centers
US 31 North, Acme, MI
938-2400

West Bay Shopping Center
947-7290

Traverse Gardens
3510 N. US 31 S.
946-6600

Village Garden
1111 S. Garfield
941-1808
(Behind Olson Food Store on Garfield)

Zimmerman Landscaping
M-72 West
947-1170

HOME BUILDERS ASSOCIATION OF GRAND TRAVERSE AREA, INC.

The HBA is a group of professionals dedicated to quality, serving the counties of Antrim, Kalkaska, Leelanau, Grand Traverse and Benzie. Their mission is to act as an advocate for the housing industry. This is accomplished by educating its members, informing the public, and monitoring government activities affecting the building industry.

For more information on the Home Builders Association or to get a copy of their current directory of members, contact them at:

3040 Sunset Lane
Traverse City, MI 49684

Phone: (616) 946-2305
or   (800) HBA-5166
FAX: 946-1051

Internet Address:
http://www.gtii.com/mahb/traverse/traverse.html

Services, Personal

Chapter 27

"An old-fashioned service station. You can trust Randy and his guys to give accurate and honest diagnosis and good service."—P.L.

Randy Schmerheim

Randy's Olde Towne Service

We have to do a good job for our customers. People trust us.

I moved here from Saginaw, and opened this station twelve years ago. I had been working in a service station there and vacationed in this area. I just fell into this line of work since I've always been the kind of person who could take something apart, fix it and put it back together again. Auto repair started as a hobby and I still enjoy it that way.

This is an old-fashioned service station. It's the only place in town where you can get anything fixed on your car. We can replace a windshield wiper blade or an entire engine. We also offer towing. I went to Delta College in Saginaw and attended their Automotive Program for two years. Today, I have four mechanics working with me and we are all certified by the State of Michigan.

One big difference in our station is how we handle problems. When they occur, we make it right for the customer, no matter what it takes. My name is on the business, and I know that I'm a big part of the success of the station. If I weren't here, it wouldn't work the same, and I'm happy when I see the repeat business we get.

People new in town won't get to know Curly Crandall. He was a great guy and I learned a lot from him about life and customer service. He was 80 when he died last year. He had been serving customers on this corner for over 60 years. Three years ago, I decided to buy his station across the street, and he came to work for me. He knew everybody in town and had a great memory for customers on a personal basis. We'd talk by the hour about customer service. I miss him.

Traverse City is a great place to raise my two young children. We live on a lake, so we do a lot of boating and water skiing. Often, I fly to my fishing cabin in Canada. Moving here was the best move I ever made. It's great to go into the supermarket or a store, run into people we know and have conversations with strangers. You don't get that in bigger cities.

Even though Traverse City is losing some of the small town feeling, it is still a great place to live. I feel that businesses like mine preserve some of that old-fashioned service feeling, and that's what keeps people coming back.

430 South Union
Traverse City, MI 49684
Phone: 947-0939

"These sisters have built a full-service salon in Old Town. The friendly staff serves your hair, nails and massage needs. "—C.L.

Tamara Vomastek & Sandra Guba

Impres Salon

We are a full-service salon, providing hair and speciality services to northwestern Michigan. Our mission is to continually improve our services and products to meet our customers' needs. How we accomplish our mission is as important as the mission itself. Fundamental to the success of Impres Salon are these basic values:

1. Quality Comes First— The quality of our services and products is our number one priority.

2. Our Customers are the Focus of Everything We Do — Our work is done with our customers' needs in mind.

3. Our People are the Source of our Strength – We are a team. Our people determine our reputation and vitality. Employee involvement is our way of life and we treat each other with trust and respect.

420 S. Union St.
Traverse City, MI 49684
Phone: 941-9094

We created Impres Salon because we had a passion for the industry and wanted the opportunity to create a salon from our shared vision. The salon is located in the heart of Olde Towne, Traverse City, in a remodeled building dating from the early 1900's.

Entering the salon, you are greeted by the buzz of high energy, spirit and a team member happy to help. The smell of flavored coffees and herbal tea arouse your temptation and almost always a goodie or two awaits you in the reception area. We are in a "look-good, feel-good" business, and that is what you will share when you visit our salon. Our twenty-member team is committed to education and continual growth, and several are national associates for REDKEN and SORBIE products.

Our community is our livelihood and we are committed to being loyal, friendly and dedicated members in the Traverse City community. With the friendships that we have made and the surroundings of our area, we have been gifted with a beautiful journey.

There is no other place more beautiful. Love it and respect it as we do!

"Maggie is adept at improving her client's image, from manners to wardrobe - from colors to presentation skills. What energy!"—P.L.

Margaret Quinn
Image By Design

In business since 1990, Image By Design offers classes and consulting services to individuals and corporations for the development and maintenance of the desired personal and professional image. We assist clients in creating the appropriate image for presenting themselves in the best possible way.

As the business world continues to become more competitive and continues to downsize, employees must develop skills that give them a competitive edge. This edge includes the ability to handle any situation with confidence and authority. Clients who have participated in our various seminar offerings comment about results they have noted, including increased self esteem, confidence and being more productive in their jobs.

Seminar offerings have increased yearly as more businesses understand the need to remain competitive. Our seminars are conducted both in Michigan and out-of-state.

No other local business offers as wide a variety of seminars and services as Image By Design. Our services include programs in wardrobe building, color charting, style, figure flattering dressing, business/social etiquette and dining skills for adults and children.

The lifestyle of Northern Michigan is perceived as being extremely casual. And many families move here to participate in a more relaxed atmosphere. They often come here from larger metropolitan areas with the expectation of being able to find the same things here as they had in their former residences. They enjoy the less formal way that business and dining are conducted here, but understand that it is important to know what is expected of them when they travel. Image By Design also provides programs to prepare youths and adults to compete if they choose to attend colleges or universities or accept positions in major metropolitan areas.

990 Pine Ridge Drive
Traverse City, MI 49686
Phone: 947-0024

"We love that drive-in window! It is good to see these folks expanding to the new locations. They also clean window blinds."—P.L.

Master Dry Cleaners
Dennis & Judy Conant

Master Dry Cleaners began operation as Meach Cleaners in 1949 at its Eighth Street location. The original name was recently changed to Master Dry Cleaners. This name change better reflects our mission and image. Although our business continues to expand and grow, we operate in a "family atmosphere" setting. In 1993, we added a store in Hickory Corners on Fourteenth Street. In 1995, we built and opened the location on Holiday Road and US 31 North. Our Eighth Street store is centrally located, affording our customers the maximum convenience possible.

Our dry-cleaning process is Sanitone. We constantly distill impurities, using only clean solvent. We offer a wide variety of other services, including expert shirt laundry. Same day service is available on dry-cleaning and shirt service. Our drapery cleaning by Adjust-A-Drape guarantees incoming length and perfect pleats. Blinds Express is our blind cleaning service. We clean all types of blinds from verticals, mini-blinds, pleated shades and woven woods. Take down and rehang service is available.

We offer deluxe wedding gown preservation, using a process that is safe for both the beads and trim. We also have a free seasonal storage service for cloth garments and a special storage vault for furs and leathers for a charge. Alterations are available on cloth garments as well as some minor repairs on furs. We strive to do the best possible work for our customers.

We have owned and operated Master Dry Cleaners since 1977. If you are new to the area, contact the Newcomers Club or Welcome Wagon for a $5.00 gift certificate. Our hours are 7:00 6:00, M-F and 9:00 to 3:00 on Saturday.

> 725 E. Eighth Street
> Traverse City, MI 49686
> Phone: 946-5620

"There isn't much they can't package and mail for you. A real convenience, especially for busy people."—P.L.

Robert Petersen
The Packaging Store

Packaging Store is a full-service packaging and shipping center, located in the 42nd Street Plaza, just off South Airport Road in Traverse City. This area has proven perfect for our unique market niche. Since purchasing the business, we have seen nearly 100% growth and we expect that growth to continue as the area grows and we add new services.

We specialize in handling fragile, large, awkward and valuable shipments that require professional packaging with quality materials and conscientious service. The inventory we keep on hand includes everything from basic corrugated boxes to custom-built crates and Foam-In-Place internal cushioning. This extensive inventory aids in our ability to package and ship anything, from a set of delicate china to an entire house full of furniture, or an office full of electronics to any destination, worldwide. This sets us apart from other shippers who typically offer only simple packaging services or ship only pre-packaged items. In addition, we offer options for mov-ing that allow customers to chose to purchase only the services they need, providing a cost-effective method for full-household moves.

There are many positives to operating a business in the Traverse City area. The people in and around Traverse City, whether visitors or residents, come from all over the world and all walks of life. That makes dealing with those individuals an interesting and educational experience that we truly enjoy.

Our business philosophy is very straightforward: "Be friendly and helpful." We want all of our customers to know that our main concern is taking care of their needs.

42nd Street Plaza
1425 South Airport Road, West
Traverse City, MI 49684
Phone: 929-7225

Transportation

Chapter 28

Transportation

Stephen R. Cassens
Airport Director, Cherry Capital Airport

Traveling to and from this region used to be quite a chore. First, there were trails developed by the Ottawas and Chippewas since travel then was by canoe and on foot. Missionaries first visited the area in 1839. Transportation for goods and passengers

between settlements to the north and cities such as Chicago and Detroit was by schooner; steamships took over the job in 1860. Railroads supplemented boat travel in the late 1800's. Eventually the automobile supplemented the railroads and the roads began to overtake the rails. In 1938, scheduled air service to the region was started by Pennsylvania Central Airways, operating out of a terminal on Garfield Avenue.

Today, there are two primary modes of travel in and out of the Grand Traverse region: automobiles and airplanes. Traverse City is approximately 250 miles from the East/West corridor connecting the

Atlantic and Pacific Oceans. In a way, you can think of us as being off on a northern spur. From Detroit and Chicago, both major centers of commerce, we are a four hour and seven hour ride by car, respectively, or approximately fifty minutes by air. The major paved arteries in and out of Traverse City are M-72 and I-75 South to Detroit, US-37 to US-115 to US-131 to Grand Rapids and beyond to Chicago, or US-31 North to the Straits of Mackinac. Four-lane roads coming to the region end at Grayling and Cadillac.

Traverse City benefits from a pattern of air travel established by the airlines in the early 1980's, during the initial years of airline deregulation. This pattern involves moving passengers through hub airports which feed the hubs with passengers from spokes such as Traverse City. The passenger then can connect to approximately 250 other cities worldwide. This method provides passengers with a high level of air service. Some examples are: one-stop service to destinations such as Florida, Europe and Asia through hub airports in Detroit and Chicago. With deregulation, fares are more competitive than ever before. For example, in 1985 there were 29 departures per day from Traverse City. In 1995, there were 32 departures per day, of which, three are DC-9 jets, with 3-4 times the passenger seats of commuter aircraft. There are even more flights available in the summer months.

1995

Year round   32 flights/day
(including 3 jets)

June-September   50 flights/day
(including 4 jets)

2000
(for airport expansion planning purposes)

Year round   40 flights/day
Summer   70 flights/day

The region benefits from an all weather jet port located at the appropriately-named Cherry Capital Airport. The airport is an important port of commerce, servicing all of northwestern lower Michigan. Services include scheduled commercial air service on both major and regional carriers, charter operators, air freight and overnight freight, taxi cabs, rental cars, travel services, aircraft maintenance and avionics.

Travel options to the Grand Traverse region have changed drastically over the century from Indian foot trails to contrails. Whatever mode of travel you choose to escape to Michigan's north may you always be rewarded by the splendor, beauty and the hospitality of the people of the Grand Traverse region.

BATA: Bay Area Transportation Authority

BATA is a regional public transportation system, providing transportation options to Leelanau and Grand Traverse Counties.

BATA has three major goals:

1. Create access (transportation) to employment, recreation, health care, human services, shopping, service organizations and education
2. Stimulate the local economy

3. Enhance the environment, reduce energy consumption, relieve congestion and parking problems

In 1995, BATA made 330,000 trips. By 1999 BATA expects to make 500,000 trips. The one-way cost is $1.50, $.75 for seniors.

To use BATA services, call 941-2324.

Volunteerism, Service Clubs & Organizations

Volunteerism, Service Clubs & Organizations

Barbara Lemcool
Executive Director, The Volunteer Center

Welcome to Traverse City. Our wonderful town IS wonderful because its citizens have a strong commitment to the welfare and prosperity of their community.

As Director of the Volunteer Center, I witness first-hand the caring and dedication of our residents. They view volunteerism as their duty for the privilege of living here. Volunteers work in the hospital, care for the elderly, tutor students at all 24 school sites, are a helping presence at our school bus stops, assist in countless environmental projects, read on Saturdays at the library, help in area food pantries, etc. Volunteers care about our community and, in return, get a feeling of accomplishment and enjoyment by making a difference.

The Volunteer Center has registered approximately 250 agencies, schools and organizations who are looking for assistance with projects and services.

Just give our office a call and we will be more than happy to help you find a fulfilling and exiting volunteer opportunity.

All human service agencies have an ongoing need for volunteer assistance. With grant funding becoming scarcer, agencies must rely on volunteer manpower to effectively do their jobs in our community. The Salvation Army, the Red Cross, Third Level Crisis Clinic, Big Brothers/Big Sisters are just a few of the many agencies in this area who perform much needed assistance to our residents.

Environmental groups are also very active and need concerned citizens to help ensure our area's beauty for generations to come. These groups, such as the Grand Traverse Area Watershed Initiative, the Land Conservancy and the Northern Michigan Environmental Action Council are always looking for dedicated people to assist them in their important work.

If you would like to use your talents by getting involved with a non profit board of directors, this office facilitates a "Board Marketplace" program and will help you find a suitable board. Area boards are always looking for new people with diversified skills and talents to serve in a governing capacity. Serving on a board is a great way to make a lasting contribution.

The Volunteer Center offers non-profit board of directors seminars and training. We explain what your responsibilities are when serving in a governance capacity and the responsibilities of the board to you as an individual. We also do strategic planning and general volunteer orientation.

If working directly with an agency is not what you think you might want to undertake, you can contribute to our community by joining one of our many service organizations. Any one of them would be eager to have you become a member. These organizations perform many community services ranging in focus from the hearing impaired, women and children at risk, environmental causes to youth initiatives. You will be able to get involved in their community projects, as well as to create new friendships through membership. Many of these organizations are affiliated with national organizations such as Rotary, Exchange Club, Quota Club, Zonta Club and Lions Club.

The Volunteer Center is available to you and will try to help make your transition to Traverse City a successful one.

Organizations

Organizations and contacts in the Grand Traverse Area

Note to the reader:
This directory is the result of the efforts of many different participants and is subject to being outdated as office holders in these organizations change. We have made a serious effort to present accurate information and apologize for any errors. If the contacts shown here are no longer correct, they should be able to put you in touch with the right contact. Please accept our apologies for any outdated information. For daily information on organizational meetings, refer to the Calendar feature in the Traverse City Record-Eagle.

AARP
American Association of Retired Persons, Jim Houdek, 941-7163

AAUW
American Association of University Women, Ann Laurimore, 946-8595

ABWA
American Business Women Association, Suzanne Sutton, (h) 946-6299 (o) 946-0550

ACADEMY FOR ECONOMIC RECOVERY OF OLDER WORKERS
Judy Shay, 947-8920

ACME CIVIC ASSOCIATION
David Kipley, 938-1000

AD CLUB OF TRAVERSE CITY
Shann Vander Leek, 947-7533

AMERICAN CIVIL LIBERTIES UNION
Paul Bare, 946-2191

AMERICAN CULINARY FEDERATION OF NW MICHIGAN
Karl Malin, 922-6285

AMERICAN HEART ASSOCIATION
Heidi Kleinfelder, 946-9524

AMERICAN MILITARY LEAGUE
Bruce Wise, 941-7253

AMERICAN GUILD OF ORGANISTS
Joyce Kloosterman, 943-4895

AMERICAN-ISRAEL PUBLIC AFFAIRS COMMITTEE
Mickey Fivenson, 946-7760

AMERICAN LEGION
Commander Donald Pratt, 223-7494

AMERICAN LUNG ASSOCIATION
946-1344 or (517) 484-4541

AMERICAN RED CROSS
947-7286

AMNESTY INTERNATIONAL
Dr. Michael McManus, 271-3127

AMVETS
Commander Doug Drake, 264-5583 or 264-5182

ANTIDEFAMATION LEAGUE
Mickey Fivenson, 946-7760

ANTIQUE AUTOMOBILE CLUB OF AMERICA NW MICHIGAN
Kay Hollis, 946-5362 or 947-3340

ANTIQUE BOAT CLUB
Marv Wittig, 946-5060

ARTISTS, NORTHWEST MICH. ARTISTS AND CRAFTSMEN
941-9488

ARTS COUNCIL
Mardi Link, 947-2282

ASSOCIATION FOR RETARDED CITIZENS
Craig Mosher, 941-0560

AUDUBON CLUB
Molly Harrigan, 269-3113

BAY LINER KITE CLUB
Steve Rutkowski, 946-5762

BAR ASSOCIATION
Dave Peterson, 941-8900

BARRIER-FREE ENVIRONMENT ADVISORY COMMITTEE
Rick Woods, 947-7207

BETA SIGMA PHI
Karen Frook, 946-2675

BICYCLE CLUB, CHERRY CAPITAL
June Thaden, 941-BIKE

BIG BROTHERS AND SISTERS
Kay Vandervort, 946-2723

BLIND, MICHIGAN ASSOCIATION OF THE
Joann Search, 947-3519

BLIND, NATIONAL FEDERATION OF THE
Marshall Houchin, 947-8717

BONSAI SOCIETY, SAKURA
Carol Carpenter, 946-2658

BOY SCOUTS OF AMERICA
938-2200

BOYS AND GIRLS CLUB
Fred Urbanski, 941-2303; John Conklin, 941-7700

BRIDGE CLUB
June Buller, 946-8778

BUSINESS AND PROFESSIONAL WOMEN'S CLUB
Tamera Thaxton, 941-0111

BUTTONS AND BOWS SQUARE AND ROUND DANCE
Ron Hensel, 938-1985

CANCER SOCIETY, AMERICAN
Barbara Barton, 947-0860

CEREBRAL PALSY ASSOCIATION, UNITED
Mrs. Harry Day, 276-9547 or 946-7132

CHAMBER OF COMMERCE, TRAVERSE CITY AREA
Hal Van Sumeren, 947-5075

CHERRY CAPITAL CHORUS
929-1396

CHERRY CAPITAL CLOWNS
Linda Lile, 938-2762; Bernard Hanchett, 946-5177

CHERRY CAPITAL CYCLING CLUB
June Thaden, 947-8476

CHERRY FESTIVAL, NATIONAL
Tom Kern, 947-4230

CHERRY GROWERS ASSOCIATION, RED TART, MACMA
(800) 292-2653

CHESS CLUB
946-7483

CHILD & FAMILY SERVICES OF NW MICHIGAN
Bernard Thompson, 946-8975

CHILD GUIDANCE CENTER, NW MICHIGAN
947-2255

CHILDRENS HOSPITALIZATION/FAMILY SERVICES
929-9700

COMMUNITY CO-ORDINATED CHILD CARE COUNCIL
(800)968-4228, 941-7767

CHORALE, GRAND TRAVERSE
922-1054

CHRISTIAN WOMENS CLUB
Lisa Annable, 941-9835

CITIZENS FOR BETTER CARE
Beth Osowski, 941-1399

CIVIC PLAYERS
947-2210

CIVIL AIR PATROL SQUADRON HO OF T.C.
256-9445 or Keith Marrow, 946-5916

CO-OP NURSERY
Jeanne Rokos, 946-1428

CONVENTION AND VISITORS BUREAU
Debra Knudsen, 947-1120

COUPLE TO COUPLE LEAGUE OF G.T. COUNTY
Steve Purdue, 938-9443

CRIME VICTIM VOLUNTEERS ASSISTANCE
Denise Schmuckal, 922-4543

DAISY CHAIN
Myrna Clement, 946-6171

DANCE, TRAVERSE BALLROOM
P.O. Box 5314

DANCE, BAYSIDE TRAVELERS COUNTY SOCIETY
Patricia Reeser, 946-9567

DANCE, INTERNATIONAL FOLK
Bob & Shelley, 946-8862 or Neila, 947-6675

DAUGHTERS OF THE AMERICAN REVOLUTION
Marian Solem, 929-3087

DEMOCRATIC COMMITTEE CHAIRPERSON
Linda Collins, 276-6525

DOULA TEEN PARENT PROGRAM
947-0067

DOWNTOWN TRAVERSE CITY ASSOCIATION
Brian Crough, 922-2090

DENTAL SOCIETY RESORT DISTRICT
Dr. Michael Lueder, 775-9797

DUCKS UNLIMITED
Steve Reicker, 946-0414

EAGLES
Lester Bannon, 947-8604

EASTER SEAL SOCIETY
Betty Reynolds, 941-1271

EASTERN STAR #147, ORDER OF
Sue Loomis, 947-6993, Gladys Liddell, 929-1564

EAST BAY BUSINESS ASSOCIATION
Randy Biggs, 947-6792

ECONOMIC CLUB OF TRAVERSE CITY
Randall Kiessel, 929-4700

ELKS, B.P.O.E., TRAVERSE CITY LODGE #323
Dan Tanis, 946-6171

EMBROIDERERS GUILD OF AMERICA
941-7616 or 929-9030 (Mondays)

EMOTIONALLY DISTURBED CHILDREN, MI ASSN. FOR
Gail Brink or Mary Little, 946-3335

ENCORE SOCIETY OF MUSIC
263-7200

EXCHANGE CLUB, TWIN BAY
John Welsh, 922-2350

EXCHANGE CLUB OF T.C.
Carl Lemcool, 947-6049

FARM BUREAU, N.W. MI
947-2941

FAMILY & FRIENDS OF PRISONERS & EX-OFFENDERS
Vennetta Wheeler, P.O. Box 193

FAIR, NORTHWESTERN MICHIGAN
943-4150

FOR ANIMALS
334-4122

GARDEN CLUB, CHERRYLAND
Dr. Louis Ursu, President 941-1130

GARDEN CLUB, IKEBANA INT. & MA ME NE INT.
Maxine Meach 947-1946, Mildred Webb, 947-1943

GARDEN CLUB, FRIENDLY
Mary Ann Pobuda, 947-7440

GARDEN CLUB, TRILLIUM
Mrs. Carlysle Rogers, 946-0616

GIDEONS INTERNATIONAL
Rex Matzinger, 947-9509

GIRL SCOUTS, CROOKED TREE COUNCIL
947-7354

GOLD WING ROAD RIDERS ASSOCIATION
Jerry and Dottie Baker 276-9267

G.T. CONVENTION & VISITORS BUREAU
947-1120 or 800-TRAVERS

G.T. AREA EMERGENCY LODGE
922-4890

G.T. AREA LITERACY COUNCIL
Carol McConnell, 941-5736

G.T. COUNTY COMMISSION ON AGING
Georgia Lopez or Betty Sutfin, 922-4688

G.T. ECUMENICAL ASSEMBLY
Sister Katherine, 946-8100

G.T. FAMILIES IN ACTION
922-4543

G.T. GENEALOGICAL SOCIETY
Lorraine Wallace, 947-8906, Jan Novak, 947-8555

G.T. HIGHLANDERS
Mrs. Doris Kusch, 616-258-6430

G.T. MINISTERIAL ASSN.
Rev. Dean Bailey, 946-5191 or 946-5750

G.T. ICE YACHT CLUB
John Russell, 947-2737 or Pete Norcross, 946-6439

**HEARING IMPAIRED, NW MI.,
PARENTS FOR THE**
Sue Braden, 275-7063

HEMOPHILIA ASSOCIATION, NORTHERN MI
Sandra Derman, 264-9053

HIGH TWELVE CHERRYLAND
Bill Morrison, 264-8212

HISTORICAL SOCIETY, G.T. PIONEER &
946-2647

HISTORICAL SOCIETY, MI
517-373-3559

HOCKEY ASSOCIATION
Cliff Kelto, 938-9022

HOME BUILDERS ASSN. OF G.T. AREA
Nancy Maxwell, 938-1130

HUMAN RIGHTS, T.C. COMMISSION ON
Lynn Larson, 946-4184

INSURANCE ASSN., BAY AREA
Don Miles, 947-6119

**IRISH-AMERICAN CLUB (ANCIENT
ORDER HIBERNIANS)**
Timothy LeJuene, 946-9138

**IRISH-AMERICAN CLUB OF G.T.
(FAMILY ORGAINIZATION)**
Maureen Titus, 267-5365

ITALIAN-AMERICAN CLUB
Angelo Vozza

JAYCEES
Wade Van Houzen, 935-1242

JUNIOR ACHIEVEMENT
Amy Whiting, 941-2211

KENNEL CLUB
Richard or Sean Smith, 264-5855

KIWANIS, G.T.
Dennis Mikkok, 947-3446

KIWANIS, T.C.
Len Gerhardt, 947-5914

KNIGHTS OF COLUMBUS
946-4104 or Paul Watkoski, 946-7000

La LECHE LEAGUE (BREAST FEEDING)
Tryna Terbrugh, 946-5296

LEADERSHIP GRAND TRAVERSE
Matt Meadors, 947-5075

LEAGUE OF WOMEN VOTERS
Luci Novak, 947-0738

LIONS CLUB
Bob Chamberlin, 271-4262, Fred Smith, 941-7269, Paul Hanrahan, 935-7241

MAKE-A-WISH
(800) 622-9474, (517) 372-4220

**MADD (MOTHERS AGAINST
DRUNK DRIVING)**
Valerie Johnson, 947-MADD

MARCH OF DIMES
947-2488

MARINE CORPS LEAGUE AUXILIARY
Mary Garber, 352-9304

MARITIME HERITAGE ALLIANCE
946-2647

MARTIAL ARTS-KUNG FU CLUB
935-4488

MASONS, MASONIC LODGE 222
Bill Rowden, 946-6863

**MEDICAL SOCIETY, GRAND TRAVERSE,
LEELANAU, BENZIE**
Dr. Rutkowski, 929-5700

MICHIGAN HEART ASSOCIATION
Marty Cotanche, 946-4414

MOTEL ASSOCIATION
Nancy Maxwell, 938-1130

MODEL A FORD CLUB
Weldon Fritch, 946-6238

MOTORWHEELS OF YESTERYEAR
P.O. Box 375

MOTHERS OF TWINS CLUB
Nancy Kivgima, 941-0174

MUNSON MEDICAL CENTER AUXILIARY
Helen Nesky, 947-4366

MUSCULAR DYSTROPHY
Paula Dibley, 616-459-4331

MSU ALUMNI
Dr. David Dean, 947-3762

**NATIONAL ASSN. OF RETIRED
FEDERAL EMPLOYEES**
Robert P. DeVol, P.O. Box 1, Old Mission

NEWCOMERS HOSTESS
Alice Beeker, 946-0188

NORTH COUNTRY TRAIL ASSOC.
Arlen C. Matson, 941-4152

NORTHERN MI DANCE COUNCIL
Ede Meyer, 947-2818(H) 947-6820(W)

NORTHERN MICHIGAN ENVIRONMENTAL ACTION COUNCIL
946-6931

NORTHERN MICHIGAN PLANNED PARENTHOOD
Alice Clayton, 929-1844

N W MICHIGAN GIFT OF LIFE
Kathy Styrk, 943-9125, Kim Hall, 947-6969

NURSES ASSOCIATION, T.C. DISTRICT
Marylee Pakieser, 947-5875

OPTIMISTS
Jerry Keelan ,929-9919 or Rod Willard 267-5045

OVEREATERS ANONYMOUS
Cindy, 941-9940, Wendy, 946-2527

PARTNERS IN EDUCATION
922-6475

PETROLEUM WOMEN'S CLUB
Sharon Moseman, 938-1648

POWER SQUADRON, G.T. BAY
Lon Deneff, 922-4104

QUOTA CLUB
Barbara Lemcool, 922-7338

RAILROAD HISTORICAL SOCIETY OF N W MI
P.O. Box 1845

RAINBOW GIRLS #55, INT. ORDER OF
Virginia Kelly, 947-1074 Sherry Wemple, 943-9561

R.E.A.C.T., G.T.
Wayne Milks, 943-3007

REBECCAS, WISTERIA LODGE #424
Mrs. Elton Bigger, 947-8698

REPUBLICAN COMMITTEE CHAIRMAN
Patricia Labelle, 946-3333

RIGHT TO LIFE
946-9469

RSVP (RETIRED SENIOR VOLUNTEER PROGRAM)
922-1136

ROCK AND MINERAL CLUB
223-7644 or Bernard Finn, 938-3092 or Victor Nelson, 271-6826

ROTARY CLUB
941-5421

RUFFED GROUSE SOCIETY
Mike Estes, 929-0827

SALVATION ARMY
Major Alvin & Shirley Clark, 946-4644

SENIOR CITIZEN CENTER
Joyce Stortz or Pat Thompson

SENIOR SOFTBALL
Jim Houdek, 941-7163, Tom Cook, 947-3664, Russ Tracey, 947-7754

SHRINE CLUB
Stan Liddell, 929-1564

SIERRA CLUB
Cathy Search, 946-7913

SINGLES GROUPS
Singles Over Sixty - 922-4911
In-Between - Support Group for loss of spouse - Bethlehem Lutheran Church, 947-9880
Singles I - Ages 18-33/Singles II - Ages 34 & up - Bayview Wesleyan Church, 947-3792
Separating & Divorcing Support Group - Bethlehem Lutheran Church, 947-9880
T.C. singles - Charlotte, 946-1553, Cathy, 922-0067

SKATING CLUBS (ARTISTIC, SPEED, JUNIOR OLYMPICS)
Robert VanEver, 941-1400

SKI CLUB, ADULT & FAMILY
Marlianne Warmbold, 276-6616

SKI CLUB & PATRONS, G.T.
P.O. Box 205

SKI PATROL
Linda Murphy, 946-6041

SKIN DISORDERS, CHRONIC
Donna Sivik, 947-9123

SLED DOG ASSOC., CAN AM TRIPLE CROWN
Ray Feagles, 946-3406

SNOWMOBILE COUNCIL, G.T.
Jill Rye, 946-8999

SOARING CLUB, NORTHWEST
352-9160

SOCCER, TRAVERSE BAY AREA YOUTH
Fred Haines, 946-1288

SOCIETY FOR MAGNETIC NORTH, THE
Jim McGee, 264-5607 or Jim McIntyre, 947-9707 or John Watkins, jr., 946-1518

SONS OF NORWAY
Bruce Hockstad, 946-2456

SPEBSOSA (BARBERSHOPPERS)
Wayne Campbell, 263-7203, Ken Forbeck, 269-3174

SPECIAL OLYMPICS
941-8937

SPORTSMANS CLUB (TRAVERSE REGION CONSERVATION CLUB)
Ron Barnes, 946-9253

SWEET ADELINES, G.T. CHAPTER
Jan, 264-8075 or Linda, 943-8077

SWIM CLUB (POSEIDON SWIM TEAM)
Chuck, 922-4819

THIRD LEVEL
(crisis intervention and counseling)
922-4800

TOASTMASTERS, CHERRY CAPITAL
941-4243 or 922-1058 or Douglas Baumgartner, 922-2177(w), 943-9082(h)

TOPS
Sharon McWethy, 947-8560 or Jean Widrig, 269-3239

TRACK CLUB OF T.C.
George Kuhn, 947-6417

TRAVERSE BAY ECONOMIC DEVELOPMENT CORP.
Charles Blankenship, 946-1596

TRAVERSE CITY BUSINESS & PROFESSIONAL WOMEN CLUB
Dorothy Crimmins, 935-1226

TRAVERSE AREA PERSONNEL ASSOCIATION
Clay Cronin, 947-3000 or Char Slater, 947-8532

TRAVERSE CITY MUSICAL
Delphine Welch, 322-6139

TROUT UNLIMITED
Bob Summers, 946-7923

UNITED WAY
947-3200

UNITED WE STAND AMERICA
Carol Ward or Dorothy Matzinger, 947 0321

UNIVERSITY OF MICHIGAN CLUB
Dan White, 941-5063

V.F.W. (VETERANS OF FOREIGN WAR)
946-7317

VASA, NORTH AMERICAN
938-4400

WELCOME WAGON
Gail Slack, 946-8253

WHEELCHAIR, BARRIER FREE INFO.
Rick Woods, 947-7207

WEIGHT WATCHERS
947-0010

WIDOW TO WIDOW, ANTRIM & KALKASKA
Cynthia Dinofrio, 947-5678

WIDOW TO WIDOWER SUPPORT GROUP
Central United Methodist Church, 922-9395

WOMENS CLUB, ACME
Linda Bruening, 938-2148

WOMENS CLUB, T.C.
Verle Arden, 946-6384

WOMENS ECONOMIC DEVELOPMENT ORGANIZATION (WEDO)
947-7190

WOMENS RESOURCE CENTER
Janis Williams, 941-1210

YACHT CLUB, GRAND TRAVERSE
946-9779

YOUNG MARINES
Don Beyer, 947-4277

YOUTH FOR CHRIST
Bob Johnson, 947-5574

ZONTA INTERNATIONAL
Virginia Watson, P.O. Box 552

ZOOLOGICAL SOCIETY
Rick Griffin, 947-9433

"This lady is a super volunteer. She loves the area and enjoys telling her friends about it."—P.O.

Bonnie Oppliger
Volunteer

I moved to Traverse City in 1984 from a town very similar in size to Traverse City. My father was born and raised in Empire (a small town west of Traverse City) and all my childhood vacations were spent in the area, where I still have many relatives.

There were, however, adjustments to be made. Coming to the Traverse City area had always meant fun and leisure. Therefore, when I moved here I thought nothing of going to the beach while 60 unpacked boxes sat in the middle of the living room floor. Eventually, reality did set in and I was able to combine caring for my home with enjoying the area as a resident, rather than a tourist.

I tend to be a joiner and had no problem getting involved in many areas. We joined the Newcomers Club and met so many great people - some who still remain friends. I became involved in political volunteerism, church and hospital auxiliary, Dennos Museum, and will soon begin volunteering at the new Visitors' Center. There is no end to the volunteer work that can be done in this area.

To me, it is very important to give back to the community that you live in as much as you receive.

Traverse City has given me so much and I feel a special need to give some of my time and energy back to the area. It is truly amazing how many organizations are viable because of the volunteers behind them. The diversity of interests is incredible and I cannot imagine that everyone cannot find something to take part in.

I have been asked how we can tolerate the noise, traffic and congestion of the Cherry Festival. We decided the first summer we lived here, that: "If you can't beat them, join them." As a result, we have enjoyed eleven years as Cherry Festival Ambassadors.

A friend of ours from downstate made the comment about Traverse City, "Well, it's a nice place in the summer, but what do you do in the winter?" Our answer was, "We spend a lot of time trying to decide which of the many available events we will attend." Yes, there is a lot to do in Traverse City twelve months of the year.

We enjoy two or three trips a year to Chicago and Atlanta to visit our children and see the big city, but are always ready to return to our beautiful, tranquil part of the world.

Weather

Chapter 30

Weather

Dave Barrons
TV 9 & 10, WWTV & WWUP TV

Weather in the Grand Traverse region can be described as exhilarating at times and tedious at times. It really is the weatherman's proverbial "mixed bag."

The best our weather pattern offers is the likelihood that we will enjoy some extended spell of beautiful weather, every year. It may come in any season, but most years offer their own fair weather lasting weeks or even months. The recent fall of 1994 comes to mind when unusually fair weather lasted from Labor Day until Christmas. Much of it was truly exhilarating with the clear, crisp air and rich blue sky the north country is known for.

The worst our weather offers is a pattern of wet, or windy, or cold weather on successive weekends. It seems, that at least every other year, we experience a period of lousy weather one weekend after another. For a population that enjoys being outdoors and an economy that relies on tourism, that is BAD weather. In the early 90's, we suffered through a summer with thirteen consecutive rainy weekends.

There are meteorological reasons for the anecdotal description given above. To begin to understand the weather of Northern Michigan, consider where our state lies within the land mass of Canada and the United States. Look at a map and you will see that we are just to the right, or east, of the center. Consider that all weather moves from west to east across our continent. That puts us squarely in line for fully-developed low pressure systems, or storms, moving in from any westerly direction. We truly sit on a very broad boundary-line in North American weather patterns, giving us the full range of conditions Mother Nature has to offer.

Look again at the map and it becomes clear that any weather system arriving in Northern Michigan, must cross the waters of Lake Michigan. That fact more than any other determines the daily weather experience for Traverse City and the surrounding area. It is called lake-effect weather and the term "lake effect" is one of the most often used phrases describing our weather.

Lake Michigan continually moderates our weather one way or another. In summer we are generally a bit cooler because the big lake acts as a giant air conditioner. It may be hot inland and downstate, but close to Lake Michigan, the on-shore breezes are cooled by the water. The on-shore breeze, known as the "lake-breeze," and so well known to sailors and pilots, is itself generated by the difference between land and water temperatures. This is not an excessively windy region, but the lake-shore winds are a steady feature of our climate and offer welcome protection from stifling heat in summer.

When it does get hot, our heat is rarely stifling. It doesn't last long, there is almost always a breeze, and we lack the excessive humidity found in Kalamazoo and Detroit. At 85° F, southern lower Michigan can routinely experience relative humidities around 50%. While at similar temperatures, the Grand Traverse region usually experiences relative humidity around 40%.

During the late fall, winter and early spring, the "lake effect" is just the opposite of summer. The relatively warm waters of Lake Michigan moderate the cold air flow coming from the north, sometimes straight from the arctic, or polar regions. While we can still experience bitter cold, our low temperature extremes are less frequent and less extreme than they would be without the warming provided by the big lakes. This same warming produces other weather phenomena as well: excessive cloudiness, increased snow potential, and protection from late spring frost.

The Grand Traverse region can be rather cloudy at times, especially in the fall and spring, when the heat and moisture given off by the lakes produces more clouds on the lee side of the lakes. We have been known to go a full month without seeing the sunshine. Factually, however, we are less cloudy than Sault St. Marie, Grand Rapids, or Muskegon.

Excessive snowfall is perhaps our most notable "lake effect". As cold air rushes across the warmer waters of Lake Michigan, it picks up moisture from the lake, and then deposits it as snow on the downwind side. Even when there is no actual storm involved, northwest lower Michigan can receive heavy snow, as much as 18 inches and more from the lake effect or lake enhancement of moisture in the air. Early in the season, lake effect snows tend to fall 15 miles or more inland from the shoreline, generally northeast of Traverse City itself, while late in the season lake effect snow tends to occur right along the shore line. In March, it is not uncommon to find heavy cloud cover and snow blanketing the shoreline while just a few miles inland there is bright blue sky. The extra snow from "lake effect" is one of the reasons we enjoy a healthy skiing and snowmobiling industry in our region.

The "lake effect" weather creates an even bigger economic impact on fruit crops. In late spring, the warmth of Lake Michigan gives the hilly, sandy soil of our shorelines protection from frosts. Nighttime

temperatures on the other side of the lake can go below freezing while on this side, very close to the shoreline, our temperatures will stay just above the frost level. This is the primary reason the orchard fruit industry exists here. The immediate Grand Traverse region has the greatest concentration of cherry orchards found anywhere in the country, and apples, plums and peaches are also grown in abundance. Thanks in part to just a little bit of lake effect warmth!

Regarding the weather, northwest lower Michigan is one of the safest places to live in the United States. During the warmest months, the cool waters of Lake Michigan offer some protection from the really large, violent storms that are born in the heat of the great plains. As those storms move east and encounter the cooler waters of Lake Michigan, they lose a significant portion of their strength. So, while we occasionally do experience tornadoes and other damaging winds, they are much less frequent here than they would be without the protection provided by the big lake. Our thunderstorms are generally smaller or weaker, so their ability to produce damaging winds of any kind is greatly reduced. We are not prone to serious flooding, hurricanes rarely make it this far north and west, our droughts don't last as long as in other parts of the country.

Some basic statistics: The all time record low for Traverse City is -37 F. Our coldest period annually, is mid January to mid February, when daytime highs average in the mid twenties. But note that we have achieved a daily record low of -11 F as early as December 11th, and every daily record low for the month of March is below zero.

The all time record high temperature is 105 F. Our hottest period annually, is early July to the end of the month when daytime highs average in the low eighties. But note that we have achieved a daily record high of 104 F as early as June 1st and 21 days in September still have daily records at or above 90 F.

Average precipitation is about 32 inches per year for Traverse City itself, but locations just 20 miles away average more than 140 inches! It is difficult to define a pattern other than the lake effect snows already mentioned. We can get big snow storms that dump heavy wet snow made from water brought all the way from the Gulf of Mexico or from the Pacific. More likely, we receive smaller amounts of a drier snow from the cold air/lake-effect. Lake effect snows are most often accompanied by wind, which means that blowing snow, drifting and difficult driving conditions are a frequent fact of life for us.

Clearly, the weather of northwest Michigan is a little of everything. Sometimes it's very little! Our one big shortcoming is in the spring when we are teased with hints of the real thing from March onward; but consistent spring weather seldom arrives for sure until the first week of May. And then, it lasts about two weeks and suddenly it's summer.

There is a saying about Michigan weather: "If you don't like it, just wait five minutes and it'll change." Truth is, that saying probably applies to other climates more than ours. Yet the beauty of our weather pattern is that it does change on a steady cycle. If the weather is bad now, at least it won't last too long. New weather systems arrive on a steady 3-5 day cycle during the extended fall and spring seasons, and can settle into shorter 5-7 day cycles mid-winter or mid-summer, especially summer. Change is the name of our weather. No two succeeding years are ever the same. The summer following that one with all the rainy weekends, for example, had near-perfect weather with gorgeous weekends, and most rains came overnight.

The Irish have many sayings about the weather. My favorite is: "When the good Lord made weather, He made plenty of it!" and we in northwest Michigan get to see nearly all of His creation at one time or another.

Seasonal Affective Disorder

FEELING SAD?

Winters are long in Northern Michigan, and that alone can be depressing, but winters are particularly trying for people with a neuro-chemical disorder called Seasonal Affective Disorder, or SAD. We asked Michael Engel, D.O., a Traverse City psychiatrist, about the condition.

WHAT IS SEASONAL AFFECTIVE DISORDER?

It is best described as a winter depression. Recurrent depression usually starts in October or November and subsides by April or May. Studies suggest a neuro-chemical imbalance in the brain. It appears that light stimulates production of these neuro-chemicals, which are related to mood, and that diminished light in winter produces the depressive symptoms.

WHAT ARE THE SYMPTOMS?

Increased appetite, weight gain, craving for carbohydrates, and excessive sleepiness (sleeping 12-16 hours a day). Persons with SAD often have extreme difficulty getting up in the morning. Other symptoms include feelings of sadness, hopelessness, or worthlessness, as well as sluggishness, low energy, social withdrawal, difficulty concentrating, decreased sexual drive, irritability, interpersonal difficulties, and impaired functioning at work. Individuals with SAD often notice that when they go to warm latitudes during the winter, the symptoms subside.

WHO IS MOST AT RISK?

Women are four times more likely than men to be affected. People whose siblings or parents have a psychiatric condition - particularly major depressive episodes, alcohol abuse or dependency - also appear to be at greater risk. One quarter of the people diagnosed have no prior history of psychiatric treatment. 41% have taken antidepressants in the past.

WHAT CAN YOU DO IF YOU SUSPECT YOU HAVE IT?

The most important thing is to rule out a medical condition, such as diabetes or blood-pressure problems, which may cause symptoms similar to this type of depression. This is usually done with a general physical assessment and specific laboratory tests. This can be done through consultation with a psychiatrist. If medical causes are ruled out and you are diagnosed with SAD, it is important to educate yourself, your family, close friends and perhaps your employer about SAD. Seek as much light as possible - a south-facing office or classroom with windows, sitting by south windows in restaurants and even in cars. Maintain a regular sleep/wake schedule and get regular exercise. Arrange winter vacations in warm, sunny places if you can.

Some new antidepressants appear to have a dramatic impact on seasonal depression. Frequently, patients need take the medication only in winter. Light therapy is effective, but dosage and distance from the light is important and should be monitored by a psychiatrist ("full-spectrum at 2500 Lux for two hours a day has been recommended). Over-stimulation can produce headaches, hyperactivity and sleeping difficulty.

WHAT RESOURCES ARE AVAILABLE IN NORTHERN MICHIGAN?

Psychiatrists have been trained to recognize and treat SAD, and psychotherapy may help individuals to develop strategies to cope with it. To learn more about SAD, contact the National Organization of Seasonal Affective Disorder, P.O. Box 451, Vienna VA, 22180. Light boxes are available at many hardware and health food stores, and some are qualified to recommend dosages.

Dr. Engel is in private practice in Traverse City and is medical director of Northern Michigan Community Mental Health Services, serving Charlevoix, Cheboygan, Emmet and Otsego counties. This article first appeared in TRAVERSE, Northern Michigan's Magazine in January, 1995, and is re-printed here with Dr. Engel's permission.

Wineries

Wineries

Ed O'Keefe III, President
Chateau Grand Traverse Winery & Vineyards

To Build a Winery

Someone once said, "If you want to make a small fortune, start with a large fortune and go into the wine business." This phrase rings so true when I reflect upon the huge undertaking and challenge my father, Ed O'Keefe, took back in 1974 to build and establish Chateau Grand Traverse Winery on Old Mission Peninsula.

When our typical suburban Detroit family moved to the area, we only knew of Traverse City as a beautiful, little town "up north" where we would go on vacation periodically throughout the year. Others knew of this area as the "Cherry Capital of the World" with its traditional July parades and pageants celebrating its claim to fame. Until recently, few people would have considered the Grand Traverse region a notable location to grow grapes and produce high quality wines.

Although Michigan has a fairly long history of wine making, spanning back well before prohibition, these activities revolved primarily around the southwestern portion of the state. Most of this grape growing and production geared itself toward the making of sweeter, high alcohol wines, as well as grape juices. By the early 1970's, some Michigan wineries were producing higher quality wines made from the hearty French/American hybrids, but nobody was willing to undertake the huge financial risk to plant the fragile European Vinifera grape varieties which were notably grown throughout the finest wine regions of the world. In fact, industry experts felt the overall climate of Michigan was simply too cold to sustain the European Vinifera grape varieties on a commercial scale.

The greatest wine regions of the world share a number of similar vineyard site criteria that must be in complete harmony to allow the growing of grapes. Some of these critical factors include: elevation, hours of sunlight, slope angle, air and water drainage, soil makeup, rainfall, and most importantly, no exceedingly cold temperatures. In most cases, these ideal growing conditions are obtained when situating a vineyard near a large body of water because of temperature moderating effects. Considering these necessary conditions, some have mirthfully stated, "Grapes like to grow where people like to live."

The Grand Traverse Bay region seemed to provide the suitable conditions to establish a new vineyard, but with one exception - the low critical temperature! Industry experts agreed. If a thermometer reading fell below -6∫F for more than a four hour period, grapevine death would most likely occur. It was common knowledge that Northern Michigan regularly achieved winter temperatures below -25∫F. Knowing this basic information and considering the substantial up front investment, most people would have been deterred from even contemplating planting grapes in such a harsh area. In retrospect, my father said, "I must have had more money than brains at that time."

In reviewing the weather data gathered by Cherry Capital Airport, as well as local farmers, it was clear that winter temperatures were simply too cold to sustain grapes. Keeping this in mind, my father questioned how it was possible that certain Old Mission Peninsula fruit growers regularly produced high quality and abundant harvests while for many other area growers, this simply was not the case. This, he felt, was due to the choice specific growing sites combined with the unique "micro-climate" generated by the effects of Grand Traverse Bay. In other words, his belief was that this mass of water surrounding Old Mission Peninsula offered a favorable, moderated temperature effect different from inland or questionable growing sites. This "lake effect" provided a slightly cooler temperature in the spring, thus maintaining plant dormancy and avoiding the possibility of early budding and freeze damage. On the inverse, this effect maintained warmer fall temperatures, thus increasing ripening time. Furthermore, the issue of lethal, cold temperatures was combated by an annual snowfall of 150+ inches that would create a virtual insulated blanket around the vine. This subjective understanding provided my father with enough incentive to be the first person to take on the risks, and commercially plant 55 acres of European Vinifera Grapes in Michigan.

Working with the late Dr. Helmut Becker from Geisenheim, Germany, and Professor Coheen from the University of California, Davis, many steps were taken before the first grapevine could be planted. First, a vineyard site was selected, located at the highest point of Old Mission Peninsula, to ensure the warmest possible temperatures while avoiding

potential frost pockets. Secondly, well over 1,000,000 cubic yards of earth were moved and reshaped to obtain an ideal, southwest gradual slope. Finally, in 1975, it was certain all the other necessary growing variables were in place. Only then could the initial 55 acres of Johannesburg Riesling, Chardonnay, and Merlot vines be planted. During the wait of an additional four years for the first, limited harvest, it was necessary to confront the ridicule of doubters who dubbed the entire project "O'Keefe's Folly."

All doubt was cast aside in 1979 when Chateau Grand Traverse entered the wine arena and won the "Best of Show Award" at the annual Michigan State Fair Wine Competition with its first ever production of Chardonnay. Since Michigan residents still wouldn't consider the wines on a serious level with that of European or California counterparts, it was necessary for Chateau Grand Traverse to develop markets in noted wine consumption areas such as San Francisco. By winning awards and critical acclaim in these markets, only then would Michigan customers consider Chateau Grand Traverse wines seriously.

Currently, there are nine wineries located in the immediate Grand Traverse region which is divided into two federally recognized Viticulture Appellations known as "Old Mission Peninsula" and "Leelanau Peninsula." Wineries located on Old Mission Peninsula include: Bowers Harbor Vineyards (est. 1991), Chateau Chantal (est. 1993), Chateau Grand Traverse Winery and Vineyards (est. 1975), and the newly-formed Old Mission Cellars (est. 1994) Wineries located on the Leelanau Peninsula include: Boskydel Vineyard (est. 1976), Good Harbor Vineyards and Winery (est. 1980), L. Mawby Vineyards (est. 1977), and Leelanau Wine Cellars (est. 1975). Today, virtually all of these wineries produce their own award-winning styled wines made from some variety of European Vinifera Grapes that Ed O'Keefe pioneered.

With continued vineyard expansion, as we have seen over the past several years, local wine production is becoming an important and integral part of the Michigan agricultural community. Who knows, maybe one day Traverse City will be thought of as the "Napa or Sonoma Valley of the Midwest."

Boskydel Vineyards
7501 E. Otto Road
Lake Leelanau, MI 49653
Phone: 256-7272

Bowers Harbor Vineyards
2896 Bowers Harbor Road, Old Mission Peninsula
Traverse City, MI 49686
Phone: 223-7615

Chateau Chantal
15900 Rue de Vin
Traverse City, MI 49686
Phone: 223-4110

Chateau Grand Traverse
12239 Center Road
Traverse City, MI 49686
Phone: 223-7355

Good Harbor Vineyards
2191 S. Manitou Trail
Leland, MI 49653
Phone: 256-7165

L. Mawby Vineyard
4519 S. Elm Valley Road
Suttons Bay, MI 49682
Phone: 271-3522

Leelanau Wine Cellars
12693 Tatch
Omena, MI 49764
Phone: 386-5201

Old Mission Cellars
2464 Kroupa Road
Old Mission, MI 49673
Phone: 223-4310

Women's Issues

Chapter 32

Women's Issues

Jo Bullis
Program Director,
Women's Resource Center

Welcome to the Traverse City area. Over the last several years, we have been fortunate to have many programs here that are directed toward the success and well-being of women. For this brief introduction to some of these programs, I will use an outline presented in recent forums sponsored by the Nokomis Found-ation. This program, "Women Matter!," identified four issues as top concerns for women in Michigan.

Participants at eight regional forums (including one held in Traverse City in June of 1995) identified Economics, Education, Health and Violence as issues that are important to them — as issues that matter. The regional groups continue to meet to develop strategies to address these issues and statewide conferences will be held once every two years. For more information about the local "Women Matter!" contact Louise Johnson, 941-0943 or Linda Kansa, 935-6202.

This is an overview of commonly-used services and some unique opportunities in the Grand Traverse Area that are related to the issues identified by

"Women Matter!." While it may not be a comprehensive listing, it will give you a good idea of some of the many programs available. If you need additional information or services, contact us at The Women's Resource Center or Third Level Crisis Center's information and referral service at 922-4800 or 800-442-7315.

Economics

In "Women and the Future of Michigan," the Michigan Women's Foundation reported that "women are making dramatic strides in entering the workforce and achieving economic self-sufficiency," but "they have a long way to go in attaining equality." According to the Michigan Women's Commission, the "declining availability of full-time work with fringe benefits such as health insurance is a growing problem for women in Michigan." (Part-time Employment: An Issue of Concern for Michigan Women, 1992).

In the Grand Traverse area, the greatest numbers of women are employed part-time in the retail and service industries, which includes medical-related employment and manufacturing assembly, requiring fine-motor skills. Wages are generally lower than, or equal to, those in other parts of Michigan's Lower Peninsula.

For women to work outside the home, they need affordable child care. The Northwest Michigan 4C (Community Coordinated Child Care) Council promotes quality child care that links children, families, caregivers and communities in the area with training, support and information. For parents, the Council provides referrals to licensed child care providers; information about choosing good child care and financial assistance if needed; parenting workshops; a "lending library" for toys, books, periodicals and audio-visual materials; and referrals to other community resources.

Currently, the Council maintains a list of over 400 child care providers. Weekend, evening and infant child care may be more difficult to locate in some communities than traditional weekday care for older children, but it is available in the area if you are able to transport your children. Currently, you can expect to pay about $2 per hour per child, although some providers charge less and may give a second child discount. The 4C Council also provides many services for child care providers, employers, and the public. For more information about 4C Council programs, call 941-7767 or 800-968-4228.

Education

Zonta's "Project 100" is an ongoing program that promotes math, science and technical career opportunities to girls. Believing there is a relationship between education in math and science, self esteem and career interests, the program works with eighth grade girls and encourages them to stay in math and science courses by sponsoring an annual "Recognition and Encouragement Day" and providing tutors and career discussions.

The Bridge Program at Northwestern Michigan College offers a unique "bridge" for area residents who want to make a smooth transition into college or back into the workplace. The program places a heavy emphasis on competence and confidence building in an atmosphere of support. Students in the program gain self-confidence while practicing basic workplace literacy skills, including computers, applied math, and applied communication. Assistance with employability and study skills is also available. Any adult learner is eligible. For more information about the Bridge Program call 922-1721 or 922-1717.

For those already in the work force, "Leadership Grand Traverse" (a Chamber of Commerce sponsored program) provides new, emerging and poten-

tial leaders with the opportunity to strengthen individual leadership abilities while encouraging active participation in the community. Some of the objectives of the program are to educate participants about community needs and leadership opportunities; to improve management and leadership skills; to develop relationships of value when working together on community projects; and to assist in matching the talents of participants with community leadership needs.

Health

Munson Medical Center provides a variety of services for women through its Women's Health Services programs. In addition to general hospitalization and emergency medical care, Munson offers childbirth classes, a family birth center, and infant mental health/parent support programs; cancer prevention, detection, treatment and support; classes and counseling related to diet and nutrition; the Vital Choice program, which helps women make positive lifestyle changes to reduce stress and other risk factors; and a Behavioral Health Program that addresses women's mental health and alcohol and drug treatment needs.

The Women's Health Network is an information system that educates and informs community members about women's health concerns. A lending library provides books, pamphlets, videos and a computer database. A registered nurse is available to assist in the research process as well as to answer questions about women's health issues. "Focus on Women" is a Munson-sponsored community lecture series presenting topics relating to women's health and well-being. For more information about these services, call 935-6678 or 800-376-1135.

Violence

The Women's Resource Center (WRC) provides 24-hour crisis intervention, including a toll-free help line and on-site advocacy; immediate safety; emergency shelter; one-on-one and group counseling; food, medical, legal, financial, transportation, housing, educational, employment and children's advocacy; information and referral; follow-up; and community education and prevention services to domestic violence and sexual assault victims and their families.

WRC's emergency shelter serves a five-county area, including Benzie, Grand Traverse, Kalkaska, Leelanau and southern Antrim counties. This is a population base of approximately 125,000 people. WRC's shelter and administrative offices are located in Traverse City and two nonresidential outreach offices are maintained in Benzie and Kalkaska counties. A re-sale store, operated by the agency, provides clothing and personal items to residential and nonresidential clients, free of charge. Bedding, furniture, large appliances, and other household items are provided to women and children leaving the shelter to assist them in obtaining and maintaining independent housing. Presently, the WRC serves approximately 4,000 people a year in its residential and nonresidential programs. For more information about WRC's services call 941-1210 or 800-554-4972.

The Grand Traverse area is also the site of "The Initiative," an innovative, community-based violence prevention project. Sponsored by the Grand Traverse/Leelanau Human Services Coordinating Council, "The Initiative" includes nine Action Teams working cooperatively to stop family and community violence. Team members have participated in two community forums and currently are implementing their initial violence prevention strategies. The Action Teams are focusing on the workplace, media, education, intervention, diversity, religious community, legislation and public policy, neighborhoods, and child abuse prevention. For more information about "The Initiative" call 941-1210.

"This description is part tongue-in-cheek and all real. A welcoming message for women moving to the area."

Carol LaPorte
Moving to Traverse City —A Woman's Viewpoint

Last December, I met a woman from California who had moved to Traverse City about three months earlier. She missed the city, she missed the warmer weather and, basically, she was just plain unhappy. It brought back lots of memories of my first winter in "God's country." For years I had thought how many women there are out there making the same adjustment. My first week here was in early November. We had moved on a bright, crisp late fall day from the Detroit suburbs, and two days later we were in the middle of the season's first Arctic gale in Traverse City. The wind was blowing, my hair was wet and straight and I was generally miserable. I knew I was in for a change!

I now love living here - in fact, I hope this is where I will stay for the rest of my life. I don't even have a desire for a condo in Florida. So, how did I get to this point? For me, it wasn't an easy transition. My children were grown and gone, and our first winter here was spent in our vacation home about 15 miles outside Traverse City. I felt isolated and lonely, and without the crutch of children's activities to meet people, I knew I'd have to do it on my own. We were building a home in the area so I made daily excursions into town to monitor the progress. That

was the beginning of some socialization. My friends laugh and say that I know every store owner in town. I got to meet lots of them that first year while I was exploring the area. That was the first indication that I was in for a change. Store owners remembered my name and took the time to chat and get to know me. When I went to the library, for the second time, I was totally shocked that Mary, the librarian, greeted me by name. I had always been anonymous in the city - this neighborliness was new and enjoyable and it continues to be one of my great pleasures in living here. The social banter in the community creates a real bond between the people here and by opening up to it, you'll have more fun and meet lots more people.

Winter up here was harsher than I was used to. That first year I did two, 180 degree spins in my car while madly pumping the brakes and going no more than 15 miles an hour. Every new snow storm caused lots of anxiety because I know I'd be too afraid to drive. We remedied that the first February when we traded in our car for a new 4-wheel drive Explorer. I love my truck. Now I know I can get around anywhere, even in the worst weather, so my feelings of isolation disappeared and I've never been stuck or done another spin. One of my friends gave me some good tips for women to remember when driving in the winter. She packs a little box every fall and puts it in her trunk. In it are a bag of kitty litter to throw under the tires if you're stuck, a fold up shovel, a couple of flares, some Granola bars, a bottle of water, a pair of heavy duty boots and mittens. All are "just-in-case" items and not a bad idea, especially the kitty litter. The warmest coat you can afford will make you more comfortable and buy the most weatherproof rubber-bottomed boot you can find. There are a few that have some style. So—a reliable car, warm coat and boots and an emergency kit for the car. That should help get you around the first winter.

Shopping in Traverse City was a notable change from the place I'd lived for over twenty years. Suddenly, there was no Jacobson's, no Hudson's, no Pier 1 - unless I drove to Grand Rapids or Detroit. The year was 1990 and the Grand Traverse Mall hadn't been built. Where were the shoe stores?! Luckily, there have been some major changes in the shopping situation here. In fact, I honestly buy almost everything here now. Women still bemoan a shortage of shoe stores and it's still hard to find a special dress in the area but we're getting there. I'm a firm believer in supporting the local economy whenever possible, so I try to purchase things in the area. Even doing a major home remodeling was accomplished by buying everything in Traverse City. With a little research, you'll be amazed what's available. In fact, sometimes I've found items here that I hadn't been able to get elsewhere. There are so many wonderful small businesses around and the service and personal care you'll get is terrific. Another thing happens after you're here awhile, especially if you come from a larger city. Shopping isn't such a big priority. Clothes are more casual and the concentration of your interests will probably shift to new areas.

Well, the next big issue for me centered around cultural activities. The first month, we were invited to the symphony. It was held at Lars Hockstad Auditorium in Central Grade School, and it was a combination of the symphony orchestra and several barbershop quartets. I was fascinated. It was so unlike going to the Ford Auditorium in Detroit and I wasn't sure how I felt about the experience. Now,

several years later, I can tell you that I respect and admire the talent in The Traverse Symphony Orchestra, and I am thankful that, in a town this size, we even have a symphony orchestra. We may not have the huge auditoriums here yet, but we have Interlochen, jazz concerts and theater. The community is so rich with cultural activity that we are never without a choice of something to do. The size of the performances may be smaller, but that's the advantage. There's an intimacy in most of the performances in the area that is often missing in a larger city. Exciting growth is going on in the cultural community of Traverse City.

I was getting more adjusted after that first winter. Spring was coming, birds were singing, beaches were beckoning and then it happened—COMPANY! It seems that every person you ever knew in your former life ends up on your doorstep. Of course, some of it is great, but it's a complaint I hear from many of my friends. They're exhausted! Company is a lot of work for women. I don't care what the women's movement says, the equality isn't here yet. We're still the ones who buy the food, cook the meals, wash the towels, change the sheets, etc., etc. So, what to do?

My first advice-if you wouldn't have them overnight in your former home, don't have them overnight here. That first summer, my place was like a B & B. I had fresh muffins, juice and coffee for breakfast, and the day continued from there with sightseeing trips to organize and a big dinner to fix at night. Not only is it exhausting, but it can really get expensive. Trust me on this one. Right from the start, set some ground rules or your summer will disappear. Everyone who visits thinks we do nothing but vacation up here. They also forget that they're not the only guests we'll have during the summer. Try to limit the time period your company will stay. We try now to keep August free for ourselves. I usually have something easy in the house for breakfast but do not spend time on other meals. I no longer pre-plan every meal. Now, it's something on the grill or a meal out. I have maps available and some brochures of activities so our visitors can go off and do their vacationing while I garden. Guests strip beds when they leave. Then I found that the problem was really of my own making. It's not that I don't want company- I just don't want to do all the work. Now, by doing less and expecting more from my guests, it works out better and I have more fun.

Now it was autumn. Time to burrow in a little and get some things done around the house. Mid-November and I'm ready to have some electrical work done. A call to the electrician revealed the Up-North phenomenon that I had totally forgotten. Hunting season! Actually, I knew it existed but didn't realize its massive scope. Be advised- if you want ANYTHING done in your home, don't plan it for the month of November. Hunters in the area talk about nothing else from October until Thanksgiving. They will promise to do the work, but you'll never see them. There are events in town just for women and there is a mass exodus of orange and camouflage out of town. The newscast every night shows deer strung up and we hear lots of statistics on racks and points. It will be over soon but one real word of caution: This isn't the time to go for a walk in the woods in the country.

Repairmen are another topic that needs to be addressed when discussing a move to Traverse City. Time seems to be a different commodity here than in the city. You'll eventually get it done, but it always seems to take longer. First of all, parts often have to be ordered. Then there's the relaxed attitude of most repairmen. They usually have time to chat and get to know you a little. You may need more patience to get your work done but, in general, I've been pretty pleased with the outcome. Pushing someone to hurry a job won't get you a better job and you may not get your work done at all. Emergencies are another story, though. We've had a few, and I've been completely impressed with the willingness of people to be there if you're in trouble. We've had frozen pipes and oil leaks and basement floods, always at strange hours, and I have always found someone to help immediately. The feeling of community is very strong here when anyone is in need.

Those are the basics. Any move is traumatic and every area has its own peculiarities. This is a wonderful area in which to live but like anyplace you go, it's up to you to do a little work. Find an interest group, work, participate in a church or your children's school activities. The key is to get out the door because I know the people in this community are warm and friendly. I moaned for about a year until a friend told me that it was time to get on with my new life here. Maybe I can save you that initial year of moaning by giving you this advice now and telling you that if you hang in there, you will never want to leave.

Paul and Carol LaPorte are both natives of Michigan and moved to Traverse City from Birmingham, Michigan in 1990, after six years of commuting to a cherry farm they still own in the area. In addition to delighting in all the things Traverse City has to offer, they both enjoy traveling and reading. They have two grown children, David and Kate, and a grandson, Jonah.

Paul's career is technically-oriented, mostly in computer software. It has taken him around the world as a communications and marketing professional. He has also taught at the college level, published articles on technical education and presented several papers around the country on technical education. Since moving to Traverse City, he has owned Mission Communications, a firm specializing in professional and technical communications. Paul holds a B.A. in English from University of Michigan.

Carol is a Master Gardener and an avid quilter. She earned her B.S. in Nursing from University of Michigan, and later, a degree in interior design. For twelve years prior to moving to Traverse City, Carol owned and operated her own design practice "Second Opinion" in Birmingham.

Paul Oppliger was born on a wheat farm in central Kansas. After high school, he served in Army Intelligence and earned a B.S. in Chemical Engineering from the University of Kansas. He joined a small high tech company, Dow Corning Corporation and experienced great personal and professional growth during the thirty years he spent there.

He and Bonnie married in 1956. They have three children: Julie, Jeff and Susan; and two grandchildren: Jonathon and Chase. Since Bonnie's father had been born and raised in nearby Empire, she had many attachments to the Traverse City area, so this was a family vacation spot and a natural retirement destination for the Oppligers.

Paul first began dealing with the "movers and shakers" of the region in his position as Executive Director of the Data Research Center, keeping track of economic and demographic trends in the region. His forecasting and planning activities allowed him a view not seen by many.

"The beauty of the area is seen by all and is remarkable," says Paul. "Less visible but equally important is the attitude and commitment of the residents to keep it clean, friendly and beautiful. It is a trust given to us when we move here and most take that trust very seriously."

Photo Credits

Thaddius Bedford
Alpine Electric, S. Anderson, J. Barrett, M. Bowie, J. Bullis, M. Carlson, D. & M. J. Censer, J. Falconer, Fitness Center, D. Folgarelli, T. Heger, V. Herman, M. Johnson, S. Kassens, L. Keenan, D. Kelly, D. Knudsen, T. Lampton, P. LaPorte, B. Lemcool, H. Lemcool, J. Lindeneau, A.J. Lorenzen, S. Loveless, Mary's Kitchen Port, J. Milliman, H. Nye, E. O'Keefe, R. Peterson, Professional Office Supply, H. Schelde, R. Schmerheim, T. Simonelli, Sound Room, E. Takayama, A. Valdmanis, G. & L. Wildman

Terry Burton
R. Portenga

Glen Graves
Impres Salon

George Underwood
J. Little/B. Riggs

John Robert Williams
B. Cole, B. Crough, J. Hooper, E. Jenniman, P. LaPorte, F. Leonard, T. Kern, K. Musson, M. Quinn, J. Williams, P. Yeager

Windborne
N. Hayward, B. McLain

All other photos were supplied as a courtesy to the publication.